SWAN DIVE

SWAN
DIVE

THE MAKING *of*
a ROGUE BALLERINA

Georgina Pazcoguin

Henry Holt and Company
New York

Henry Holt and Company
Publishers since 1866
120 Broadway
New York, NY 10271
www.henryholt.com

Henry Holt® and ⓗ® are registered trademarks of Macmillan Publishing Group, LLC.

Distributed in Canada by Raincoast Book Distribution Limited

Library of Congress Cataloging-in-Publication Data

Names: Pazcoguin, Georgina, author.
Title: Swan dive : the making of a rogue ballerina / Georgina Pazcoguin.
Description: First edition. | New York, N.Y. : Henry Holt and Company, 2021.
Identifiers: LCCN 2021006372 (print) | LCCN 2021006373 (ebook) |
    ISBN 9781250244307 (hardcover) | ISBN 9781250244291 (ebook)
Subjects: LCSH: Pazcoguin, Georgina. | Ballet dancers—Biography. | New York
    City Ballet.
Classification: LCC GV1785.P33 A3 2021 (print) | LCC GV1785.P33 (ebook) |
    DDC 792.802/8092 [B]—dc23
LC record available at https://lccn.loc.gov/2021006372
LC ebook record available at https://lccn.loc.gov/2021006373

Our books may be purchased in bulk for promotional, educational, or business use. Please
contact your local bookseller or the Macmillan Corporate and Premium Sales Department at
(800) 221-7945, extension 5442, or by e-mail at MacmillanSpecialMarkets@macmillan.com.

First Edition 2021

Designed by Meryl Sussman Levavi

Printed in the United States of America

1   3   5   7   9   10   8   6   4   2

This book is lovingly dedicated to
artists both distinguished and unrecognized
and to the blessed unrest . . .

Author's Note

Before we embark on this journey together, there are a couple of things you need to know. I've changed the names of some people (and okay, also some dogs) throughout the book. And while my brain and body have memorized countless ballets, I wouldn't say that I can recall each word of every conversation I've had or overheard with the same level of precision. Read on knowing I've recaptured dialogue and scenarios to the extent my memory allows. In the pages that follow, I'll be sharing my experience as a dancer at New York City Ballet with you. While much of it is exciting, moving, hilarious/ridiculous—there is a darkness too. You'll see that I'm not going to hold back when it comes to discussing my experiences, notably with several people who have at times been negative forces in my life.

I'd like to say that while I share a deep love and passion for ballet with many, we've all been impacted by intense scrutiny and pressure that have been passed down through generations like dysfunction within a family. We've grown up in a flawed world that celebrates great personal sacrifice, as well as an inherent bias about what a ballerina looks like.

But where my commonalities with the cast I'll soon introduce end is that I am a mixed-race woman who has succeeded despite this outdated ideal. How these individuals at NYCB view the ballet world is different from mine, largely for this reason. Their experiences as dancers, and now administrators, do not and cannot match mine.

SWAN DIVE

A MEMOIR IN FOUR PARTS
AND INTRODUCTION

Based on the life of New York City ballerina Georgina Pazcoguin

You've never been to City Ballet . . . or any ballet? NO PROBLEM, I've got you. And even if you do occasionally drop your backside into the plush, red velvet seats at the David H. Koch Theater at Lincoln Center . . . there are a few things you may not know. Brace yourselves.

Once upon a time—in 1948, to be precise—a former dancer/genius choreographer from Saint Petersburg, Russia, named George Balanchine and his partner, Lincoln Kirstein, founded a ballet company. They called it the New York City Ballet (NYCB). Please don't be confused and think I dance with American Ballet Theatre (ABT).

Another genius choreographer named Jerome Robbins (*West Side Story* or *Fiddler on the Roof*, anyone?) was also a founding choreographer of NYCB. Balanchine created his very own training style, which is taught at the ultraprestigious School of American Ballet (SAB), founded with the same cohort in 1934. "But first, a school" was Balanchine's edict. And now we know why: he had BIG, BIG plans for ballet in America. SAB is the first stop on the wild train ride that is becoming a professional dancer with NYCB.

City Ballet has also produced and been home to some of the most iconic American dancers EVER. Maria Tallchief and Tanaquil Le Clercq (both of them were married to Balanchine at one point, by the way), Suzanne Farrell . . . and of course, the one dancer just about everyone has heard of: Mikhail Baryshnikov.

ACT ONE: 1989–2000

A rogue ballerina is born. Ballet lessons, a typical childhood rite of passage, unexpectedly prove to be an actual career choice. Most people find their purpose after college. I found mine at the age of four.

ACT TWO: 2001–2003

Behold the unique growing pains of a working child turned young professional turned actual adult turned legal drinker in the city of instant gratification.

ACT THREE: 2003–2016

If you've ever seen *The Nutcracker*, whether your six-year-old niece was playing an angel, or you got all Christmassy and posed with your family in front of the iconic fountain before a Lincoln Center performance . . . you have Balanchine to thank for that. *The Nutcracker* was the first big production Balanchine created . . . spreading ballet-themed Christmas joy all over America. Other favorite Balanchine productions (I mean, if you ask me) include *Symphony in Three Movements*, *Agon*, and *Serenade*. You have my full support to skip *The Nutcracker* for these glorious works of art.

ACT FOUR: 2016 to present

It has been the greatest honor of my life to be a part of this company, but recently things have been dicey in the house that Balanchine built. The last few years have been marked by drama, scandal, and a whole lot of heartache.

THE CAST

In the following pages, I share my experience as a ballerina onstage and offstage. The good, the bad, and the totally crazy. As you join me on my ballet-fueled journey, you're going to encounter the following characters:

Peter Martins:

former dancer turned artistic director who retired amid an investigation into allegations of sexual harassment and verbal and physical abuse (which he denied).

Rosemary Dunleavy:

senior repertory director, keeper of all things Balanchine (she has all the steps of every production memorized), stern matriarch when you're a dancer in the corps.

Jean-Pierre Frohlich:

repertory director, the Larry David of the ballet.

Thomas A. Lemanski:

director of rehearsal administration, keeper of schedule, giver of insults.

GEORGINA'S COMPANY

The brothers Angle, Jared and Tyler:

Jared, young heartthrob, and Tyler, first dancing partner and childhood friend. Both principal dancers at the NYCB.

Savannah Lowery:

former soloist at NYCB, best friend, and if that wasn't enough, now she's becoming a doctor.

Miranda Grove:

best friend since age four, beaches buddy (literally and figuratively, à la the movie with Barbara Hershey and Bette Midler). Also a professional ballerina, albeit sadly never in the same company.

SWAN DIVE

Adrenaline

Adrenaline is a great fucking drug. It was the perfect top-off to the full range of emotions I had clawed my way through during the past twenty-four hours. I rode the 1 train downtown to the David H. Koch Theater in silence, believing my next performance as a dancer with the New York City Ballet would also be my last.

Two weeks earlier Peter and I had a yelling match of epic proportions. It ended with me screaming as I ran down the hallway, easily within earshot of anyone in the dressing rooms and the administrative offices. One of my stagehand buddies came running to my rescue to see what was up and make sure I was okay. Now Peter had requested to meet with me. I was sure I was getting fired. I was burning inside as I walked into the office, bracing myself for whatever unjustifiable abuse I was sure was going to be thrown my way: Fat shaming? Maybe I'd be accused of not being fully committed to the company I had danced with since I was a teenager? I was ready to defend myself this time, and my last words to Peter would be as sharp as daggers. I walked into the office, and Peter gestured toward the couch, where Rosemary, the ballet mistress, was seated. I had really grown to love her over all these years. Her passion and wisdom brought its own form of comfort, strictly unique to Rosemary. She was more stern stepmom than warm nurturer, but my feelings for her were solid despite her devotion to the man who continually caused me pain. I was glad she was in the room for this moment, even if just to witness whatever happened next.

The couch was absurdly low. Peter had positioned his six-feet-four-inch frame in a tall chair right across from me. It felt like he had me exactly where he wanted me, at his feet, prone before his throne. Like I was paying homage. I was weighed down by dread but still picked up on a feeling of calm in the room. This is exactly the kind of fuckery that drove my anxiety through the roof.

Peter finally spoke: "Georgina, I don't see us ever agreeing or seeing eye to eye."

His emphasis on the word "ever" was like a quick but sharp jab to my gut. A clear and painful reminder that he seemed to know exactly which buttons to push, and to remind me that not agreeing with him brought consequences.

He continued casually, as if we were roommates who disagreed about who washed the dishes last and weren't talking about the end of my life as a ballerina.

"We have differences of opinion."

The sadness rushed at me like a wave. I was twenty-nine years old, and my career was about to be over in a snap. This man, whose mere presence in the rehearsal studio loomed over us like a threatening storm cloud—who could take a dancer down with one sharp look or cutting comment—had the supreme power to cut me loose. And it was going to happen right now. I was struck silent, immobile.

"You have danced so strongly over this season. That is undeniable." Peter took a deep, concerning breath before he said, "I've decided to promote you."

His words did not compute. What did that fucker just say? He repeated it, "Gina, I'm promoting you." My rage starts to dissipate, and I am flushed with euphoria. *Wait, I'm a soloist? I'm a fucking soloist?* Part of me was in disbelief; did this just happen? Tears of gratitude were about to spill. I didn't really care if he saw me cry, but I wasn't going to reward him with a display of emotion. After our last blowout, I promised I'd never let him see me get emotional again.

Rosemary stood up and gave me a look of approval. I had earned some mutual respect over the years from this woman, who was a very tough nut to crack. Rosemary's career as a ballet mistress began under Balanchine and continued with Peter—in other words, she's dealt with some shit. It was like a strong woman who had been beaten down extending a hand to another strong-willed woman who had been freshly killed. Peter was standing now, towering over me, looking expectant. *Oh, Jesus. C'mon . . . he wants me to hug him?* I tried to find the will to push aside the disgust I felt from this weird peace offering, to just do it. To hug my boss—my abuser.*

I blurted out, "Thank you, Peter, for this recognition."

I stuck my arms stiffly out to the side and went in for a hug, but at the last second my body betrayed me. It's like as I got closer to my boss, I was confronted with an imaginary force field. The attempted hug between us became more like a chest bump between two rivals who were reluctantly attempting a truce. I kind of ricocheted off Peter's chest and instantly checked myself from laughing at this mutual fail. Taking in Peter's stiff body language and strained expression of approval, I thought, *Yeah, for a guy in his sixties, you are still solidly classified in the "brawny-brute" category, especially when standing directly next to my five-foot-five frame.* It was the best I could manage without cracking up in his face. I had won this battle of wills, and he knew it.

---

* To be clear, abuse comes in many forms: verbal, mental, and physical. I also want to be clear that my abuser did not hit me. Nothing I say in this book should be interpreted otherwise. The harm he has inflicted on me is psychological, and its effect on me has been devastating.

"Gina. One more thing." I stopped cold. *Oh, so here comes the axe.* Was this a cruel joke? I slowly turned toward him. "Your Carabosse," he continued. I played the role of the evil fairy in Peter's version of *The Sleeping Beauty*, the first in a growing number of character roles that allowed me to channel my complicated emotions into wickedness. "She just seems a little too mean."

The irony of his statement was not lost on me. At least he got the message. That's one thing I gotta hand him: Peter is not stupid. For the last two weeks I had been channeling every ounce of anger and angst into my role.

"Okay, I can tone it down."

The conversation was over; I was reeling from the unexpected twist. I walked out of the office, no longer a member of the corps de ballet but the first Asian American woman soloist in the history of the company. And I had also just agreed to dial back my rage. I headed up to the dressing room to get ready. I had a show in an hour.

Tchaikovsky's score was swelling grandly, sounding like a celebration. In thirty seconds, I'd be performing for the very first time as a soloist for the New York City Ballet. I rotated roles in this run of *Sleeping Beauty*, and by a stroke of fate, instead of acting Carabosse, I'd grace the stage tonight dancing the Fairy of Courage. This role was a pleasant departure from my usual rep at City Ballet. I often danced the strong female roles, but this time I was playing a strong female that would require classical ballet technique while wearing a very classical tutu. It was the kind of role I knew I could nail if only given the chance, and finally, my advocacy for myself had come through. Waiting in the wings to go on, Canary Fairy's theme had started—each tinkling note of her song was like a piece of glass shattering in the ceiling I had been trying to break for years. Now I had my title—I was about to grace that stage as a *motherfucking soloist*. Canary Fairy hit her last pose and disappeared off into the wings. The orchestra transitioned into Fairy of Courage's vamp—my energy pulsing, my body ready to soar with each BOMP

BOMP. I flew like I had been released from a cage—the conductor and I sharing one heart. I was completely in sync with the rhythm and energy of the orchestra. The same tenacity and grit that freed me from the fist of my boss transformed into power and technical precision . . . the ultimate badass ballerina combo. The audience was with me for every point and turn, grand jeté, chaîné, and battu. There were a few parts of this variation that had always been a pain in the ass to execute well. Peter's choreography here was crazy-fast, a by-product of the time-honored tradition of men who choreograph things never taking into account what it would be like to execute the movements en pointe. Female ballerinas always rising to the breakneck challenge for fear of saying, "Hey, can we take it down a notch?" Imagine telling Jesus that while it's great he turned water into wine, you'd prefer your water be a Syrah blend, not a cabernet. You have a solo, lady. Shut up and twirl. But today those struggles didn't exist. I was lit. This was my victory dance. The high-octane ninety-second variation was choreographed to impress—it ended with a set of diagonal piqué turns and sauts de basque. This is the kind of shit that seriously wears a ballerina out, but today I had a turbo boost in the form of vindication.

I'm right in it; the momentum I have is insane. But suddenly I realize I'm not headed in the right direction. I'm supposed to dance off into the wing, but I'm not lined up right to do that. *Shit.* I'm headed toward the proscenium at the edge of the stage. I need to decide in a split second whether I should correct myself by sacrificing the momentum, or do I keep going and hope I find a way to stop? I felt amazing. It was kind of like riding your bike down a big hill as a kid. You're speeding along with abandon and it's pure freedom . . . hair flying, stomach dropping, a huge smile plastered on your face as you defy gravity. But then you realize the hill is about to end in the middle of a busy intersection, and you're moving at breakneck speed. Do you hop off? Do you slam on the brakes? Do you just hang on for dear life and hope you'll be spared somehow? I land the saut de basque and decide to hang on. I start the chaîné turns and dance with so much fever that I'm on the marley clearing all the way onto the apron where the rehearsal pianist normally sits. If this was a rehearsal, I'd be sitting in her lap right now (after crashing into her piano). I've reached the last piece of real estate on the stage, and I have to put on the brakes somehow or I'll hit the wall. As I end the final turn, I stretch out my leg and pop my foot right onto the wall. And dink! I've stopped moving just in time.

The pose I'm standing in is not exactly picture call–worthy. It looks like I'm about to whip out a razor and shave my goddamn leg. I'm aware that professional ballerinas don't generally cling to the wall like Spider-Man in a tutu. So I dramatically throw my arms into the air in a desperate attempt to add a prima flourish.

The applause was EPIC. Perhaps in part because no one had seen a ballerina get this close to breaking her neck by crashing into a brick wall and then tumbling into the orchestra pit—but I didn't care. With every clap, my soul expanded, and my entire body was flushed with adrenaline. I felt like the audience had just taken this wild ride with me, and we were sharing this moment. My leg was still planted on the wall for balance, and now I have to get off the stage. This presented another interesting challenge, as I wasn't even technically on the stage. The wing was behind me. I pushed myself off the wall with my pointe shoe and gave a quick nod to the audience. *Thank you for this beautiful exchange!* I did a complete about-face, running off the stage with yet another over-the-top Vasiliev-style flourish. First show as a soloist and I nailed it. And fuck you, glass ceiling. Sometimes the act of performing is so powerful it carries you off. I had thought I had felt it all before, my first *Nutcracker*, my first performance on the State Theater stage—but I had never felt a high like this. Now I was a soloist in the New York City Ballet, and this was the real stuff. Those baby highs had nothing on this feeling. I wanted more.

The Gateway Drug

CHAPTER 1

Welcome to the School
of American Ballet

The city was revealing itself to me in all its urban glory as our minivan sailed down the Henry Hudson Parkway. The early summer sun was high above the buildings, and the river to my right glistened with promise. I was quiet in the middle of the middle seat, sandwiched between my two younger siblings, who were dragged along for the epic journey from Altoona, Pennsylvania, to Lincoln Center, where I'd be spending the next five weeks of my life. I barely even registered annoyance as Cory rummaged through a bucket of fried chicken, then shoved it past my face over to Christina.

"Christina, that last leg was supposed to be for me! What did you do with it?" Christina snatched up the bucket. "Chickens only have two legs. You ate them both, asshole."

My mother pushed her oversized sunglasses to the top of her head, leaning forward into the middle row. Mom was a sassy Italian who conjured up images of a young Liza Minnelli. But you'd be more likely to find my mom splitting a late-night cheesecake with the *Golden Girls* than hanging around Studio 54 in a Halston dress. Mom's realm was family, friends, food, and conversation, and her reign was supreme.

Mom always sat in the back on any long drives, and this was not our first lengthy ballet-related road trip. My parents had dutifully hauled me to ballet "conventions" all over the country, including one especially ass-numbing trip to Jackson, Mississippi. Mom had some anxiety around driving, and the car was the one place my mother let my dad take full control. My father may have been a colonel in the army reserve and a revered general ER surgeon, but there was no doubt that it was my mother who ruled the family. The car was the one place in the Pazcoguin family jurisdiction where my dad could relish some authority. To this day, if you need a ride, you can count on Silvino Ben Pazcoguin. He will drive anyone in my family anywhere at any time with pride and love.

"Gina, you are going to dance in this big city. This is it!"

My mom said this with genuine excitement, but with a side dose of something I couldn't quite recognize. Maybe it was sadness or worry about leaving me alone in this enormous and anonymous city, but before I could give it further thought, she shouted loudly over all of our heads, "Ben! You're gonna miss the exit if you don't get in the left lane. Pronto!"

We lurched forward as Dad made a harrowing three-lane switch so he wouldn't miss the exit. As our minivan made a left onto Fifty-Ninth Street, turning up Amsterdam Avenue, Dad, attempting to navigate the busy city traffic while reading his AAA TripTik notes, announced that the Rose Building, my new home, should be just up ahead. The Rose Building housed the School of American Ballet started by George Balanchine and his partner in artistic crime, Lincoln Kirstein, years before the New York City Ballet was even born. SAB is prestigious AF, and the crazy-competitive summer program draws two hundred of the country's finest young dancers, many of whom have been dreaming about being a professional dancer as long as they had memories. SAB is also the only way a dancer gets into New York City Ballet. There's no auditioning for the company at the ripe old age of eighteen. The corps de ballet is like an elitist cult, and all of its young, moldable members are plucked right from the school. That first summer, my only knowledge of SAB came from a school report I did on Maria Tallchief, a ballerina who at one time was married to Balanchine. I knew that 1) some Russian guy named Balanchine invented an interesting ballet technique, and he started a ballet company in New York City; 2) Maria Tallchief is obviously the coolest name a ballerina could ever have; and 3) for some reason this institution gave me a full scholarship.

My dad pulled over, and taxis buzzed past us like a swarm of killer bees. My sister opened the door and scooted out. I followed suit, getting my foot stuck in a half-full bag of Doritos.

"Dude, I was gonna eat those on the way home. Thanks, Grace."

My brother laughed, then nimbly hopped over our mountain of road-trip debris and leapt gracefully onto the sidewalk. Mom shimmied out of the back back, popped a Jolly Rancher into her mouth, and efficiently snatched my trunk out of the minivan and hauled it to the curb with a thud. Car horns blared as if issuing a warning, "Watch yourself, Midwestern lady. You're not in Altoona, PA, anymore!" We waved goodbye to my father, who was venturing forth into the wilds of the Upper West Side to find parking. We stood awkwardly on the corner, all of us just staring as our minivan got smaller and smaller, eaten up by the mass of traffic, buildings, and crowds.

It didn't take long for me to notice my people. Up ahead snaked a long line of nearly identical-looking, long-legged girls who might as well have been deposited on the plaza from outer space. The alien-like limbs and gigantic smiles were topped off with the ultimate ballerina giveaway, the perpetual bun. I considered my own thick, straight, and extra-long ponytail and wondered why anyone would bother with a bun if they weren't in class. I always struggled to get my bun tight enough, and I hated all the fumbling with bobby pins. Did their mothers do this for them? Were they actually capable of pulling this off on their own? I made a note to myself to befriend a good bun maker as soon as possible. How else was I going to keep up with this level of slicked-back crazy? My raven horse mane swung freely between my shoulder blades as we made our way to the end of the line. I stood nervously and quietly while my brother teased and fake-anime-battled my unwilling baby sister. My mom was already chatting up the line, talking to the girls ahead of us. "Where are you from? You drove all the way from Chicago! Oh, really? How long was your drive? Did you hit much traffic?"

Her friendly questioning made me unbearably uncomfortable. "Mom, quit it," I hissed. "I don't even know if these girls are in my level."

My mom stopped talking, but only to wave down my father, who was slowly making his way across the plaza. "Oh, there you are. I was starting to worry." My father mumbled something under his breath, and that was only the beginning. My Filipino dad speaks perfectly fluent English. However, friends have mentioned that my dad has a rather particular accent. It's not something I'm usually ever aware of. If he's really angry or really frustrated, then I do clock it. Dad's regular speech had just morphed into the special combo of Spanish and French accents, peppered with a few words he just made up on the fly. This is something we only heard when Dad was truly livid. When he's angry on this level, it's like he transforms into an Asian version of Ricky Ricardo. His anger increases, he becomes nearly impossible to understand, and eventually people just stop listening—his own family included. If I had to guess, his mutterings were likely related to the fact that parking for two hours in New York City costs more than outfitting all six of his children with new back-to-school clothes and still money left over for a golf club.

The line was moving forward. The summer sun was eclipsed by darkness as we shuffled into a narrow hallway. Small batches of ballerinas and their families were being loaded onto the freight elevator. My family, plus four other little aliens and their parents, remained silent as the large steel door was pulled down and we started moving up. The elevator came to an abrupt stop on the seventeenth floor, and we were greeted by an enthusiastic teenager wielding a clipboard.

"Welcome to the School of American Ballet! Let's see—Pazcooogin? You're in suite 1702, and your roommate has not checked in yet."

This moment represents the first time—out of thousands if I had to guess—that my last name would be emphatically mispronounced by someone associated with the New York City Ballet. My family followed me into my dorm room, my siblings staring out the window at the fountain while my mom laid my foam egg crate on the bottom bunk and covered it up with a worn set of freshly washed sheets. She folded me into her arms and gently kissed my forehead. She smelled like home. It suddenly hit me that we wouldn't be taking trips to Value City together this summer. And I wouldn't be around to help her plant tomatoes in the family garden, kneeling side by side on our knees, our hands busy in the warm dirt. My father hugged me. "We'll call you when we get home, Gina." My siblings turned from the window, said goodbye, and that was that. I wouldn't say it was a clinical goodbye. There were some feelings expressed by each member of the family. But our departure didn't necessarily feature the outpouring of emotion you might expect from parents about to leave their barely teen daughter in the hands of strangers in Manhattan. I wouldn't learn about the walk back to the car for several years, when my sister brought it up. A horse-drawn carriage trotted by, causing my mom to stop in her tracks and say, "Oh, Gina would have just loved that horse." And with that comment she burst into tears.

I plopped down on my bed and felt a ball of emotion taking root in my gut, and I had no clue how to untangle it. I was fourteen years old and about to spend a good chunk of my summer away from everything I knew. I'd be apart from my five siblings. I'd be separated from the puppies the family brought home to replace our beloved dog Ebony. Ebony's death was so hard on me I had actually landed in therapy, and now I'd be away from the puppies, too. I'd miss swim team practices and reading books in my very own bed as I fell asleep to the summery sound of crickets chirping. Until now, summer had meant a glimpse of the regular kid freedoms I didn't usually experience during the school year. There was a ritual transformation as soon as school ended and before my five-week ballet camp started. My leotards were swapped out for swimsuits and goggles as I joined other local kids at the country club for early-morning swim team practice. Those days I was just another kid on the country club swim team—but I was always the first one to dive into the chilly water at 7:30 a.m. when practice started.

The rest of the day was spent with my best ballet school friends or with my brothers at the pool. We'd tramp around our field of a backyard and surrounding rural neighborhood, my hands stained from eating mulberries right off the tree. If that wasn't idyllic enough, we'd actually suck on the honeysuckle blossoms that were dotted through the yard like prizes. We acted like honest-to-God tree-climbing, rhubarb-stealing, getting-dirty kinds of kids. I'm talking about some serious *Goonies*-style adventure shit. There were also the requisite midweek sleepovers with ballet pals. We made up skits and elaborate dance routines for our pretend hit TV show, *Jammin' in Jammies!!* I'd act furious each time my older brother scared the shit out of us—popping out in a Michael Myers mask and wielding a kitchen knife, but I was secretly giving him props. Although locking us in the basement and stabbing a knife through a wall during one particularly harrowing *Halloween* re-enactment was a bit much. Fun times, the '80s. But my siblings were back home, and Miranda and Tyler were taking class in San Francisco that summer—and with me in New York City, nothing felt the same. New people, new sounds, even darkness falling was different and required getting used to. Darkness never really came in New York City, not like it did in Altoona. There were no fireflies or stars to help transition the evening into a peaceful night. There was just light and life. It never ended in the city, and the brightly lit buildings did nothing to quell the big anxiety I felt every night at bedtime.

I was unmoored, but it didn't keep me from feeling excited. I was at SAB because I truly loved ballet—and my love for ballet permeated everything I did. How I spent my afternoons after school, what I wore, who I hung out with on weekends, and the confusing twinge that hit my heart when I chose rehearsal over another school dance. My love for the craft grew when I mastered a new challenge, like earning my first pair of pointe shoes, and blossomed when I performed new roles in my ballet school's annual production of *The Nutcracker*.

Those moments surrounded me with a feeling I recognized as love, but there were no expectations, no preconceived notions of how this relationship would unfold. Ballet and I would be together for the long haul, or maybe we wouldn't. Maybe I'd be a doctor like my dad . . . Who the hell knows? Until now this love was pure and innocent, and my relationship with dance was unfolding naturally without any outside pressures. I had been given the gift of the world's best stage parents. I was offered full support, my parents happily paying for the expensive lessons, shoes, and leos. They were dutifully present for every perform-ance from my first role as an angel (I fell) to my very first professional show. But they never pushed me too hard; they never once forced me to take a cold, hard look at the realities of ballet—they never pressured me to work harder. I was an intense kid, and they very well may have intrin-sically understood that I was already putting this pressure on myself. Ballet was accepted as just the thing I do, like how other kids played volleyball or video games. Once in a while my mom would casually trot out the temptation of a day off to me and Miranda. "Gina, how about instead of class today, we go shopping or have dinner? A movie!" It could have been anything at all . . . just doing something else was the point. I always chose ballet. What masked itself as a childhood hobby was already a deeply embedded passion . . . and there was no stopping it. I'd always pick ballet over a John Hughes movie; plus, my dad had the most impressive collection of what would become '80s cult movies on VHS around. I figured I could catch up anytime.

Dad applied pressure just once, and he used the lightest touch. He woke me up extra early one Saturday morning the previous February. It was the time of year in Pennsylvania when the cold stings like a slap in the face. Grey days fall in line one after the other, and it's hard to remember that a bright blue sky or sunshine ever existed.

"Hey, Gina, so we're going to drive to that audition. It's time to get up, okay?" I was tired and content to stay in bed, but the idea of driving to Pittsburgh with my dad to audition for the SAB summer course was almost enough to lure me out from under the covers. We had never had a discussion about this audition as a family—it wasn't something we all agreed would be "important for my future." I didn't spend extra hours training for it. I never devoted energy to thinking what it could mean if I was actually accepted. My family was simply aware the audition was happening, and apparently my dad thought driving to Pittsburgh was a good way to kill a Saturday afternoon in the ice-cold guts of winter.

"C'mon, Gina, get up. We're going to go to this audition. We can get spaghetti at your favorite place on our drive back home." There was an Italian restaurant inside of an old train car that I loved in Pittsburgh. I always ordered the spaghetti. I tossed aside the covers and put on my favorite black leo. This one was my armor; when I slipped it on, I always felt smooth and sleek. It had black horizontal slits down the entire back, a badass but defining feature that helped me distinguish myself ever so slightly from every other dancer in a black leo. Even then I was slightly rogue. I strove to stand out.

It was just Dad and me, driving under a ribbon of grey sky for hours. When we got to the audition, we were immediately confronted with a never-ending supply of enthusiastic young ballerinas. I checked in and my number was pinned on by the smallest of safety pins. We were lined up in groups. I was asked to do a tendu à la seconde, développé à la seconde, and an arabesque. My ability to execute these movements properly would demonstrate my facility for turnout, arch, and flexibility. SAB auditions are famous for this prescreen. Line and physical aesthetic are essential in ballet. It can be developed to a certain degree, but

to become a professional ballet dancer, male or female, ultimately re[s]
upon your God-given traits. The first obstacle to becoming a profe[s]
sional dancer is a big one—it's determining if fate gave you a body tha[t]
can be molded into "perfection."

After the prescreen we were all to take part in a class where we'd
undoubtedly be observed and judged. Did we have something truly special? Or was ballet just meant to be an after-school hobby, eventually
swapped out for Pilates or yoga when we got older? There was something about being around so many other dancers that fostered a desire
to shine. Now that I was here, I wanted to do really well. I wouldn't let
my dad watch. I made him wait in the hallway. I felt nervous, but I was
in my zone. The class was fun, and I liked the corrections the teacher
was giving me. I have never loved adagio, but I did it. The last part of
the class was jumps—grand allegro. I knew this was where I could stand
out because even though I was a fourteen-year-old girl from small-town
Pennsylvania, I had developed the ability to fly. My ability to take flight
that day was enhanced by the live musician playing the piano. I loved
music, and dancing to a live musician was an unexpected treat. Adding
live music turns the art of ballet into a conversation. To me a dancer
is the personification of music. It's like a siren call. Hearing live music
awakens something deep inside of me, even if I'm just in class. This feeling is not limited to the stage on performance night. The interaction
between a musician and a dancer is otherworldly, a synergy of artistic
power. If you watched the cartoon *Captain Planet* from the '90s, you'll
get this: Five teens from different continents combine their unique powers together in order to summon this ultra being who magnifies their
gifts tenfold, which are then used to save the earth from environmental
disaster! Combining my gift with another artist's gift is exponentially
increasing the impact we can make. So, for that reason, live music is
much more than someone sitting at a piano during class or rehearsal.
Music is my rock, my partner, my trusty sidekick. And at that audition,
it was the match to my fuse—it gave me liftoff.

After the class was over, I walked past a group of girls who were furiously asking questions of a tiny woman with red hair hanging to her shoulders like a river of fire. Susie Hendl was a former Balanchine ballerina who was sent out to Pittsburgh to lead the audition and teach the class. In other words, to ballet nerds auditioning for SAB on a random Saturday afternoon, she was an A-list celebrity on a New Kids on the Block level. I didn't know who she was the day that she separated herself from the girls and approached me. With all the hopeful eyes now staring directly at me, she asked, "Your name is Georgina, right? I can't say anything officially, but I can basically tell you you're going to get a scholarship. Do you have any plans to audition anywhere else?" I stood there trying to comprehend what I had just heard, and I had no idea how to respond, "Huh. I don't know. Ask my dad?" I said thank you politely and left the room and went into the hallway, where Dad was waiting. He smiled when he saw me. "How'd it go? I heard other girls talking about how good you did in there." I didn't fully understand what had just happened, and I masked my excitement. I relished having a secret but didn't want to draw attention to myself. Once I was safely out of earshot of the other girls and in the car, I told him, "I think she said I might have gotten a scholarship, but I don't know." It was snowing again. The sky was heavy with grey and the promise of more winter. We set off to get spaghetti, but we got lost. We never found the restaurant.

In late February an official letter of acceptance arrived. I had been offered a full scholarship to the summer program at the School of American Ballet. *Holy shit.* My acceptance at SAB was the very first hint that this passion of mine could shape the course of my life. It was the first solid indication that I had promise, that maybe ballet and I were headed somewhere together. It was like waking up to discover the little boy I had been playing with since preschool had suddenly blossomed into George Clooney. I didn't know what it all meant, but I was definitely interested in finding out.

CHAPTER 2

Saved by the Bell
and John Lithgow

The cafeteria at the Rose Building is unlike any school cafeteria. Imagine something like a college campus cafeteria—it's used by Juilliard students and faculty, and anyone involved in a production at the Walter Reade Theater and the Clark Studio Theater, as well as by the Lincoln Center constituent offices. The line in the cafeteria is likely to include Juilliard students grabbing a bagel between classes, the ladies who work in various offices picking up a salad, John Lithgow eyeing the desserts, or, God rest his soul, Philip Seymour Hoffman picking up a coffee before heading back upstairs to rehearse *Death of a Salesman*.

Then summer hits. And these half-dressed young men and women swirl in and take it all over. Imagine if the food court at your local mall was suddenly held hostage by the cast of *Fame*. However, like any cafeteria anywhere in the world, the Rose Building cafeteria is also a palace of teenage awkwardness come summer. Ballerinas are absolutely everywhere, sporting tights and leos, limbs too long and braces too bright. Each girl is crowned with a perfect bun.

On that first day my hair was in a bun, too, but I had regular clothes on over my ballet clothes. It was breakfast time, for Christ's sake. The smattering of male dancers present was completely outnumbered by the female persuasion—a common occurrence anywhere young ballet dancers gather. I stood alone and nervous, unaccustomed to all the newness. I was used to the togetherness that comes from six kids fighting at the breakfast table about who gets the last slice of Ellio's pizza or the last of the ramen soup. We were never a cornflakes and Cheerios kind of family.

I got in line behind a group of slightly older girls. They were pulsing with a confidence that only comes from familiarity. Their comfort level practically screamed, "We've been here before and we own level six." I was in level six, but my newness overshadowed any confidence I would have gathered from being placed in such a high level at such a young age. As I waited, I looked down and noticed they were all wearing what looked like Christmas stockings on their feet. Chunky, thick, bright red stockings that went all the way up to the knee, with leather sewn on for a sole. They were cute and cozy but seemed like an odd choice, seeing that we were in the middle of a cafeteria in July. The tallest girl picked up on my curiosity and acknowledged me with an explanation: "They're mukluks. Everyone here wears them," as if the group mentality behind their weirdo shoe choice made them look less ridiculous. Did they realize they were shuffling around on the concrete floor in stockings that have no grip? I watched as the tall girl slid her tray right past the towers of carbs—triangles of toast, pancakes, waffles—and continued pushing it past the bacon and sausage, coming to a halt in front of big bowls of pink and white yogurt. The pink yogurt was unnaturally bright and supremely unappealing. The white yogurt was the winner. She spooned enough yogurt to feed an infant into her bowl, moved a few inches down the line to add fruit, then finally topped it off with an impossibly small sprinkle of granola. The other mukluk chicas followed suit, each ballerina slowly adding yogurt, fruit, and granola into her bowl. I wanted a bowl of ramen desperately, but instead I filled my bowl with yogurt, fruit, and granola—the portions I'd chosen seemed humongous in comparison. Behind me stood the Juilliard kids—they were so obvious. They wore regular clothes and ate whatever the hell they felt like. I guess excessive waffle consumption has no direct impact on how well you perform in front of your peers during violin class. Lucky bastards.

I heaved my dance bag higher onto my shoulder, balanced my tray, and whipped out my meal card. I chose the nearest empty table; it seemed like the safest and least conspicuous move I could make. The mukluk girls were a few tables over, eating together, slowly spooning tiny amounts of yogurt past their lips, silently and practically in unison. Another group of dancers left their food mostly untouched. It was as if they were too excited to eat. Too busy chatting, hugging each other, and pulling their legs up behind their heads in absurd acts of flexibility. They exuded familiarity and closeness, too. I thought about Tyler and Miranda—far away at the San Francisco Ballet's summer intensive; I was envious that they had each other. If they were here, we'd be sitting together, wondering where you score a pair of those weird shoes and maybe even sharing a breakfast sandwich. The wicked mixture of anxiety, discomfort, and uncertainty I was feeling would be watered down by their presence. I might have been surrounded by other ballet aliens, but I was alone and I was the newbie. This was a difficult combination to conquer. I wasn't necessarily afraid of being alone—even as a member of a big family, I had always managed to find a way to spend plenty of time solo. But this was a lot to take in . . . the different, the good. What were the rules here? Who was my competition? Did Tyler and Miranda feel as unmoored as I did? Were they able to help each other figure out what was what?

This was the first summer we were apart. The three of us had operated our own nerdy ballet posse since we met as tiny people at the Allegheny Ballet Academy. I landed at Allegheny because my first experience with ballet had ended before it began. The ballet school most conveniently located to our house expected my mom to be present during the entire time I was in class. My mom wasn't having that. She was holding my brother by the hand, had my baby sis high on her hip, and had three other kids who would be getting home from school soon. Basically, as a mother of six, she had a lot of other shit to do. She couldn't stick around for this and paraded me right back to the car. A few days later I was incessantly twirling around in the kitchen making a real nuisance of myself while Mom was trying to make dinner and dealing with all the kids alone. My father was stationed at Fort Benning and would remain there for the duration of the Gulf War. The TV was blaring in the background, and my younger siblings were running around like maniacs following my lead. My mom stepped away from the stove and grabbed the phone book from the cabinet. She plopped it on the counter and gave her index finger a lick, impatiently flicking past pages until she landed at "DANCE." The very first listing was the Allegheny Ballet Academy. She dialed the number as the sauce bubbled on the stove.

"Hi. So, I have this girl who is constantly moving and twirling. I want to sign her up—"

Deborah Anthony cut Mom off and informed her that she teaches "a well-rounded hybrid of Vaganova and Cecchetti ballet styles."

Mom got right to the point. "Debbie. Tell me. Do I have to stay and watch?" From the look on Mom's face, it was clear that she didn't. No parental guidance required. Debbie wanted the parents and all of the distractions they brought out of her way. We had a win!

The next day she dropped me off at the Allegheny Ballet Academy. It was really just a repurposed old church, but in my mind the barre and the mirrors had transformed it into something miraculous. We were placed at the split-level barre that frames the large wood-floored room, most of us only able to reach the lower level. The music started, and we were guided into a simple series of pliés and relevés. Next were explanations of the classical ballet positions, the six basic positions that are the foundation of barre work and the center work that came after. My little, not-yet-there muscles fired right up, and I liked the feeling—the strength that came from it. I disappeared out of myself and clicked into something bigger than my tiny four-year-old body. Something let loose inside of me, and I felt simultaneously freed and focused. I didn't know what I was doing, but I knew one thing. I wanted to move this way all the time. Even the ballet shoes had their own magical qualities. They started out firm, but then the leather softened as my body heat warmed them up. Eventually they conformed to my feet—memorizing the specific shape of my tiny pointed toes. My normal shoes didn't do that! The wooden barre felt like a protector in my hands. I felt safe just touching it. The mirrors were like a friend that echoed my exact feelings back to me without ever speaking. I even loved the record player—letting myself get lost in the tempos, rhythm, and movement. I dug all of this shit, and it absolutely blew my four-year-old mind.

Over the next few years Allegheny would become my second home. I'd meet Miranda, Tyler, Rebecca, and more, who would become life-long friends—forever bonded by ballet and our childhood antics. Those one-and-a-half-hour weekly lessons would eventually be stretched out to longer hours and more days per week as we got older and more serious. Even as kids, even in middle-of-nowhere Altoona, ballet meant making sacrifices. Regular kid activities like going to football games were rare, and getting dropped off at the mall to spend an afternoon messing around looking at clothes and eating pizza with friends wasn't a thing for me. Having Tyler and Miranda in my life made missing these coming-of-age rites of passage much easier. They didn't think I was a freak—that weird ballerina chick who never hung out with anyone else. They understood the commitment. They also chose ballet class every day from 4 p.m. to 9 p.m. because they felt the same love I did. And when we were out of class, we were normal kids (relatively), sending my dad out to Blockbuster for movies, running around in my family's giant backyard. We shared those normal kid moments, but more importantly we all knew that ultimately, we didn't want to be "normal." We were young artists at heart, and there was no need to defend or explain what that meant to each other. We had all been in the same crazy, ballet-themed boat since were practically babies. For me, ballet was always connected to them, but now that was changing. My breakfast ramen was gone; my safety nets were gone. I did still have the barre, though. Would the solidness of it soothe me even though I was away from everything I knew? I heard the sound of chairs shuffling, silverware clanging. I pushed aside all homesick feelings about my friends, the puppies, my family, and post–swim meet ice cream cones and dropped into ballet-class mode and focused. My first level-six class was about to begin, and this is why I was here.

Swan Dive #1

"Debbie, is she okay?" Mom had been watching backstage as she was assigned baby-ballerina chaperone for the evening. It was my first *Nutcracker* run, aka the very first time this ballerina fell on her ass, onstage, *during a performance*. Mom was concerned but slightly embarrassed—her daughter had just gone down. With several decades of *Nutcracker* performances under my belt, I can tell you that if I had to bet on who is most likely to go down (or pee) during a show, I'd pick an angel every time. Those Hula-Hoop skirts can be unwieldy, and the dry ice creating special-effect clouds can make for a very slippery floor. I can imagine how it was for me—the curtain rising for the second act, the excitement as the twinkly music of the overture begins and the darling little angels move onto the stage . . . Candlestick up! Candlestick down! Spin around . . . Now do it twice. Smile! *I am in the land of sweets and I am a star!* Time to cross over to the next formation now . . . those trills in the score revving me up and bam! I'm down. *Well, that was unexpected.* I popped right back up and didn't so much as miss a raising of my candlestick.

"Oh, she's fine, Mrs. Pazcoguin. She got right back up! She did exactly what she was supposed to do. She really played it off."

Mom looked visibly relieved. Debbie continued, "Well, she's pretty small. I'd suggest tacking up her Hula-Hoop skirt for the remaining performances. She probably tripped over it." "Of course!" Mom responded quickly, not knowing that the tacking-up of that angel skirt was the gateway to her becoming the full-on costume lady for the entire school.

CHAPTER 3

The Mother Ship

Dance bags of all shapes and sizes bursting with everything from extra T-shirts and tights, skirts, pale pink ribbons, sewing kits, and pairs of sewn and unsewn pointe shoes were strewn all over the room. Steely puffs of lambswool dotted the floor in random places. This artsy mess was meant to send a message . . . *This spot at the barre is spoken for; do not even think about dropping your shit here.* Dancers just coming in were nervously seeking out a spot for themselves. I quickly grabbed a place at one of the center barres. As I looked around, I could feel the corners of my lips cracking into a smile. The ceilings of the studio were massive, the polished floor stretched out like a field—everything was so new it almost felt space age; it was the ballet mother ship. Just standing in that room made me feel like I could fly higher. It was the first time I was moved by the sheer grandness of a space. The vast room felt like a blank canvas just waiting for me to fill the space with movement.

Even now, while traveling or just on a date, I am hard-pressed to resist busting out with a giant manège when confronted with a big open space. A wine cave in Chile, the floor of the old retired Chicago Stock

Exchange—these are just a couple of places where I dropped the veneer of "tourist" or "date material" to let my superpowers show. I might look like a regular chick from the outside, but when I let the pent-up energy fly free, the resulting display of life force can be spectacular. I have to fly, even if only for a second. The heavy-duty center barres, just like the one I was resting a hand on, were made of finished oak. It would take two ultrafit ballerina bodies to roll them back and forth from their storage place before and after class. Then there was the piano. The beautiful Baldwin, shiny and proud, made that record player I had loved so much in the studio of the Allegheny ballet school look like yard sale scraps. You know who else played a Baldwin? Liberace, *that's who*. This was some seriously state-of-the-art shit. I closed my eyes, took a breath, and tried to let the atmosphere crank my consternation down a few notches. My angst never leaves completely. It whirs inside of me constantly, not unlike a high-powered blender. I'm always revving, but sometimes I have to control the intensity. It can be an incredible tool, yet at the same time it can interfere with my instinct of movement. Ballet is a mind game. Level six was the highest level at SAB, and I was younger than most of the other dancers in the room. I didn't know if this should quell my fears or send my anxiety straight into red-zone emergency levels.

All heads turned as a mass of black fabric scurried into class and took a seat at the piano. The expression on her face was semiapologetic, as if she had committed some kind of faux pas known only to herself. Katarina Batist announced herself with a side order of Russian flair. Dramatic, somewhat foreboding, semidetached. I was immediately intrigued by her and would remain so well into my adulthood. She always managed to appear somewhat disengaged, never revealing an ounce of interest in what was going on in the room. Balanchine's ghost himself could have walked in, slapped her over the head, and she would have dutifully kept playing, adjusting the music to whatever pop song she deemed ideal for a ghostly encounter. Katarina's magic was that she could always be counted on to come up with the right tempo for any exercise we were doing. She would dazzle me with Chopin one minute, then effortlessly transition into a Whitesnake song for center work. She understood how important the music was to our movement and seamlessly blended the classical with the contemporary. Katarina Batist was a model of tenacity and grit, two qualities that are oddly crucial to one's success as a class pianist. In a city like New York, where there are more aspiring musicians than there are pigeons, you'd think a good class pianist would be easy to come by. But they're not, even in the blessed halls of the New York City Ballet and SAB.

There is a bizarre dynamic involving cattiness and barely under-the-radar resentment that exists between some pianists and the teachers. It's deeply embedded, almost like a multigenerational feud that's gone on so long no one remembers what the beef was about in the first place. We'll never know what sparked it, but the first blow was obviously unforgivable, with repercussions reverberating through the decades. In New York City, these unforgettable actions could stem from any-thing . . . cutting the line at Zabar's and getting the last of the smoked nova salmon. Or maybe stealing a taxi on a cold, rainy afternoon—who knows? I've witnessed the pianist/teacher drama playing out for years, and I've noticed it manifests in a few unique forms.

Weird dynamic #1:
Piano vs. ballet drama.

Most commonly you'll have the perfectly fine pianist being berated unreasonably by a teacher, in front of everyone. We could be at the barre, Bach pouring out beautifully from the piano, our bodies flowing into the movement, when Peter would bark out, "No. no. Stop. Too many notes! I don't want so many notes! Just chords." Here sits a concert-level pianist who can play the shit out of anything, but the teacher isn't going to let them play what they want. With one command they're reduced to playing "just chords" or even "Twinkle, Twinkle, Little Star." On the flip side, I am absolutely mortified—offended, really—when a pianist bangs out "Twinkle, Twinkle, Little Star" for tendu work. *What the fuck?* One could argue that the strictness of class and the necessity of certain musical structure for class exercises relegate the pianist's art form to a lower status so ours can be elevated. But ultimately the two work so beautifully paired. And my body may be conditioned to appear like the body of an adolescent, but I am a thirty-four-year-old woman, for Christ's sake. I do not want to listen to a nursery song while I'm trying to warm my ass up. Give me Michael Jackson, AC/DC, Prince, Mozart, Billy Joel!—anything else, please.

Weird dynamic #2:
You say tomato, I say SHUT UP.

I should point out that the piano/teacher dynamic isn't strictly limited to the New York City Ballet. Flora, one of the pianists at Steps on Broadway, where I sometimes take class, likes to rock an eccentric necklace. Flora's necklaces are effing enormous and feature Christmas-ornament-sized baubles that can easily be seen from the other side of the room. One of her more notable necklaces consisted of a toothbrush. A full-on, adult-sized toothbrush was hanging around her neck as she played the piano. *Flora does Flora.* I've been in the game long enough to know Flora is a good pianist, but neither her skill nor her sizable necklaces are enough to shield her from ultrabitchy and uncalled-for comments such as, "Flora! You're playing so heavy-handed that I swear to God it's like an elephant is playing the piano!" Such behavior makes me cringe. I know it's done for show. It's a ploy to instill the fear of God into the students and to raise the status of the teacher to create the power dynamic of master/minion. I know what it feels like to be an outlier, and it's as if I'm a sponge for all the embarrassment in the room. Moments like this make me want to pick up my bag, click my pointe-shoe-clad heels together, and disappear.

Weird dynamic #3:
You play, we dance. NO joy, please.

I dig Joe and his piano playing well enough. I appreciate his style and the unique contribution he makes to the class, but apparently my feelings aren't shared by the rest of the company. Joe has fun. He plays music that works well with whatever combination we're doing. Then if he's feeling superinspired, he'll take it to another level and bust out with some acoustics in the form of banging on the top of the piano with his hands. There's Joe, happily pounding out the beat when heads start to turn his way. Some of the dancers have perfected a look that manages to convey, "Oh my God, this is so weird; why are you doing that? And lastly, my beautiful ballerina vibe is being destroyed by your spirited drumming!" All of these sentiments are rolled into one supermean but admittedly efficient look. Think Blue Steel with a side of Medusa's stone-cold stare. I never hated on Joe. From my perspective, at least this guy's got passion. Props for passion!

To be fair, not all pianists are cut out to be pianists for company class.

Not every pianist has the ability or desire to rearrange music on the fly from a standard measure to an eight count. You've got to be comfortable with all the weird tempo changes and be prepared to adjust the music along with the teacher's whims. When you're a class pianist, it's like you're a human playlist. Using an *actual playlist* would require the teacher planning out ninety minutes of movement in advance and following the plan perfectly. Having a human playlist in the form of a *human* piano player allows the teacher to have some flexibility with the combinations. As the movements change, there's no time for the pianist to pause and think, "Huh, what catchy pop tune should I play now that they're about to transition into center work? I know, Bruno Mars!" A pause disrupts the class, makes it difficult to execute a combination, and pisses everyone off. There was a Russian pianist who was always playing the wrong tempo, seemingly on purpose. It was in Kramy's class. Andrei Kramarevsky was one of my favorite teachers. He was an expert on the art of partnering and teaching character, and we often shared the stage together in *The Nutcracker*. I was busting my ass in the corps as a maid, while he played a spectacular Drosselmeyer. If Kramy needed the tempo to increase to match the combination, the pianist would take it down to a slow death march. When the teacher actually needed the tempo to be slower? He'd start playing something crazy-fast like we were backup dancers for Beyoncé. Getting your body to move along with tempos that aren't conducive to a combination feels wrong. Think jackhammer sex or the terrible sound of grinding the gears while driving a Porsche 911. Something beautiful is being completely spoiled by someone else's incompetence. Class is ninety minutes, but it's an important part of our day—and this guy turned those precious ninety minutes into an out-of-control circus. In the end, he got fired. We dancers banded together and had him voted off the island.

So many pianists have come and gone; the no-nonsense pianist who used to play the right tempo even though the ballet master had called out the wrong one. Why play the wrong thing when *she knows what he means*? The one who had a penchant for playing jazz, which never ever seemed to match up with our combinations. But any piano player is better than no piano player. Showing up in class to discover there's no pianist is like arriving at the gym and realizing you forgot your headphones. Who wants to run on the treadmill to the soundtrack of their own dark thoughts? No pianist means someone shouting out a beat, maybe a few songs played on an iPad. Ultimately something is missing, and my body knows it. Those classes are the ones you just get through, and tomorrow, hopefully, another pianist will be at that bench, and they'll have enough tenacity and grit to get us through.

CHAPTER 4

Carnage

A few seconds later the door opened, and a tiny old lady came walking in, leaning on a cane. Her loose-fitting black dress, gold earrings, and the artsy scarf poured over her shoulders didn't commit her to any one particular era. She managed to appear timeless and ancient at the same time. She looked frail, but her eyes gleamed with a comforting warmth and generosity. Her age and stature made me want to scoop up this adorable little lady in my arms and gently deposit her in the chair that waited for her. The charge of nervous energy in the room shifted to awe and terror with a healthy side dose of amazement. Is this who we think it is? Is this really happening? One dancer broke the silence, "Holy crap. That's Tumey!" There were audible gasps and murmurs. Everyone in the room had heard somewhere, somehow about the legendary Antonina Tumkovsky. Stories of her spectacularly difficult classes floated around the ballet world—an urban legend wrapped in pink tulle and tights. Dancers might have heard about her impossible combinations from visiting guest teachers who had taken her class and survived—repeating the tale to rural ballet school students all over the Midwest. Older siblings of ballet school friends may have come back from the summer course talking about how they had been "totally wrecked" by a tiny old Russian lady. The lore goes that just about anything could happen to a dancer in Tumey's class. You could pass out, throw up, shit yourself, or just drop dead from exhaustion.

Madame Tumkovsky was born in Kiev in 1905, which put her solidly in her nineties by the time I was in her charge. She was a soloist in the Kiev Ballet and eventually ended up in New York City in the late 1940s. Part of her folklore was that both of her precious feet were broken in her attempt to defect. No one knew how or exactly why. One broken foot is a ballerina's worst nightmare, but two broken feet? That's a dance tragedy of epic proportions. The story goes that Tumey (as we affectionately called her) approached Balanchine and asked him for a teaching gig. But first, she felt she must confess to him that she had only been a soloist, and never a "prima ballerina"! Balanchine, who was "only a soloist" himself, observed her teaching a class, liked what he saw, and hired her on the spot. Tumey went on to teach at SAB for over fifty years.

Ask any dancer, current or former, at any level, corps, soloist, or principal, about Tumey's class, and they will give you their own version of the same answer—it was motherfucking hard. The amount of strength, balance, technique, and jumping she loved to have us do pushed our bodies to the absolute limit. It wasn't just that the steps were hard, but they were strung together in absolutely brutal combinations that required serious grit of spirit. The physical exertion this entailed was extraordinary. Imagine running the New York City Marathon—you cross over the finish line. You're totally wiped, but hell yes, you made it! You're about to let yourself succumb to the pain and exhaustion, but then you're marched over to the starting line of a tough mudder. Now you'll scurry under barbed wire, hurl your body over walls, and leap through a ring of fire. Okay, you've finished that? Great. Now you can cool down by giving birth to twins. Did I mention that your face should be a picture of complete serenity during all of this? Ballerinas do not show pain, ever.

Sometimes Tumey's class would get the best of a dancer, and they'd decide to "take one for the team" and just fall. Drop to the ground, stage a slip—anything for a moment of respite from the brutal combination. When a ballerina lands on her ass during class, there's a pause. First, you're distracted. Oh, wait, who fell? The music stops and we make sure whoever went down is okay. The staged fall gave everyone a brief moment to recover. We always suspected Tumey knew the falls were fake, but she never said anything. During one extrapainful combo, my dorm mate Olivia and I tried to take the trickery up a notch. Our legs felt like overcooked spaghetti, so we moved across the floor just doing the arm movements, giving our legs a few precious seconds of recovery. We were busted immediately. "Get back to corner DO again!" Each word punctuated by an extra-heavy pounding of the cane. We might have messed around a little bit in Tumey's class (we were desperate), but you wouldn't dare show up at the last minute. You got there early and warmed up. You got your mind straight before it started. You mentally and physically prepared for what was to come. Only a fool would show up cold. Waltz in on time? You'd pay, with pain.

The bottom line? Every dancer in level six was just about pissing their pants to ride the roller-coaster ride that was Tumey's class. We all knew she was old, but that didn't stop us from being startled by her appearance. Tumey's spine was permanently curved, undoubtedly from years of burden, and her wrinkles were set so deeply they resembled thick, dark lines. Tumey was slow to move, but we watched her labored steps with awe. It was like Grandmother Willow, the all-knowing willow tree from *Pocahontas*, had just materialized in the middle of the goddamn rehearsal studio. Tumey's tiny frame was a vessel for everything we wanted to know. To be near her was to be near history, greatness, legacy, talent, excellence, and most of all . . . Balanchine. It felt like the seasons could change in the amount of time it took Tumey to get to her chair. One dancer wondered, quite reasonably, "Can she even see us?" As excited as we all were, I think it's possible we were all somewhat comforted by Tumey's ancient appearance. Tumey's impossible age combined with her smallness fooled each of us in level six into thinking we'd just blow right through her class. Look at her, obviously it couldn't be as challenging as we were led to believe! This sigh of relief was the last easy breath taken before the massive ass-handing that was about to occur. Tumey tossed a quick but knowing glance over to Katarina. Katarina started stroking those ivories, her sly grin suggesting she was incredibly excited to witness the torture to come. Tumey started tapping her cane. At that moment we were introduced to Tumey's own personal definition of hard, and it was like nothing any of us had ever felt before.

Tumey commanded the class with her cane; she barely needed to speak. She tapped out our marching orders, guiding the rhythm. She'd call out the combinations, her heavy Russian accent spread out over the French ballet terms, requiring almost a double translation in my head. I was keeping up, but just barely. It was fast and difficult. I scanned the room, honing my "fish-eye" skill—quickly seeking out the dancers who were more experienced, knew the combos, and whom I could safely use as a guide. As soon as we made it through one movement, Tumey would say, "Again. Again. Again," her commands punctuated with the pounding of that cane. This was a legit ballet class—actually a legit Russian ballet class. It wasn't just that the steps were hard, but the combinations she called out seemed intent on making us execute every single step known to the ballet in ninety minutes.

These exercises were meant to humble our bodies and build strength—all in sync with the speed of the music. The Balanchine style is always fused to music. That's because Balanchine's technique differed from other European styles of ballet. He was less concerned with plot and more concerned with the human body. His movements are quick; they require more speed, height, and length. Everything about the Balanchine technique is more. Use all the space! Move faster, plié deeper.

I willed my body to keep moving, and eventually the anxiety and lone-liness started to slide off my shoulders. The combination she was call-ing out was crazy-intense, like nothing I'd ever done before—but my body and soul were buzzing from delight. My homesickness faded. I no longer cared about who was taller, longer, more experienced, more talented, or had the right weird shoes. I wanted to throw myself all in. I was here to learn Balanchine's way, and if that meant busting my ass for the Michael "Mickey" Goldmill of ballet, well then, I was down. I wasn't going to crash, even though my legs felt like jelly. My body felt obliterated. My legs have never burned so hard.

When it was over, the relief was palpable. Dancers were stumbling all around the room. A few ballerinas had been reduced to tears—possibly from pain, or maybe sheer joy that it was finally over. Others seethed in what I imagined was a deep rage about what we were just put through, as if we were all being tested or shoved toward failure. My body was wiped out completely, and I *was* humbled. Just an hour and a half ago I wouldn't have believed I was capable of what I had just done. If I didn't drop dead from that, what else is possible? I acknowledged the dancer next to me with a pathetic limp of a wave. Our eyes locked for a quick second as if to say, "Holy shit, that was amazing," because neither of us was capable of speech yet. My classmates were splayed out all over the room and in different displays of shock and awe, like the eye of a hurricane had just swept over the rehearsal room. As my breath-ing returned to normal, I couldn't help but be humored by this crazy display of ballet carnage. I didn't cry, I wasn't enraged, but I was able to recognize those feelings as understandable. People react differently when pushed to the limit. Our ultrafit young bodies had just been torn apart by a woman who had more wrinkles than an ancient redwood had lines inside its trunk. I didn't cry then. I'd cry many times throughout my career, but this was one of those moments where I could stand back and say, This is just ballet class. It's just ballet. One class down, two more to go today. I didn't feel I had the luxury for tears quite yet.

I was still breathing heavily while I stuffed my belongings back into my bag, when the other dancers started to discreetly yet quickly wipe away their tears. I walked into the hallway, sweat still dripping from my body as the energy shifted from exhaustion to nervousness, and the whispering started. An incredibly tall man with blond hair loomed over two other people who were clearly dancers.

"That's Peter Martins!" a girl whispered, "and Darci Kistler and Jock Soto!" I got the feeling I was supposed to feel starstruck by this sighting, but I just moved on to my next class. I was ready to dance again.

Swan Dive #2

The scene is Mass at my Catholic middle school. If you haven't been to a Catholic Mass, you've probably seen enough movies to know that there is a lot of standing up. Followed by sitting down, only to stand up again—and of course there's plenty of kneeling thrown in as well. Father Desabito was getting ready for the ritual of transubstantiation, but during one of the ups and downs, I clipped my knee on the hymnal rack, where they keep the missalettes. I'm trying to recover and refocus on the Mass when the scene kaleidoscopes to black. I wake up sprawled out in the middle of the center aisle, my legs every which way and my Catholic uniform skirt in a very immodest mess, bringing the Mass to a dead halt.

Based on the shock-and-awe reaction from the parishioners, you'd think Jesus himself had just appeared. *Wow, how did I manage to pull focus from Jesus?* After I was helped up, I was given the option to receive the Eucharist. I accepted, even though I felt like I had usurped God's moment. The nurse called my mom after Mass and insisted I go home to rest. After a solid nap and a head start on homework, I was cleared by my mom to go to ballet class that night since I seemed no worse for wear. However, to this day I still pass out if my knee is nailed in that same spot. It doesn't take much. It doesn't even have to hurt, but clip me in the knee and it's a TKO. Sorry, Jesus . . .

CHAPTER 5

Home

Dogs? Love them. Food? Sometimes it's better than sex, if I'm being brutally honest. And people? The jury is still out on whether or not I qualify as a people person. While that verdict remains outstanding, I nevertheless seem to exude the sort of energy that announces, "I am approachable. Please feel free to interrupt my rushed commute to ask me for directions, restaurant recommendations, relationship advice, or just go ahead and share your entire life story." Maybe it's the Catholic girl in me, but I stop to help or listen. I also have the ability to dial up the charm when I need to. If I have an opportunity to flash my wit, even better. Shove me in a room with a dozen of the ballet's biggest donors and I'll shine. Members of the board, little kids, choreographers, the elderly, celebrities, stagehands, dog owners, bartenders, or random people I encounter on the street—I can manage a chat with any of them.

But I was noticeably quiet at SAB. I wasn't there to bewitch anyone with my sparkling personality. At that point, any personality I had was about as loud as a polite whisper—barely audible. I wasn't trying to be mean either; this was about self-protection. Intuition has always been one of my sharpest secret weapons. I understood that strength, both mental and physical, was the key ingredient for learning the Balanchine technique. The competition was the heaviest I had encountered, and if I wanted to survive, I needed to set my default to introvert.

Focus, Gina was my mantra. It was the fucking ballet summer *intensive*, after all, so I got intense about it. Everything was on the line, yet nothing was on the line. I was dancing with the best of the best—intense! But in reality, I was a fourteen-year-old girl who would soon return to her comfortable suburban home, where she would be welcomed by loving parents even if she was the biggest embarrassment the School of American Ballet had ever seen. Everything and nothing. I knew this was true, but I chose to turn up the volume on the drama and dance like my life depended on it. This wasn't a studio in a repurposed church in Pennsylvania—this was the real deal. Ballerinas were christened here! The pressure *was on*. I became a blank canvas, wiping my personality clean away in the process. I was all about ballet (and attacking that summer reading list). I got myself to bed at 10:30 so I could wake up and get to class early. I'd be the first one to arrive in the empty studio at 9 a.m. for a 10:30 plié start time. I'd plop down on the floor and crack open my copy of *War and Peace*. I'd absorb as much as I could of Natasha, Pierre, and the Prince until it was time to strip off my T-shirt and claim my favorite place at the barre. Once class started, I was enthralled. Every day was another lesson in how my body could do new things if asked.

Variation class blew my mind. Learning a variation means you're learning a solo from an actual ballet. I got to dance the principal woman's solo from Balanchine's ballet aptly entitled *Theme and Variations*. It's performed to the last movement of Tchaikovsky's Suite no. 3 for Orchestra in G Major, and it's a short, dynamic little ditty. The variation starts off with some bourrées and then gradually increases in speed as the orchestra really starts to swell. Then there's a diagonal combination of Italian grands pas de chat that move into switch crossed fourths en pointe that change directions so fast you could easily tear an adductor muscle. This feisty combo repeats itself three times. The final portion of the variation has one last shift in direction into regular pas de chat—and then oh, watch out! . . . because here comes a fifth double turn repeated another three times! And hold on to your hats, bitches, because now I'm traveling directly across the front of the room, and this is all going to get wrapped up in a glorious sequence of piqué turns, then a chaîné step-up double turn—and then I'm going to land in a regal fourth. It's basically Nancy Sinatra's "These Boots Are Made for Walkin'" come to life, except instead of boots, pointe shoes. This variation is a spectacular display of technique for the female principal of this ballet. Executing the moves made the hair on the back of my neck stand up faster than any sweet whispers into my ear from any lover ever would these days.

After successfully completing this variation in a group with two other dancers, I walked over to the barre. I needed a minute to recover. I closed my eyes, completely giving myself over to the experience, letting my body revel in what it had just accomplished. At that moment, Balanchine equaled pure bliss for me.

Then I felt something behind me. When I opened my eyes, I jumped. A fantastically tall and pale dancer stood behind me in the mirror like a ghost. I got the feeling she had been standing there for a while. I was completely immersed in my own ballet-induced euphoria. *Did everyone have this same feeling?* I was just starting to make my way back to earth so I could evaluate the next group of dancers who were going to take a stab at the variation. Pale ghost girl, whom I recognized from the cafeteria, spoke, "Hey. I just wanted to tell you that those turns at the end of your variation were really amazing and spot-on. You really nailed it." In stunned silence, I stared back at her perfect ectomorph limbs and wide smile that was noticeably free of braces. *Did this chick just pay me a compliment?* I really wasn't trying to be a dick, but I was definitely on high alert. Was there a hidden subtext? What's the etiquette here? Is it my turn to pay her a compliment? She does have really good-looking feet. What's stuck in my braces? Is that an apple peel? *Shit*. I was instantly self-conscious about the garden growing across my teeth, and I closed my mouth. I never complimented her on her wonderful croissant-shaped feet. I might have muttered a thank-you at the very least, but the thick layer of competitiveness I wore like a parka kept me from accepting a simple and sincere compliment. Instead my instincts told me to get over to the other side of the room before this crazy-good ballerina made me look less-than. Or maybe her true intentions were to cut me down. I just felt plain distrustful. What kind of girl wears a bun every single day, avoids solid foods, and carries around a bike tire at all times in case they want to stop what they're doing and use it to stretch their body in a manner that suggests they were born without ligaments? I moved away before this gorgeous creature could whip out her bike tire and transform her stretch-a-tron into some sort of slingshot that could take me out in a ballet-themed version of Tonya versus Nancy.

The name of the game for me that summer was survival. I was too busy wondering how these alien ladies might try to thwart me to even think about making friends.

I knew I had acted icy around the other girls, but after class when I told them where I was going that night, they still responded with wide eyes and giggling.

"You're going to dinner with Jared tonight? Shut up!" We were gathered in front of the mirror in the communal bathroom. I was getting ready, which consisted of plucking food scraps out of my gigantic braces, sweeping my hair into a ponytail, and putting on my coolest top and kicks. I slipped on my black halter, which was dotted with red cherries, and inserted my sore feet into a pair of tie-dyed Keds. Another dancer, freshly showered, was combing through her wet hair while bouncing up and down on the balls of her feet with excitement. "He's soooo cute!" Correction. Jared is not cute. Jared Angle is as dapper as they come. He is positively drop-dead movie-star gorgeous, and here I must pause and send a heartfelt thanks to any of those dancers who were present in the bathroom that day: that swoon-worthy Jared Angle was taking my ugly-duckling ass out on the town was actually hilarious, but no one laughed.

To me Jared was my best friend Tyler's big brother. He was taking me to dinner out of the kindness of his heart and most likely out of some sense of obligation. We were both from Altoona, and we both trained at Allegheny. Over the years, my mom had gone from wanting as little to do with the Allegheny ballet school as possible to devoting her spare time to being a den mother to everyone in our preprofessional Motley Dance Crue. She was also an unofficial seamstress of the ballet, along with Tyler and Jared's mom, Barb, and Miranda's mom, Judy. My mom surely called Barb and asked, "Would your son please make sure my little vampire of a daughter actually leaves the studio and sees the light of day while she's in New York?"

Jared was talented, handsome, and an easy first crush for the girls of SAB. He was also the living embodiment of a ballerina's dream—he had arrived at SAB a few years ago just like us and was now a bona fide member of the New York City Ballet. To me, he existed in a different universe—he was Prince Albrecht in our ballet's version of *Giselle*. He was bound for greatness! When he left Altoona for SAB, it was like he was going to another planet. What he was accomplishing with his talent seemed unreachable to me. And now his status as an honest-to-God professional dancer put him in an entirely new category. Even more mind-blowing to me, Jared lived in Manhattan. He was away from home, living like an adult. Buying groceries, paying bills, making meals, cleaning up—ballet was hard enough without the added pressures of regular life. During a break between his rehearsal and that night's show, Jared picked me up outside of the dorm and walked me over to Pomodoro, an Italian joint nearby. This was something I could barely comprehend. How do you go out for a casual Italian meal when you're going to be dancing in front of an audience in just a couple of hours? We sat down, ordered our food, and I immediately felt the relief that comes from familiarity. Jared might have been hot by traditional standards, and he might have been a professional ballet dancer, but at that moment he was exactly what I needed: a friend from home.

Jared took a bite of his salad and looked at me. "How's your summer going, Gina?" I finally felt like I was able to talk. "It's been, well, it's been eye-opening. I'm learning a lot. The classes are wicked hard and fast, and my inner thighs still burn from Tumey's class. I love it!" I felt myself blush in the most minor way. *Was it weird that I mentioned my thighs?* I quickly jumped back into our conversation, adding an emphatic, "The teachers here are so great!" It felt like I hadn't talked to anyone in ages. Now that I'd started, I couldn't seem to stop. I muted myself by inserting a large forkful of spaghetti into my metal-laden mouth. It was like the bowl of spaghetti in front of me represented freedom. There were no other dancers around; no one was watching me. No one was staring at me and my pasta like we were prey to be pounced on by a pack of starving hyenas. Some of the young women in the summer program were clearly battling the classic power duo of the ballet world: body dysmorphia and her sidekick, the eating disorder. Witnessing their tension around food made me doubt if I was built for this kind of pressure.

Jared gestured for the check and paid the bill like a real live adult. On the walk back I grilled him about the different roles he was learning and which ones he'd soon be performing. He was brimming with positivity, opportunity, and potential. I felt a twinge of jealousy. I wanted to be where he was. But could I ever make it in New York City, much less as a dancer? The subway tokens jingling along in my pocket were a constant reminder that I couldn't even summon the inner courage to ride the subway. Was it possible to exist in New York City and never leave the few blocks surrounding Lincoln Center? Who needs to go downtown anyway? Jared dropped me back off at the dorms and went to get ready for his performance. It was early enough that the sky was still light. Sharing a meal and chatting with someone I could trust was like a balm. I was temporarily soothed. I slipped into my pajamas and plopped on my bed. I was still working my way through my summer reading list from school. I opened up *To Kill a Mockingbird* and out dropped a Post-it with a quote I had written down from the text: "Courage is not a man with a gun in his hand. It's knowing you're licked before you begin but you begin anyway and you see it through no matter what. You rarely win, but sometimes you do." On some level I understood what he was saying. Was I going to win? Right now, all these years later? I still don't know that answer. But it's not really about winning, is it? I read as many pages as I could before my exhausted body fell into a heavy sleep.

* * *

The carefully planned excursions were meant to be a fun addition to an exciting summer learning ballet in New York City. Soon we'd all be heading home, and our friends and family weren't likely to be wowed solely by the trials and tribulations from our five weeks of studying the Balanchine technique. But oh, you walked all the way to the top of the Statue of Liberty? That's so cool. The excursions gave us a taste of some of New York City's classic tourist attractions like Ellis Island and a Yankees game. I skipped the baseball game; two decades later and I have still not crossed "attend baseball game" off the life list. I grew up watching Benny Hill, Mr. Bean, and Lucille Ball with my dad, so being the little oddball that I was I opted for the excursion to Rodney Dangerfield's comedy club. "Just because nobody complains doesn't mean all parachutes are perfect," said Benny Hill. I figured since I was batting zero in the making-friends department, I could at least connect with the other smart-asses who might be hanging at a comedy club. I was by far the youngest person in the group of eight, and none of the other attendees were dancers, just chaperones and volunteers from the SAB summer program. In other words, I tried to have fun with the other dancers, but once again I missed the mark (but I did laugh a lot).

SAB wanted us to have fun when we weren't in the studio dancing. The thought of focusing on fun was a relief for me. I was being forced out of my shell at a rate that was much faster than I had anticipated, and fun sounded like just the right medicine. The excursions also likely helped curb the temptation for any of us (or at least those who weren't terrified of the city) to step out-of-bounds. Students under eighteen at the summer course had a curfew of 9 p.m., and my mom made me swear I'd stay in the confines of Seventy-Second Street and Fifty-Ninth Street. Surely nothing could go wrong for a young girl alone in New York City as long as she stayed within those thirteen blocks. My mom had no idea that one of the roughest tenement houses was situated within the "safe" boundaries right off Amsterdam and Sixty-Fifth Street. Just a few years ago, a dancer had been mugged and punched in the eye, which seems not only awful but also unfair. Why the eye?! The person can still identify your ass with one functioning cornea. I also made a point to never ever mention the characters that were sprinkled along Columbus Circle. Despite her fear of highway driving, my mom would have jumped in the minivan and picked me up faster than you can say "gentrification" or "seven-figure condo." Those excursions were the only times I left our designated little square of Manhattan that summer. I rarely left Lincoln Center, and the only place I felt comfortable going alone was to see the soup cart guy because he was known to the other dancers, and it was safely confined in bounds.

The Statue of Liberty was going to be our last excursion for the summer. As the ferry cut through the water of New York Harbor toward Liberty Island, my ponytail repeatedly whipped me in the face, causing my eyes to well up with tears. I relished in the poetic nature of this minor sacrifice on my voyage into history. The other dancers sat up straight around me; their tidy buns kept their hair perfectly restrained. Ellis Island is an incredible history lesson, and I'm into history. However, as any semiseasoned New Yorker can tell you, this is the wrong activity to do in late July. It's high tourist season, which means it's crazy-crowded. The air is sticky and thick with a permanent smell of crotch. But as we got closer to Lady Liberty, I was filled with awe and thought, *That is one hell of a gift*. I suddenly wanted to get closer. My body had taught me it could take a beating or two over the past few weeks, so surely the climb up to her crown would be easy-peasy. Twenty stories? No problem. I started up the 354 steps to the top. The stairway is only nineteen inches wide and the ceiling is just a titch over six feet high. The journey to the top is like a deadly cocktail of heat stroke, claustrophobia, and vertigo, topped off with a big fat garnish of regret. There's really nothing to exalt at the crown; there's just a tiny, dirty sliver of a window that's almost impossible to see out of. If you're seeking a view perched above the river, this attraction *just does not deliver*.

By the time I made it out, I was just happy I didn't bust a classic Gina fall on my way down, breaking every single bone in my promising young body. I could imagine the sad headline in the *New York Post*, with a picture of my six-year-old self in a bedazzled tutu that would become the face of unspeakable tragedy: "Swan Dive: Baby Ballerina Trips to Her Death in New York City Tourist Attraction." The thought of stairwells or close quarters with strangers gives me chills to this day. I was rattled by the journey, but I made it out alive. Standing back down at the pedestal, I looked up toward the crown, where I had just been. It looked impossibly high. I could barely even see it, the sun was so bright. It had been unpleasant at times—the quarters were tight, it smelled, I was scared, but I had made it there and back. And now I had another story to tell, and some Polish tourists had taught me a few good swear words. "O, kurwa!"

I was exhausted on the boat ride back, and I looked out at the skyline while the other dancers chatted and laughed. Yesterday afternoon, Kay Mazzo, one of the teachers and heads of the school, had asked to speak to me in her office. I was petrified that I accidentally didn't pay for that second bagel I took in the cafeteria yesterday. Maybe she saw? Or maybe this had to do with my stretching the SAB dress code by wearing the requisite black leo, but one with flashy red trim? I must have done something else wrong. She's a fine teacher, but I found her condescending in class. When she gave us corrections, her delivery and tone of voice made it sound like she was scolding a group of kindergartners, so I wasn't sure to expect when I sat down.

"Georgina, it's been great having you here. You've really absorbed the Balanchine technique even in this very short time. You've worked hard and you show great promise. We'd like to offer you a scholarship to stay for the winter term."

So, this wasn't about the bagel. My heart and stomach flip-flopped in unison—and I realized how much I wanted this, how absolutely in love I was with ballet. The Balanchine technique had taken this love to a deeper level that I couldn't have anticipated in my basement classroom in Altoona. I was so flattered, I was overwhelmed, and I didn't know what to do.

A day later, as the ferry tore through the water, blowing cool wind across my hot face, I thought about what the future might hold. My parents wouldn't understand most of my ballet triumphs this summer, but they would be excited to hear about my 354-step perilous climb up to the crown. This summer had been different—no swim team ribbons, no gardening and running wild until darkness fell, and certainly no missions to steal rhubarb from the neighbors. But I felt a sense of accomplishment like I had never felt before. Completing Tumey's class, alone, was a feat to be acknowledged. For the first time in my life, I was tearing through pointe shoes. I knew nothing of Tumey's past, and I didn't understand a word of the Russian phrases she tossed around liberally, almost as if she were speaking to herself. But it was clear she was a fantastically strong woman. I felt drawn to her. I loved her intensity because she matched my intensity. More importantly, it was clear that the intensity of the School of American Ballet matched my intensity, and this was weirdly comforting.

It turned out that Tyler, Miranda, and I weren't the only little freaks who put ballet on a pedestal—the School of American Ballet had an entire factory of young hopefuls who felt the exact same way. There was no question; nothing was taken more seriously here than ballet. I looked at the girls around me, and while I didn't easily fit in with them, I knew that we shared one common bond—none of us viewed ballet as an after-school hobby. Ballet came first for all of us. I was buzzing all over with a warm feeling. I was in a place where people could provide me with a direct path to a career as a ballerina, and I was starting to suspect this might be what I wanted. It was like I had gotten a sense of what my hard crush would be like later on as a true life partner, and I liked it. The stakes were starting to mount for me in this relationship, and I was ready to give it my all. We got back to the dorms right before dinner that night, and I wanted to find Kay. I wanted to tell her how much I appreciated their offer, and that this summer opened my mind (and body) to a new world of dance. I was going to keep pushing, striving, and growing, but I was going to do it at home near my family and friends. New York City and the School of American Ballet would have to wait for me. I wasn't ready to settle down just yet.

Swan Dive #3

"Ya dead, mon?" I asked, hoping our inside joke would elicit a response from Miranda and indicate in fact that she wasn't dead. The last sound I heard from my best friend as I was frantically trying to grab the sheet that had come untied from my twin bed while she was rappelling herself down from the second-story window was "Oh, shit!" followed by a crash and a thud. Of course, our first-ever attempt at mischief would end in one of us dying tragically. The second-floor window of the beach condo our family had rented really wasn't that high! As soon as I felt the panic start to rise up in my throat, I heard Miranda's voice reciting the next line from *Cool Runnings*, "Nah, mon." *Oh, thank effing God*. I did not want to have to wake up my trauma-surgeon father to tell him my best friend had severed her spine while we were trying to sneak out to a lifeguard's house party.

"But Gina"—she stood up slowly, assessing the miraculously minimal number of flesh wounds—"I smashed a plastic lawn chair with my body. Quit pussyfooting and get down here so we can go."

I had just finished my second summer course at SAB and had brought Miranda, basically an adopted family member whom I had been danc- ing with since I was *tiny*-tiny, along on the family vacation. The August trip to Bethany Beach, Delaware, is a treasured Pazcoguin tradition. Long days at the beach, giant buckets of warm caramel corn, even bigger buckets of salty boardwalk fries, and of course, bushels of blue crab. The entire Pazcoguin family (as well as spouses and friends for a ridiculous grand total of people) were packed into a three-bedroom condo—sand strewn and wall-to-wall covered in sleeping bags. That summer, Miranda and I were as boy crazy as ever. I slid out of the win- dow as agile as a cat but then froze. Hanging on with my chin hovering just above the window, I was suddenly afraid to move.

"Dude, you gonna catch me?"

"Just let go, Spider-Woman." Miranda was laughing at my predicament. I released my grip and flew backward into the air, landing directly on top of Miranda and a pile of destroyed lawn furniture.

We were on the prowl. I was seventeen years old, adventurous and charged, and ready to shed the label of "virgin." We walked along the beach, the moonlight practically providing our very own path to the party. Once we arrived, we got situated among strangers. Miranda was instantly approached by the indie bohemian hottie she'd scouted earlier in the week. I had my eye on the poster boy for all lifeguards. He liked *SNL* and football. But what he lacked in charm he made up for with a gorgeous six-foot-four physique. When we told them we studied ballet, did they smirk—exchange glances? I can't recall. But later in the evening we were invited by Miranda's new chap to his grandparents' two-bedroom condo overlooking the ocean, and we all had the same goal in mind.

Miranda and I were a team in this venture. She was more experienced in this field. She had mentored me on how to handle the basics but insisted I keep her posted. As things started to heat up, I tore myself away from my lifeguard to check in with Miranda, who was zeroing in on her bull's-eye. I knocked on the closed door and heard "One sec!" Miranda appeared at the door wrapped in a sheet.

"Hey, Casanova, how ya doing over there?"

I laughed nervously.

"Hey," she said. "It's going to be okay. I'm literally right here if anything should happen. I'm serious; knock three times and we'll scoot."

She handed me a few condoms. "Make him wrap it up. Now go, my little flower! Blossom!" She sent me off armed with prophylactics and encouragement.

Getting back IN to our condo and past all the sleeping Pazcoguins was another story . . . but, finally home, we threw ourselves into our twin beds. As I was falling asleep, my best friend pissed from our harrowing return home but still sticking beside me, I felt ready for what was next. I had decided to pass on the rest of a normal high school experience. I was moving to New York City to study ballet full-time in the fall. I'd sure as hell made the most of my last summer as a relatively normal teen. When I got back to SAB, on the first day of fall class, one of my male dancer friends said to me, "You look different, Gina." Mission accomplished.

CHAPTER 6

You Don't Fit In
(from Here to There)

The waiting room was quiet. I was the only one there. The chairs were made of soft leather that nestled my body, tempering my anxiety just the slightest bit. The magazines were glossy and crisp, as if they'd never been opened. There weren't any whining, sniffling kids or harried moms sitting around like there would have been at the doctor's office I went to in Altoona. When I told Mel about the conversation I had just had with Peter and Rosemary, she shot me a sympathetic look and said, "Oh, you need to go see Dr. Wilcox right on West Sixty-Fourth Street.* He's helped some other dancers."

Doc Wil had the power to solve my problem. It was a problem I had no idea even existed until my January 2002 midyear review with Peter and Rosemary. Since apprentices are by definition on a trial run, we had reviews to discuss our progress. At that time, apprentices were the only people in the company to have an official review. If a dancer wanted an *unofficial review*, Peter claimed that his door was "always open." But

---

* This is not his real name, FYI. You don't need his real name.

it was generally understood that if you walked through that door, you had somehow effed up. "No word was good word" was the line we were supposed to follow, but I have found that "no word" in general does not work for a) women, or b) artists, and lastly, c) people who want to excel at their jobs. If you entered his office for a conversation about your dancing, it was at your own risk. If you were *summoned* by Peter, that was a sign of dark things to come. But all my eighteen-year-old self knew going into that meeting was that there were nine other apprentices, and no one had come out of their meeting ugly-crying, swearing, or throwing objects. As far as I knew, everyone else's review went great, so shouldn't mine go the same way?

* * *

"Are you happy here, Georgina?" The question was asked by a stone-faced Rosemary. She had the ability to flip between guardian and adversary watchdog in a snap. Each word she spoke suggested grave concern for my well-being. I was too young to know better. I had worked hard and was learning how to handle the demands of being a dancer and an almost adult. Just a few months ago I had bid adieu to Altoona, my family, and my Catholic high school to become a full-time student at SAB. As an apprentice, the next step for me would be a contract to be in the corps de ballet. Getting into the corps would mean I was an official member of the company. This club I so desperately wanted to join was so exclusive it was akin to the secret society Skull and Bones. You could do your best to work all the gifts you've naturally got, but ultimately no one really knew why some got tapped on the shoulder and others were passed over. The level of competition to get into the corps isn't normal—it's not conducive to operating with a regular amount of human spirit. You've got to fight for respect, fight for a chance to show your value. You can't stand in another dancer's shadow and hope you'll still shine.

Being in the corps at City Ballet is extra special in that Balanchine's choreography leans heavily on the corps dancers. This specialized group of dancers aren't used as just a backdrop. Other companies might relegate corps dancers to basic roles like "elderly peasant person wearing burlap sack" or "blade of grass," but that wasn't the case at all at City Ballet. Balanchine knew the corps could be the company's secret sauce. Imagine eating a big, fat, juicy burger that's bursting with umami flavor. Sure, it's possible the burger would be pretty effing good on its own with your basic ketchup and mustard situation, hell, maybe a sliced pickle. But you know damn well that it's umami flavor that's responsible for that party in your mouth, making you want to take one big bite after the other until it's gone. Remove the spirit of the corps from a Balanchine production, and what you'll get is bravura without context.

Whether dancing myself, or the few times I get to watch from the audience, the heroism of the corps de ballet is awe-inspiring to me—the corps is dancing their asses off for the full forty-minute ballet that makes Balanchine ballets so gratifying to watch (and to perform). Yes, the principal work and choreography can be stunning, too (and hard AF), but I swear to God it is much easier to dance as a single unit or as part of a couple than it is to dance in an ensemble. For example, you can't just make up an arm or hold balance when you are dancing in the corps of *Concerto Barocco*. The eight corps ladies stay onstage for a full twenty minutes of dancing—there's no popping offstage to dab the sweat off your face, or once, in my case, to pull the nail out of my motherfucking foot.

I have always loved *Concerto Barocco*. The simplicity of the costuming—plain white leo with a skirt and pink tights—coupled with the beauty of Bach's violin concerto and Balanchine's genius syncopated choreography is the perfect mix of classical and modern. The corps dancers start onstage and begin dancing as soon as the curtain goes up. It's classical—the choreography is strenuous, or as we like to say, *It's puffy*. The second act gives the dancers an opportunity to regain their stamina because then the third movement is all grand allegro in different formation changes. In other words, we are hopping all over the place en pointe. It's a mesmerizing series.

I am tenduing on the four count, when I'm like, *What the hell is that?* This is hurting way more than it should. My brain is quickly flipping through my catalog of pain as I continue to hop on the very tips of my toes, not missing a single beat . . . *This isn't joint pain, and it doesn't feel like a stress fracture.* I am still moving when it occurs to me what this fresh helluva new pain is . . . some sort of foreign object. It is in my shoe, and whatever it is has embedded itself into the flesh (highly callused, mind you) between my big toe and the next piggy.

I don't have time to think about what it is because the principal dancers are now onstage and that series of hops has to be REPEATED. A single slow tear falls from the corner of my eye, and I swear something is now puncturing bone. At the end of the movement, which marks the end of the ballet, I'm supposed to walk en pointe crossing fifth and execute one final entrechat six jump that takes me to a pose on the knee. I manage to finish the dance, and the curtain mercifully closes. There isn't enough time to fix whatever it is before curtain call, so in an act of desperation I remove the heel from my shoe for the bow.

That's when I see what it is—an effing nail. With every hop en pointe, I have essentially been hammering a nail directly into my foot.

The shanks of our beautifully handmade pointe shoes (our shoes are crafted for the needs of our own unique feet—my shoemaker's symbol is the Maltese cross, which is stamped on the bottom of all of my shoes) are held together by a series of tacks. When I broke my shoe in, I must have done it in a way that loosened a tack. God bless my calluses. I can't imagine how this would have felt if I had the tender feet of a nondancer. Once curtain call was finally over, I cut the threads holding my ribbons neatly tucked at my ankle, sat down, and guffawed at what I just lived through. I pulled that nail out of my flesh; "You bitch!" I yelled at it as I threw it into the garbage and grabbed an individual pack of Advil from the massive Costco-sized box backstage.

Freak pointe-shoe accidents aside, the corps really is the heart of City Ballet; they are the tour de force that supports the soloists and principal dancers. Take *Serenade*: it's a beautiful ballet, and it's that umami flavor of the corps that makes it so delectable. *Serenade* is the first Balanchine ballet ever presented in America, debuting in 1934. The ballet starts off with twenty-eight dancers, and some of the antics with the corps were worked right into the piece. When Balanchine started out, he was working with a somewhat ragtag group of dancers. As the rehearsal period went on, fewer dancers showed up. I guess they either threw in the towel or just had something better to do. *Who knows?* As the ballet progresses the number of dancers on the stage is reduced. But that's not all. The legend goes that one day a dancer showed up late, and one time a dancer fell on her ass. Both of these moments were worked into *Serenade* in a gloriously graceful way. Balanchine let the corps inspire this piece, and there's undeniably something special about it. When I would finally dance the role of one of the Russian girls, I found it immensely empowering. Just making it through those dances is a true test of wills. What a push to finish! But back then, just the thought of being in the corps at City Ballet was deliciously appealing because it meant I would actually get to use my talents; it involved honest-to-God dancing! That ballet could be my actual job blew my mind. I couldn't imagine an alternative. More traditional paths like *high-school-college-law-school-pass-the-bar-work-at-a-huge-firm-get-married-have-kids* just didn't seem like a path I could walk down. I was meant to move and perform and doing so in a courtroom or a boardroom held no appeal at all, even though my parents continually reminded me that these were valid options. If either of those paths involved raucous applause after defying the laws of physics, well then, maybe. But I'd rather machete my way through the path forged by so few.*

---

* There is a maximum of ten apprenticeships, but guess what? Some years no one is selected.

Rosemary's question, "Are you happy here?" hung heavy in the air, and I sensed a darkness in her tone. Foreboding. I was suddenly very, very uncomfortable. It was like the sudden descent of fog when the young couple parks their car in the woods during a horror film. You know their make-out session will be interrupted by a crazed serial killer who just escaped from the local mental hospital and made a beeline to the first parked car they saw, pausing only to obtain a sharp knife.

Was I happy here? The question took me by surprise. I was one of the youngest members of one of the best ballet companies in the world. I had been dancing since I was four years old, living *the dream* of any young girl who had ever slipped on a pair of pointe shoes. It was beyond tough: the competition and stress, the jealousy and judgment, and living in a big city on my own without my family around to provide comfort and continuity. I had also been force-fed a big-ass piece of humble pie. I had been happily perched on top of the totem pole at my school in Pennsylvania and then again at SAB only to be plucked out and tossed into an ocean of talent with a set of starkly different and severe rules. It often felt like I was swimming with sharks. On top of all this, September 11 had completely unnerved me. I had a stress fracture in my foot—even though I didn't let it stop me from performing in a workshop. I was up against a wall of challenges and trying to keep it all under the radar. All of this change took its toll and required adjustment. Still, I knew there was no other place I'd rather be.

"Why yes, I'm very happy here." I smiled big, hoping to put an immediate end to the conversation, but Rosemary persisted.

"Well. Georgina, it just doesn't seem like you fit in."

It felt like my heart was beating right out of my black leo. *Holy shit, am I going to get kicked out? Have I reached the pinnacle of my career at the age of eighteen?* My mind was racing, as I thought I had been dancing really well. I had won the Wein Award for outstanding promise! It suddenly seemed haughty of me to think this mattered so much. How could I have believed that if I could just learn to dance my parts, never get injured or miss a class or rehearsal, I'd be just fine? I could practically hear my parents slowly chanting, "Georgina! Go to college. Law school, Georgina. Anything with a degree!" The idea of swapping work at the barre for studying *for* the bar made me queasy; it just wasn't who I was. Self-doubt had tackled me to the ground, and questions about where I went wrong kept flying around in my brain. But Peter's next comment put an end to my inner questioning.

"Georgina." The low baritone of his voice was unmistakable, and the way he pronounced my name always felt heavy, like I should listen very carefully to what he said next. His voice always came like a rolling wave of thunder—imagine being scolded by Zeus and Satan simultaneously.

"It's that you don't really fit in from here"—he pointed to my knee with an unusually long index finger—"to there," he said, pointing to what I only could interpret to be my ass.

His comment delivered a jolt to my system, and I finally saw with complete clarity what this conversation was really about. It was definitely not about my happiness . . . it was about my thighs. *Oh damn, Gina, welcome to your first fat talk!*

The arrival of my first fat talk was a shock. You know those effortlessly chic women you see running loose here on the streets of New York City? Hair and makeup are perfect in that natural, I-don't-really-even-need-to-try kind of way. Her clothes are artsy but expensive, and she carries a hardcover copy of *Ulysses* in one hand and a fucking baguette in the other. But just as you're taking in the entire pretty picture of this creature, a speeding taxi turns the corner and runs her over flat. There goes that baguette!

This is what that conversation was like. It was a full-on *What the hell, is this actually happening?* moment. I was an apprentice with nine other dancers, and their reviews all went fine! How am I being singled out for being the fatty?

Fat talks are almost a rite of passage at the New York City Ballet and come with alarming regularity. I had certainly heard the chatter about fat talks in the rehearsal studio. I had heard of ballerinas being admonished for not snapping back to pre-baby weight just weeks after giving birth. I'd seen the reediest of dancers crying after rehearsal because they've been conditioned to believe that all that stood between them and a promotion, or their dream role, were two to three pesky pounds. Einstein was right when he said, "Dancers are the athletes of God." Members of the New York City Ballet are as fit as—if not fitter than—any professional sports athlete. Tom Brady? We could totally take him. It's just that no one thinks about ballerinas that way, since we don't make big salaries or get lucrative contracts to put our name on trendy athleisure wear. Well, at least most of us ... Misty is an exception, and good on her. And here I was being told that the part of my body that allows me to leap and soar kept me from "fitting in." And suddenly I'm not an athlete of God. I'm a lazy woman with too much flesh who is in jeopardy of watching her career, as fragile as a bubble, just pop. Poof. Game over. I was never told, "Lose weight, or you're done." But the suggestion came through loud and clear when Peter drew a line in the air, highlighting my upper thighs.

At this point it is necessary for me to say that ballet is an aesthetic art form. Ballet is about *line*. Ballet and the honing of the instrument, which in this case is one's own body, requires an absolute specificity. In the training of a young dancer, every fiber of muscle is toned, working toward creating a beautiful "line." This does not simply mean that the skin and bones are a stick-straight line—this isn't about having amazing posture that would make any mother proud, although that is a by-product. In ballet, the beauty of the line encompasses the complete picture from the tip of the toe to the turn of the cheek, aura included. The line is meant to be a full-on experience of the human body, designed in a way that is pleasing to the eye, but beyond the cognitive response of your brain thinking, *Huh. I don't think having your foot that close to your ear is normal.* Beautiful line makes watching ballet seamless. It encompasses that just-perfect combination that makes the experience unforgettable. Think the loud crack of a baseball bat that charges the stadium with an energy that signals, *Whoa, dude just hit a home run*. Your body is out of the seat cheering, your beer splashing before the ball lands in the bleachers (and nope, I still haven't gone to a game). Perfect line is like Maria Callas belting out, "Tu tu! Piccolo Iddio!" The little hairs on the back of your neck stand up, and you can completely ignore the fact that Madame Butterfly just blindfolded her child, snuck behind a screen, and stabbed herself in the heart after telling her kid to go play. Perfect line is Yma Sumac hitting F#6—making you forget what you had for breakfast that morning. When I experience beautiful line, it truly, truly moves me. I've always imagined it's the equivalent of what a man feels when the love of his life walks into a room. Rendered speechless? Overcome? Beautiful line casts a spell—it's emotional, romantic, powerful. It's everything.

But make no mistake, line is not a universal thing. Line is specific to the individual and should not be compared to anyone else. However, it is a quantifiable thing to each individual dancer. And because aesthetics is an important component to line, that can mean a weight talk is necessary if you're not looking your best. To be clear, I don't mean a dancer should get a fat talk if they went hog wild and ate a grilled cheese sandwich after a show on a Friday night. We can handle the occasional grilled cheese. But if your line is off, really *really* off—and this happens to the best of us—then a conversation could be in order. It's part of the job; it comes with the territory of being a professional ballerina. But fat talks at City Ballet under Peter's reign had a deeper meaning. What actions you took after your fat talk were a measurement of your loyalty. How badly do you want it and how far are you willing to go for it? Peter had a type—the most ethereal, Eurocentric attributes wrapped up in an "all-American" package.

He seemed to want a plain Jane he could mold into some sort of Super Ballerina, a caricature. Taking steps to manage your weight on top of all the other demands of being a professional dancer was proof you could handle your place in the company. Extra pounds, an illness, or, God forbid, an injury was proof you didn't have the wherewithal to stick around. Normal human experiences such as temporary period bloat or having a baby were understood by the dancers to be a blatant defiance impacting Peter's ability to have the ultimate control over your artistic life. But if you managed to morph yourself into one of Peter's Super Ballerinas (and had been further blessed with blonde hair, blue eyes, and long limbs), City Ballet was your oyster. You'd keep getting the good roles as long as you stayed in his good graces. The irony here is that although Peter only controlled the artistic side of a dancer's life, just being a dancer informs your life choices by default.

What's so wrong about this is that Balanchine himself appreciated diversity of line. Balanchine was before my time, and I never had the opportunity to work with him directly. Was he perfect when it came to his attitudes toward women's bodies? Very probably not. Actually, I'm just going to go ahead and say no. I mean, he gave each of his ballerinas a specific perfume to wear so he could smell them coming and going. Romantic? HA. Whatever your allegiance to the genius, we are definitely crossing over into a dark grey area there.

But I believe he understood that a ballerina's body was only comparable *to that body*. It's impossible to match the line of another dancer. The Balanchine technique we've all honed is used to create a semblance in movement quality, but each dancer has their own damn line. We are not all ectomorphs; we are not all tall or blonde—but every single dancer at City Ballet is a force of nature.

At seventeen, my dream was right there for the taking—but as far as I understood in Peter's office that day, it was only mine for the taking if I could slim down, match an idealized version of a ballerina who looked nothing like me. I thought about Savannah and Maria, Wendy and Merrill, the reediest, longest, and thinnest ballerinas. Is this who I needed to be? Did I need to erase my ethnicity, my hair, my coloring, and now my body to be deemed acceptable? I had no idea that Peter and Rosemary were word-vomiting their inherent body biases to me as a biracial teenager. I looked at them, mouth agape. From "here to there" was pretty specific, and I was certainly aware of the fact that spot-losing weight isn't a thing.

"Do you have any specific feedback for me so I can try to address this?" Barring some sort of mythical magic eraser, I had no idea how to solve this problem.

"You should turn out more," Peter said.

"Oh, okay."

Turning out more wasn't much to go on. What they bought at workshop was the same shit I was selling eight months later! They knew what my form and technique was, so what's the problem now? Why wasn't there coaching? Why wasn't anyone in class correcting me? I understood at that moment that being an apprentice might be less about being mentored and trained. It was more akin to a battle to the death—no one was looking out for me but me. No one was going to announce at the beginning of rehearsal, "May the odds be ever in your favor!" But the odds would never be in my favor. I needed to figure this shit out on my own.

Peter spoke again, "How committed are you to this company, Georgina?"

Committed? It seemed impossible that my commitment could be an issue, but I knew instantly what Peter was referring to. Just weeks before I had asked for a single day off to attend my brother's wedding. My brother had just completed basic training, and the army was deploying him to Iraq. Before he was being shipped off to serve his country, he decided to marry his girlfriend. I was informed that taking the time off for that would be unwise. It wouldn't demonstrate my commitment to the company. I went to the wedding. I saw my brother get married and kissed him goodbye, hoping it wasn't the last time we'd see each other. I was back in New York City the very next day ready to get back to work.

Yet I got up and actually apologized for my lack of "commitment." I somehow made it through rehearsal. When I got home that night, I stood under the shower and tried to wash away the day. I thought about the conversation with Rosemary and Peter—in the few short hours since it occurred, I had recognized it for what it was: an attack on my appearance and a notice that I'd better assimilate.

I thought about the moment when Peter announced I had won the Wein Award for Outstanding Promise. It had meant so much to win, to be recognized. It gave me a boost of confidence and a big dose of hopefulness. But now my thighs were my burden—and my ambition, hard work, and dedication couldn't do anything about that. And then I remembered that Peter had pronounced my name wrong in the presentation. And by wrong, I mean he made it up, *Pascovich*. It stung all over again. I could be recognized, but that didn't mean I was visible.

The next day I was performing in *Firebird*, dancing the role of one of the monsters. Along with this performance came the great privilege of wearing one of Chagall's original costume designs for the production. It needs to be said that the monster costumes, especially the surreal yellow watercolor-painted monster that I had the honor of wearing that night, are a NYCB treasure. I must also clarify that at the age of eighteen, I was not appreciative of this privilege. Putting on what was essentially a well-worn, sweat-soaked, masterfully painted comforter (albeit beautifully painted by Chagall) felt like a ritual hazing. Once I accepted that I'd be inhaling the funky aroma of many dancers past, I had to navigate the logistics of performing abstract ballet movement while wearing a body pillow that impaired my vision. At least I didn't have to bother with stage makeup!

In this performance, my monster, whom I liked to call "Old Yeller," and his monster kin are sent to their demise by the titular heroine. If that weren't dramatic enough, my fellow dancers dared me to dial up the drama even further. *Dare accepted!* Being a serious artist and a classical ballerina, I decided to really own the moment of my poetic death by taking advantage of my extra padding and doing a full-on belly slide across the stage. While I was lying on the ground lifeless, but conveniently burritoed in a comforter, I realized that I was in the unique position to watch the action onstage without being seen. This is something that rarely happens in ballet. I had the best spot in the house for watching the ballerina dancing the role of the Firebird. Her fire-red tutu and feather headdress were catching a touch of the blue light just beautifully. The Firebird's defiance and wildness were palpable, even through the regal choreography. This is the part in the ballet where the Firebird clears away all the evil monsters to save her Prince. She sent us away with an almost somber effect; she is, in essence, as much of an outlier, too—a pretty monster, but one of us all the same. We may represent her home, but her loyalties lie with the Prince. As we were being pushed away, we ugly creatures shoved aside, a fire lit inside me. *No wonder they think I'm fucking fat. I'm wearing a GODDAMN DUVET. Fuck you guys. I AM the Firebird. I'm the Phoenix. Don't threaten me.* I knew I would do whatever it took to prove them wrong.

Swan Dive #4

The crappy wet, grey weather did not make for a magical morning on the Disney cruise—especially when hungover. Fast-forward a few years to 2012 (I am of legal drinking age here, readers!), my sister Christina had landed a gig performing in one of their Broadway-caliber musicals, and my mom and I booked a cruise to watch her show and soak up some sun. *Sunshine, why art thou forsaking me?* I sprang for the wine package plus a package of Dramamine—ensuring plenty of booze with my cruise (hence the hangover). Mom sipped her coffee as sea mist danced over the deck.

"Ugh, I know what I need—fries."

My mom looked at me like I had announced I was going to eat the entire goddamn buffet as well as anyone standing within five feet of it.

"Gina. You think that's a wise choice?" I looked at my mother. *How dare she shame me on a Disney Cruise?!*

"You know what? I'll just go enjoy my fries on the children's deck! No one is going to bat an eye at me there!" I stomped up to the next level, the water on the stairs squishing about my very cute (but not boat-friendly) Bernardo sandals.

I got my fries. The combo of heat and the smell of the freshly fried potatoes instantly comforted me as I made my way to a pool chair to eat my breakfast of champs in a shame-free environment. I'm almost there! And then I feel it, I'm hydroplaning on these bullshit sandals like Bambi on an iced-over lake. Activate core stability, Gina! *Oh, shit.* I'm flat on my back, my life-sustaining fries strewn haphazardly about . . . *Now that I think about it, was there a warning about wearing non-rubbered shoes on deck?*

I start to sit up and collect myself, when I see a large figure quickly lumbering toward me. An enormous white-gloved hand/paw is extended toward me, and I realize that Goofy has come to my rescue. Before I can compute this, Goofy has expertly scooped me up off the floor (yeah, the training for looking after kiddos, basically tiny drunk people, comes in handy for actual hungover people) and has seated me in a chair.

Um, thank you so much? He can't talk. That would be breaking character. I'm thinking about how embarrassing it's going to be to get back in line for more fries, when Mickey Mouse himself appears. He, too, is silent—but his overexaggerated gestures suggest next-level jolliness, and more importantly he's holding an extra-large order of fries. He sets them down in front of me, bows gallantly, and dashes off. I am left alone to eat my French fries in peace. Dreams do fucking come true.

CHAPTER 7

720

Doc Wilcox gestured toward an ancient grandfather of a scale prominently displayed in the otherwise barren exam room. I had expected something top of the line and futuristic. A device that would scan my body and spit out its scientific findings, including a detailed road map about how to get to my athletic supreme. As I tiptoed toward the scale, I tried to push away thoughts admonishing myself for being too stressed out to take my regular morning shit. This would impact the number displayed, right? *Should I try to use the bathroom again right now?* As I climbed aboard that beast of a scale, a mini–existential crisis was beginning to unfold. I didn't want to be reduced to a number. A number that represented what, exactly? No matter what it said, I wasn't going to be pleased. Did I really need to add a number to my growing list of things to worry about? I sucked in my breath in a futile attempt to defy gravity and stared at the diplomas that inevitably grace the walls of such places. This was a low, miserable memory in the making. Standing there felt like a judgment. I felt like less of an artist, even less of a woman. I'd go so far as to say that for a moment I felt subhuman.

I hopped off the scale with a thwack of metal scraping metal, waiting for what came next. But there were no discussions of my BMI or what healthy eating looked like. I needed to disappear into the perfect line of ballerinas, and this doctor had helped my much fairer counterpart who had given me his phone number. When she placed the piece of paper in my palm, all I could see was an impossible assembly of bones and skin. Whatever he had suggested she do had clearly worked. I didn't think it mattered that she was nearly three inches taller than me with longer limbs and a different body type. I figured if she can do it, hell—I'll raise you!

Dr. Wilcox referred to a chart, "Well, it really appears you are in top shape. But you could lose four to five pounds. Given your small frame, that would make a huge difference." He looked at me with encouragement. Huge difference in my small frame . . . it would be years before I could see the irony in that statement. Four to five pounds sounded reasonable. "Will I look like a wisp? Nothing but a straight line?" I asked, only half joking with equal parts hope and hesitancy. Dr. Wilcox looked at me, acknowledging that he'd heard my question, but he didn't say anything. He wrote down a number on a piece of paper: "720." That was the number of calories I could have each day until I reached the mythological weight that would save my career. I felt the telltale wooziness that indicated my blood sugar was getting low. My eyes scanned the room for the big jar of Dum-Dums lollipops often found in the offices of medical professionals. Seeing nothing edible anywhere, my brain quickly snapped back to reality. *You're not at the orthopedist; you're at the fucking fat doctor—and there are no snacks to be had at the fat doctor!*

The doctor opened a drawer and pulled out a bunch of small packets. I was to mix packets with water and drink them three times per day. I didn't ask what was in them, and he didn't tell me. I picked one up and looked at the back. There were no ingredients listed. This registered as suspect to me; however, this also predated a time when questions like, "Kind sir, pray tell, is this mystery powder organic, gluten-free, and ethically sourced?" were as hip as "Did you see the latest *Dawson's Creek*?" or "Who was number one on *Total Request Live* today?" If I had to describe the taste, I'd have to say something along the lines of chalk with a hint of chemically manufactured mint and chocolate flavoring. There was a heft to the sip, which I assume came from the addition of some kind of protein. It wasn't *terrible*. But it also wasn't food, and it provided nothing for the senses like a good meal prepared with love and care. In other words, this was not my mom's chicken soup. In addition to the chalk-dust packets, I would eat one—just one—plain chicken breast and two pounds of spinach or lettuce for dinner. This would be my menu for the next four months. End of discussion, folks! I spent eight hours every day dancing hard, and this was the diet that was deemed fit for *this* athlete of God.

At nineteen, I believed committing to eating only those 720 calories would be my express ticket to Slimsville, and from there I'd hail a cab straight to the top! Hello, success! On some level it was simple. I wanted this job so badly that I was willing to do whatever it took. Apparently, what it would take was nothing short of sheer misery. I spent the next few months of my life in a state of unprecedented "hanger," which was often unleashed in fiery rage at other dancers and other random humans I encountered throughout the day. The level of provocation varied greatly: A casual comment about disco fries or puppies could set me off. But company class was like a minefield of emotion. Getting through a Balanchine class on my three packets of nasty was practically impossible. At barre I couldn't even keep my shit together enough to get through frappés. "Frappé" means "to strike"—it's a series of jab cross jab–style movements—as sharp and quick as a punch except that the punch happens with your foot striking the floor instead of your fist hitting someone's face. The theory behind the movement seems simple, but they are usually given out in a challenging combination—in some sort of mind-bending brain teaser of complicated counts, holds, directional changes, double/triple frappés, and petits battements. And just a casual and relaxing test of balance is the cherry-on-top-of-dance sundae. Your body needs to be free enough to do the movements, but your brain has to be along for the ride and set in the right gear for it all to come together. This is made exponentially harder when a) one's response time is compromised due to hangover, and b) one's response time is compromised due to lack of proper fuel. Although I've spent time in both groups simultaneously, it's the latter I was in, since I was underage at the time.* Merrill Ashley, one of Balanchine's dancers and muses, who was known as a technical machine and was now a teacher, walked up to me to give me a correction.

"Your frappé has to be sharper, Gina! Shocking, even!" She stopped for a second, a pause coated in drama. The entire class was silent and awaiting her next words. "Think of the zap that slices through the air as a cow is sent to its fate at the slaughterhouse!"

I stared blankly at her. *The zap? Cow? Slaughter?* I fish-eyed some of my older principal dancer friends; they were angling themselves away, trying to mask quaking bodies and muffled bursts of laughter. It was only 10 a.m., and I was standing there thinking this might be the one time in my life it was appropriate to say I was . . . flummoxed. *Okay, Merrill, I get what a frappé is, but what is not clear to me at this very moment is when exactly you lost your goddamn mind. You are one weird mamma jamma.*

Merrill was a spectacular dancer of the Balanchine era—remarkable. But she was now responsible for passing down Balanchine's genius to the next generation, and I was coming to realize that her relationship to ballet was on a completely different level. *Firecracker? So cliché. Crack of a whip? Show me an idiot who can't crack a whip! But the electric current zapping a bovine causing its instant demise?* Now that's a comparison she can get behind!

---

* This is a true statement, as I had not yet been tempted into the lifestyle of the young and restless club-going folk. However, please prepare yourself for underage drinking to come.

But hey, she was just helping me perfect my craft. I looked at Merrill in all her awkwardness and remembered that she saw my talent from the moment she met me. By pushing me to do a better frappé, she was making an honest attempt to keep improving upon the work I did when I was a student in the summer program at SAB. But my hunger was so overwhelming in that moment. This talk of cows had me daydreaming about how great it would be to eat a big, fat steak right there in the studio with my bare hands (sorry, vegans!).

* * *

As we moved to center work, my brain was puttering along on fumes. My body recognized it was being deprived and started to revolt with cramps and spastic reactions as I went into a fight-or-flight response. I was navigating an impossible task. Company class is crazy—it's not unlike Grand Central Station. There is constant movement and people everywhere, but there's a flow to it. As long as people keep moving along like they're supposed to, following the unwritten rules of navigating a busy transit hub, everything will be just fine, people! When it comes to the massive displays of technique, the atmosphere in the studio morphs into an air show vibe—think the Blue Angels. Just stay in formation! But some overly enthusiastic dancer always goes AWOL, and that's when you can end up with a spectacular crash. When you've got a roomful of ballet dancers doing fouettés en masse, you can't go rogue. For Christ's sake!

"Fouetté" means "whipped turn"—the idea of it is that you stay in place. You don't go whipping across the floor tearing everything down in your path like a category-five tornado. I realize this is easier said than done. I myself have had to fight to get back on track in many a performance where I'm fouettéing onstage. I've had to regain control over my flight path, but since I'm usually onstage solo during these times, I have a wide berth for error. In a classroom setting, the second you start letting yourself move all over the place, you're going to ram into someone. There's no avoiding it.

I am so fantastically hungry that I feel like I have vertigo before I even get into my turns. I am trying to execute, essentially on a dime. I am spotting myself, glancing into the mirror with each whip, when I perceive not one but *two* kamikazes encroaching on me from both sides in wild displays of questionable technique and bad taste. These hungry* fools are two turns away from taking me down. At fouetté twenty of an attempt at the famous thirty-two, I decide to pull the brakes and get out of the way. If I don't, they will both career into me. I snap in a hangry-fueled fit, and it isn't pretty.

There is an instant change in body carriage that happens when one shifts from ballet dancing back into civilian mode. It's a classic Superman-reverting-into-Clark-Kent moment. The characteristics of normal person and superhuman both exist in that same body—but really, you only get to see one at a time. Back in my civilian mode, I was enraged; all lightness and grace was pushed aside. I went for extra drama, throwing my arms in the air and shouting obscenities before I stamped to the back of the room to grab my bag, glaring at the two assholes who were still spinning like tops (still with questionable technique and definitely in bad taste). Only a few of the other dancers had noticed the near miss; everyone else was just spinning away. This realization that practically the entire effing class was infected with narcissism just added another layer to my fury. Combine that with the grand coda of *Black Swan* being played with vigor and passion, and I was out of there! My dance bag in hand, I sulked out of the room in defeat.

Ballet: 1, Gina: 0!

I had just recovered from my stress fracture, and now I was so hungry I couldn't handle the stress of dancing among these spatially compromised dingbats. What did these people want from me?

---

* While chances are that these dancers had eaten, they were also very hungry. In this case, hungry for attention and validation.

CHAPTER 8

If You Can't Join 'Em . . .
Beat Them (at Their Game)

I popped into a bodega on Broadway before heading uptown, fighting off rancid thoughts as I looked past rolls of toilet paper and boxes of sun-faded mac and cheese until finally—I located a box of saltines. I felt like shit. My emotions were shifting from enraged to depressed. *This is not how I anticipated the initiation into my dream job. Everything seems stacked against me. How can I fit in when I feel so isolated? How can I begin to compete when I don't know how to feed myself in a way that results in my meeting their bullshit ideal?* I paid for the crackers and shoved them in my dance bag along with sweaty leos and my swimsuit, giving off hits of chlorine. I had taken up swimming again in an attempt to slim myself down. Dancing alone apparently wasn't enough to stay in the game. When I got off the Metro North with Tyler and entered the hospital, my thoughts went back to Miranda. Miranda was in the dance program at SUNY Purchase, and Tyler had just started his second winter session at SAB.

Miranda had been admitted to intensive care after a very serious bout of E. coli. She had decided to top off her salad at the school cafeteria with some nutritious, vitamin K and C–packed alfalfa sprouts. That was an unfortunate decision—though we couldn't help but wonder, *Could someone have poisoned her on purpose to get all her parts?* Miranda's salad nearly killed her. Now, isn't that the rub. I almost lost my best and dearest friend to a goddamn salad.

After days of being deathly ill and eating nothing whatsoever, she had conjured up enough of an appetite to request saltine crackers. Saltines were a questionable choice for good reason, but I was to smuggle them in anyway. Miranda was on an ultra–low sodium diet due to her body's autoimmune response of swelling her up to the approximate size of the Stay Puft Marshmallow Man. But who was I to argue with someone who'd had a brush with death? I agreed to sneak her salt-laden crackers into the hospital. I sat down on her bed, so happy to see her and to put my less life-threatening problems aside. She looked less swollen since leaving the ICU but pale and tired from the fight her body was waging. But the Miranda I loved was still there, her beauty still fierce in those strong eyes of hers. Her feisty nature remained large and in charge, too. When we arrived, she was chatting with the nurse who was waiting patiently for her to finish her red-flavored Jell-O cup. Miranda made conversation, smiling at me standing in the doorway, her sweet expression laced with an undertone only I could decipher of *Bitch, better have brought the stuff.* That look of hers made me chuckle, and the reality of almost losing my best friend hit me hard. I couldn't imagine my life without Miranda in it.

"Thank you, Nurse Bettina," Miranda said, handing her a half-empty Jell-O cup. "I'm finished with my lunch. These are my best friends, Tyler and Gina." She nodded in our direction. Nurse Bettina fussed with Miranda's lunch tray for what felt like an eternity. I started to feel freakishly conspicuous, like that box of crackers in my bag was actually a homemade pressure cooker bomb. Doesn't this nurse have any other patients? She finally left. "GINA. DID. YOU. BRING. THEM?" Even in her weakened state, Miranda easily conveyed that I'd be in big-ass trouble if I didn't have the goods. I reached past my pointe shoes and ribbons and pulled out the box.

"Original label shit, girl. OG recipe. Better than cola made with real sugar. And I checked out that expiration date. This shit is *fresh*."

"Damn! A Coke! I should have asked you to bring one of those, too!"

Tyler laughed. "Don't push your luck, woman. Weren't you two hundred pounds, like, just a few days ago?" he chided.

We were all being silly, trying to laugh off the seriousness of her NDE. But it was all too much.

Miranda ripped open the sleeve and then gently, almost *with reverence*, lifted a salt-crusted cracker to her dry lips and took a bite. I wanted to scream. I wanted to snatch my own sleeve out of my sick friend's box of crackers and start shoving saltines into my mouth by the handful. As Miranda chewed and talked, I had a hard time focusing on what she was saying. Crumbs were falling; food was being eaten in my presence—I could barely handle it. I was fantasizing about eating Miranda's celebratory "I'm alive!" saltine crackers. This was next-level fucked-up. What kind of craziness is this? I am actively not eating again for the sake of a job, and how did we get here? Key word: "again." This was not my first skirmish with an eating disorder. Dancing seriously from such a young age, I had certainly been exposed to eating disorders. One of my suitemates that very first summer at SAB was seriously struggling. And every visit to the cafeteria during both the summer courses and winter term was, if one observed closely, a virtual master class in how to fake-eat a meal or binge one. I witnessed other dancers sporting their own methodologies in what I always felt was a dismal public display of self-worth, and I felt fortunate to not be taking part in it.

Thankfully, until recently, growing up in the dance world hadn't had much of an impact on how I ate. My mom cooked balanced meals, keeping my portion wrapped in the fridge so I could eat it when I got home from class (unless my brothers gobbled down my portion).

I generally made good choices, and as I've mentioned before, those choices also included spaghetti, pizza, and ramen. But my ability to eat properly went right out the window shortly after arriving in New York City for my immersive Balanchine intensive.

At the end of summer in 2001, I took the big plunge. I moved into the dorms at the School of American Ballet to finish my training full-time. I had said goodbye to my Catholic high school in Altoona, PA, and was enrolled at the Professional Children's School on Sixtieth Street, where I would earn my diploma. The Professional Children's School catered to the unique needs (i.e., not having time to actually attend school) of children who already had full-fledged careers but still needed to check off "attend school from sixth grade to twelfth grade" on the big to-do list of life. I'd attend "high school" from 8 a.m. to 9:45 a.m., then walk back over to the Rose Building to take ballet classes from 10:30 to noon. Then back over to PCS for more standard high school fare. As far as I could tell, the only significant difference between PCS and Our Lady of Lourdes in Altoona was that instead of cheerleaders and nuns, we had a professional horse jumper and Scarlett Johansson. The overall crew consisted of child actors, child athletes, and the kids of a bunch of investment bankers and diplomats. The list of alumni sparkled with names like Sidney Lumet, Carrie Fisher, Rita Moreno, Milton Berle (and presumably his giant penis), as well as multiple Culkins and several *Cosby Show* cast members. A few other dancers from SAB were there, too, but I still didn't feel like I fit in. I wanted to make myself as unremarkable as possible. I did my best to blend. This wasn't especially hard since I'd been a straight-A nerd in Catholic school, and I was the same nerd trying to ace PCS while simultaneously trying to get myself into a professional dance company. I had to focus! I had no interest (or time) to hang out with Paris Hilton (she attended but did not graduate, BTW) and her cocktail-swigging, red-velvet-rope-hopping posse. Spending several summers at SAB prepared me for what to expect from living in the metropolis. I was adapting to the change well enough, but we could never have anticipated on our first day of school, September 10, 2001, that the entire world would be changed the very next day.

Ask anyone who was in New York City that day, and they'll say the same thing: *The sky was so clear*. I followed my new semiroutine of breakfast in the cafeteria with friends, followed by the quick five-block walk to PCS. Mid–first period, we were all called to the cafeteria. This being pre-smartphone, none of us knew why we were there. But then the principal made an announcement, "Planes have hit the World Trade Center. New York City seems to be under att . . ."

Quickly, another adult rushed up to whisper in her ear, and the principal told us in a shaky voice that another plane had flown into the Pentagon. The room was instantly filled with stress and emotion. Kids with investment-banker parents were intensely distressed—as their parents worked in those very towers. The sadness I felt for them struck my soul and cut to the bone.

The dancer contingent was told to go back to SAB. We left as a minitribe, walking the five blocks quickly—noting the eeriness of a city gone silent. No traffic. No horns. No voices or construction noise. Nothing at all. I have been and always will be a clutch player. I won't necessarily assert myself to lead, but I'm good in an emergency, and I found myself leading our little pack of us at a very brisk pace "home." My demeanor presented a certain stoicism, but I was terrified, my mind unable to process the brutality of what was happening. Arriving back at Lincoln Center, we saw everyone standing out on the patio area in front of the Walter Reade Theater. The head of the school was there, and the dorm supervisors were cooking up a quick evacuation plan. The mission was to get us all out ASAP; who knew if America's cultural heart in New York City would be the next target? The head of the school and the dorm supervisors were frantically but effectively putting together a plan to keep all of us, us *kids*, safe. Local parents, teachers, and even donors were asked to step up and help. We were told to pack a bag and prepare to leave the premises. I felt a wash of fear when it was my turn to enter the elevator of the large tower that is the Rose Building, then riding up to the sixteenth floor, not knowing whether or not it was safe. As I was stuffing jeans, a T-shirt, and underwear into my bag, I looked south toward the World Trade Center. I looked just long enough to register two towers under smoke and fire, and in an instant that first tower *was gone*. I was stunned.

Coming out of it on the way back down to the street was when I first registered the noise. Sirens and more sirens. My roommate Olivia's uncle took us in at his West Side apartment. I don't remember how we got there. I just remember none of the phones worked, and I had no way of reaching my parents. By now we could faintly smell the smoke as well as see it—five miles uptown from ground zero. We switched back and forth from staring at the TV to craning our necks off the terrace, trying to catch a glimpse of the horror show unfolding downtown. There was a knock on the door, but we barely registered the sound. "Gina. Your uncle is here for you." My uncle Tem had tracked me down! How he found me I have no idea. I flew into his arms, feeling like I had been saved. He managed to get me out of Manhattan before the island was shut down, and I hunkered down with him and my aunt in New Jersey. When I finally did talk to my mother, her voice was shaky.

"Gina. Maybe you should come home."

My mother recalls my response, though I don't: "No, the world needs art more than ever now." I was shaky, too, more than I'd ever been—and I wasn't prepared to manage all of these feelings. But I did sense that my art would be a North Star through all the turmoil.

Just one week later, we were back at Lincoln Center to resume ballet and high school. Guidance counselors were called in, and we were urged to talk about what we saw, how we felt—about what had happened. The strain and heartache permeated everything. The counseling was no help to me—at that time I couldn't fathom talking about my feelings with my own parents. I couldn't let myself be that vulnerable with a stranger.

I thought I could handle things on my own, compartmentalize it all. It's what I'd always done, pretty successfully.

In an attempt to encourage togetherness and hominess, the dorms started featuring snack nights. I'm not sure of the rationale behind it, but something along the lines of *if there are Doritos, they will come—and possibly watch a movie together in a comforting act of domestic solidarity*. Friday night became *FOOD NIGHT*. Bowls of brightly colored gummy bears, Teddy Grahams, giant tubs of Fluff, and any other junk-foodesque thing you could imagine appeared in large quantities. I couldn't control what horrors we humans could inflict upon each other and our newly adopted city, but I could control my food intake. I'd eat well all week, everything healthy for me! Then Food Night came around, and I'd practically attack those snacks. The first time, I ate so much that I got sick and threw up. It was a purge of more than junk food. It was a release of epic proportion—it was a way to get rid of ALL the junk: general discomfort, despair, anxiety, fear I was dragging around with me all the time. Eureka, I had stumbled upon a handy new coping tactic. If I wanted, I could literally purge this *crap* from my body every time I ate a meal. The relief I felt afterward was almost intoxicating in its effectiveness. Emotions? No need—I'll just stuff them down via gummy bear and purge. It wasn't long before I was getting thin. Very, very thin. I know it was noticeable, but no one said a thing except for my mother when I came home for a quick visit to do a local performance with Tyler.

"Georgina, what's going on with you?" I assured her I was fine.

For six months following September 11, I didn't eat dinner without purging. I'd let myself release the pain of it all, but only after I had finished training for the day. I thought I was clever. This shall keep me "safe"—shielded from the competitive nature of the other girls' eating habits. It wasn't about getting thin for me. This was about expelling the demons that still haunted me, even beyond my daily dance exorcism. After a while I didn't feel as clever. I felt dull, my light dimmed, and it got to a point where I didn't care about anything. I was, at last, numb. A small voice inside of me said, *If this is a real problem, one of the adult women surrounding you will say something. You will be nurtured back to health.* No rescue was planned. My façade was ironclad—presenting a picture of happiness and health. The pattern continued. The truth was I was getting the same attention, if not more, in ballet class.

The house of cards eventually fell through when my failure to take care of my mind resulted in my body breaking. I fractured my foot. An aptly named stress fracture—or a hairline crack in a bone, in this case my second metatarsal. This kind of injury comes from repetitive activity and overuse. Candidates of such injuries include high-impact-sports athletes, people who suffer from osteoporosis, and . . . wait for it! . . . young, otherwise healthy women who exercise excessively, causing irregular or absent menstrual cycles, which directly affect the strength of their bones. I was seventeen, but I had not been initiated into the crimson tide club quite yet (I would later that year). The point I'm making is that I was walking around with a target on my back—I fell into just about every single risk category.

Generally, this is the situation when a dancer suffers from a stress fracture: the healing process requires five weeks in the dreaded boot with *no dancing*. I liken the boot to the cone of shame for dogs— ballerinas look especially pitiful with crutches and a boot. Also, those things are absolute havoc on the hips no matter what your age. In my case the "situation" was a hard NO. It was workshop weekend, which is a big deal. Everyone who had the power to give me a contract to be an official member of the company would be paying attention. The stakes were the highest they'd been yet. I had to showcase my entire spectrum of artistry in a seventy-two-hour span. I was dancing two leads, and I'd be damned if I was missing my shot to get into the company. I only went to PT when absolutely necessary during the double load of class- work and rehearsal in the weeks leading up to the biggest moment of my almost career.

The Thursday before the big weekend, I had an MRI, and the doctor delivered the news.

I was slated to dance the lead of *Ballo della Regina* on Saturday
evening of workshop weekend. It's a powerhouse role that gave me the
chance to show off my new Balanchine technical prowess. Merrill was
coaching, absolutely shredding me as she prepared me to dance this
beautiful role that Balanchine had created just for her. On the coveted
Monday workshop night, I was to perform the lead ballerina role in
the *Brahms-Schoenberg Quartet*'s fourth movement. Monday workshop
was the coveted slot because it was the same night as the gala—meaning
Peter Martins would be there, plus the principal dancers and the rest of
the illustrious donors of the school.

Another tour de force role that exemplified my ability to embody
the queen. It required less straightforward technique than *Ballo*, but it
required much more gravitas and complete understanding of a certain
style of bravura. The only way for me to stay in the game long enough
to perform at the gala was for me to forfeit the Saturday-night show of
Ballo.

I was crushed and so disappointed in myself. I had already given
the role countless hours of hard work and tears, followed by secret
bone stimulator sessions* and countless small victories as I slowly made
improvements and mastered the technique required to nail the powerhouse solos of *Ballo*. Now that work would never be seen. Realizing I had
sabotaged myself was the last straw. This moment represents something
much bigger in my career than not performing in a gala. Decades later,
I can tell you that this moment impacted the trajectory of my entire
career, and it still hurts my soul to think about it. Ballo was *Merrill's
role*—Balanchine created it for her, which is like having Degas paint

---

* Sounds dramatic, but it's a device that delivers electromagnetic currents to promote
 bone healing. I had the device from my last stress fracture. I was using it in secret
 because I didn't want people to figure out that I was hurt.

you . . . and it's an insanely hard role. Now I had ruined my chance to dance it . . .

It was the moment when I was supposed to show everyone a different side of myself, that I can handle the harder, more technical roles with aplomb. I have never had the chance to prove myself like this again—that moment came and went. I blamed myself for a long time—and then I have flashes when I think about how young and hungry I was. Should someone have stepped in to keep me healthy?

But there was no alternative. I would deliver the show of my life in *Brahms* on gala night. There was a consolation prize of sorts, though. I was awarded the prestigious Mae L. Wein Award for Outstanding Promise, with $10,000 and a trophy, presented to me by Peter Martins, along with an invitation to join the company as an apprentice* on gala night, even as he wildly mispronounced my name. This is the first big step toward becoming a real ballerina—it was a trial run. As I took my bow that night on the stage in Juilliard's Peter Jay Sharp Theater, wiping tears of joy along with my stage makeup, I made a promise to the ever-shrinking girl I had been seeing in the mirror. I promised that girl I'd figure out a healthier way to manage my human condition. It would be my first endeavor as a *professional* ballerina.

It's undeniable that my form is an instrument of objectification. In some cases, displaying my body in movement results in an act of great and powerful emotion. Other times, my form is simply the source material of objectification. Ultimately, displaying my body is part of my job, and this will never change. Being a professional dancer is admittedly one of the more narcissistic things a person can set out to do. Being aware of and critiquing every muscle twitch in a mirror is part of my job on a daily basis. My focus rests solely on myself, in class, in rehearsal, and also in the choices I make outside of the studio.

---

* An apprenticeship is the first step toward professional status, but you're not a full-fledged member of the company yet. It's kind of like being engaged to be engaged. It's looking good, but the whole thing could be called off!

Whether I made "bad" choices or "good" choices will be revealed to me in the mirror the very next day. I'm trained to find and correct all of those imperfections. The reality of this hits me harder at some moments than others. Case in point: if the cards deal in my favor to dance the role of Coffee on opening night of *The Nutcracker*, I'll have to be very deliberate about my Thanksgiving meal. It's like learning less than/greater than in grade school math. What do I want *more than* what? This equation is my current breakdown of preferences, FYI, subject to change:

> wine > turkey
> turkey > pie
> pie > potatoes
> potatoes > cranberry sauce

Dancing Coffee (the day after fucking Thanksgiving) means I'll be showing off a lot of skin (including my midsection) and every blessed inch of my legs in a suggestive belly dance that Balanchine allegedly choreographed "for the dads." To be fair, I think he was joking, but let's not rip open that can of worms just yet. Stay with me. I perform a two-minute solo sporting ankle bells that declare, "Here I am!" with a light jingle every time I move or take a breath. If you're thinking, *Wait, how does this half-naked costume really differ from wearing just tights and a leo as one does in Balanchine's famous black-and-white ballets? Are they not both equally revealing?* Aha! There is one very major difference between the two, and the difference is skin. Ladies, think one-piece swimsuit versus a bikini. Gents, imagine trading in those swim trunks for a speedo. And how does that feel? Getting rid of that thin layer of tactile nylon/spandex and exposing actual skin in that Coffee costume has a more intense vulnerability factor, and it takes up extra space in this artist's mind. This is especially true when my body is supposed to express the sensual aroma of coffee through dance . . . This is a perfect example of narcissism making herself extra comfortable. Find me one person—*one*—who feels sexy the day after Thanksgiving.

These days I prefer to remain unspoken in social situations about what I do until my hand is forced. I get a little kick out of seeing someone's reaction after an entire conversation about the best way to roast a chicken or what I think of the genocide occurring in Myanmar. Most people get quiet for a second when they learn I'm a ballerina with the New York City Ballet. They usually admit my appearance clearly affirms this, but more often than not I'm met with, "Well, you sat on that keynote for a while, miss. If I were you, I'd shout about that from the rooftops!" Well, I do. *Onstage*. I've worked hard to separate what I do from who I am at my core. I can understand to some degree what it would have been like to be Marilyn Monroe, Diana Ross, or Warren Beatty: American icons of beauty, sensuality, and sexuality often and in different ways reduced to their countenance and appearance. All three struggled with being pegged for one sole attribute rather than cherished for the sum total of their individual talent, beauty, and soul. Being a ballerina, for both sexes, can feel that way sometimes. I joke about being an "athlete of God," but only because there are equal parts grandiosity and truth to that statement. I'm not just a body, even though that's what is celebrated about my craft. I'm a woman and an artist building a life. Sure, I've made some questionable choices about my body—but there are sacrifices to be made for my art form. But as I've grown older and wiser, I can see that the younger me twisted sacrifice into something darker. Especially when it came to Peter's subjective view of what my body should look like. My single-focused pursuit of securing a place in the greatest ballet company in the United States had become a battle about control. Who ultimately controlled me? Was it me or was it going to be Peter Martins?

It was a long time before I had the courage to answer this question, even after the stress fracture, after the Wein Award night. One day I was standing at the edge of the pool at the YMCA, about to swim off the extra calories and take my mind off all of the madness. I noticed a woman getting out of the pool. It was hard to tell her age because she was so emaciated. If I had to guess, I'd say she was in her late fifties. In other words, young enough to have lots of living left to do. She was *suffering* thin. Whether it was from battling cancer or more likely an eating disorder, this was not a thinness to be admired; it was a cause for concern. As she walked past me toward the changing room, the pain in her aura was palpable. She was a wake-up call. My heart broke for her, but it also broke for me. I was suffering, too. And if I wasn't careful, would my unhappiness look like this?

I realized I could make a choice to do this differently. I wanted my presence to be felt, I wanted to be empowered by my art form and use it to elevate the world. I wanted to feel joy again. I dove into the pool. The water rushed around me, and I knew it would be a long time before I swam again. I just wanted to dance, on my terms, in harmony with *my* body. On the walk back home, I wasn't haunted by what Peter and Rosemary had suggested all those months ago about how my thighs did not fit in. I was haunted by the vision of a woman who was quietly fading away. I was done with this bullshit. I would not be reduced by this man no matter how much power he wielded. My body was mine, and I was reclaiming it. I walked into the grocery store, grabbed the makings of a salad, and chose a New York strip. I was going home to cook for myself; then I'd go to bed—and in the morning I'd have breakfast, and then I'd dance.

Corps de Ballet

CHAPTER 9

House of Upsets

Ah, Saratoga.

Home to twenty-one public mineral springs, most naturally carbonated. The springs are like nature's SodaStream meets a traveling snake oil salesman. Each spring boasts health benefits ranging from clearing skin to "blood strengthening," and that's not all. Saratoga urges you to taste your way through them all! Enjoy each unique flavor profile! Most dancers, including myself, opt to only drink bottled water. One of the less-mentioned qualities of the magical health waters is that they will give you the shits. Who wants to be shitting and fighting off mosquitoes? No, thank you.

Of course, you've also got the Saratoga Race Course, aka House of Upsets or Graveyard of Champions, where the great Secretariat was beaten by a horse named Onion. Then there's the outdoor amphitheater, SPAC—Saratoga Performing Arts Center. Recent shows include the Dave Matthews Band (to my knowledge, the biggest crowd in SPAC history), the Goo Goo Dolls, Hootie and the Blowfish, and something questionable-sounding called Kidz Bop. And every single summer you can go right ahead and add the New York City Ballet to the roster.

Tradition still holds that the entire company hauls ass up to Saratoga to swat away mosquitoes and sweat buckets while dancing on a decrepit, rocker-abused stage that has no air-conditioning, in the middle of the goddamn summer. Apparently, Balanchine himself was positively smitten with Saratoga. Maybe he drank the waters; who knows? But ever since the early 1960s, for several weeks in the summer, we all leave New York City to essentially go to camp together. Back in the day, when Balanchine was first taken with the place, the ballet would do a whopping month-long residence. Now sometimes we are only subjected to Saratoga for up to fourteen days.*

My first visit to Saratoga was in 2003, and it so happens I felt like the dejected, miserable kid at camp who wasn't excited about Popsicle-stick crafts and didn't want to swim in the lake. For the dear readers who are cult classic film lovers, I was basically Rudy in *Meatballs*, and not even Bill Murray could have lifted my spirits.† If you don't know the reference, do yourself a favor and watch it. I was definitely not "ready for the summer." This is likely because there is another tradition at Saratoga, and this tradition would result in a) all my hard work paying off to make my dream come true, or b) my putting on an Oscar-winning-level performance to feign being happy for my colleagues who received contracts, while simultaneously trying not to throw up/scream/fling my body in front of the starting lineup at the racetrack, resulting in my being dramatically trampled to death by champion thoroughbreds. That would show 'em!

The other tradition at Saratoga was that it was the time and place Peter chose to inform the apprentices whether or not they would be

---

* To the lovely people of Saratoga: You and your fine town are wonderful. Please understand that any issues I have with Saratoga are deeply personal, and I mean no offense.

† Although funnily he would succeed in that exact venture many years later, accepting my challenge for an epic Christmas party dance-off that may or may not have involved licking ornaments.

receiving a contract to join the corps de ballet and become full-fledged members of the "family." Either you became a member of the company, or you finished out the week knowing that your blood, sweat, and tears were used, abused, and would be discarded in an unintentional but absolutely brutal public shaming.

Everyone would know you didn't make the cut. People would tiptoe around you those last few days, not wanting to set you off into another hysterical crying spell. It's like Peter could snap his fingers, and you're instantly transformed from a vessel of promise to a piece of festering garbage. *Thanks, but we just can't get over how you don't fit in from "here to here." Don't let the steaming piles of manure that surround you and your thighs keep you from getting back in the saddle, but your ride here, with us, is done. Good luck to you, ma'am!*

It was the last day of a rigorous three-week season, and the heat and humidity were as thick as my own malaise. Peter had requested to meet with me between performances of *Coppélia*, and while I knew to expect this meeting, my stomach was heavy. I was percolating somewhere between trepidation and despondence. My confidence had been rocked to the wrong side once again when J. P., who had been a soloist in the company in the late '70s and was now the head ballet master for the Jerome Robbins repertory, offered me some unsolicited advice, "Wow! You look good. Just a few more pounds to go!"

When it comes to my working relationship with J. P., I feel like he's always been a champion of me, or tried to be . . . *to a certain point.* As my career moved forward, it became clear that I fit into the category of Robbins rep dancer, so J. P. and I work together a lot. I think J. P. saw how much of a sponge for knowledge I was about Robbins and how I greatly appreciated his work. When Balanchine started City Ballet, Jerome Robbins was not only a choreographer but also associate artistic director, who created an incredible body of work, including sixty ballets that we still perform (although you are probably most familiar with his work on Broadway . . . *West Side Story, On the Town, Gypsy, The King and I,* and

Fiddler on the Roof). Robbins's style had a really great way of relating dancers to each other as people onstage beyond being muses of form.

J. P. has truly seen something special in my artistry and was one of the first to hand me a megaphone to broadcast my magic to an audience. He has a warm temperament and sometimes can deliver a dad joke well. He also possesses the wherewithal to meaningfully account for his actions.

But one thing about working with J. P. is that he has a tendency to say things that should have passed through his mental filter and never hit the outside world. J. P. is like a less-curmudgeony Larry David of the New York City Ballet: you want to believe he's a good person at heart, but sometimes what he says makes it very challenging.

One beautiful late spring day, J. P. was rehearsing us in *The Concert*, a comedic ballet. In this ballet, spring arrives! And this becomes evident to the audience when we all stop what we're doing to don butterfly wings—and are then chased about the stage by the pianist, who has whipped out a giant net. In the middle of his coaching, J. P. thought it would inspire us if he talked about the beautiful spring day that was happening right outside.

"You're butterflies! It's spring! It's beautiful! Think about it . . . women walking around in tank tops and short dresses, shorts! You know . . ." J. P seemed to be staring wistfully into space as he mused. He ended his long pause with this crazy bomb: "It's amazing more women aren't raped these days." *Jesus, J. P., patriarchy much?*

But I think J. P.'s first-prize display of toxic masculinity occurred in a rehearsal of *Fancy Free* during the Robbins festival. *Fancy Free* is basically a silent play told through dance and music, so the cast has to have some pretty great chemistry. Our cast had the benefit of being actual friends and veteran performers of our roles in this ballet, which included two women, three male sailors, and the classic Jerry run-on. Tyler Angle was dancing the pas de deux with Tiler Peck (whom I will henceforth refer to as T2).

At the end of this dance, the choreography has Tyler, who is playing the shy sailor, throwing T2 up in the air. He catches her, slowly lowering her until he gives her a cute, sweet kiss. We are running through a tech rehearsal, and J. P. is in a nitpicking kind of mood. I should clarify that the entire point of a ballet master is to be critical—we expect criticism and corrections, it's a huge part of our jobs! But during this rehearsal J. P. is definitely nitpicking . . . That's what we call it when there's not much to correct and the ballet master is excavating things to correct.*

It seems that he is trying to keep the youth humble in this case because 1) our cast is bomb.com, and 2) he needs to remind us that he is the only one in the room to have actually worked with Jerome Robbins. There's something about the angle at which Tyler caught T2, in midair above his head, that J. P. feels isn't quite right. Even though J. P. has never performed this role, he is apparently convinced that HE can show one of the best partner dancers the world has seen how to execute this move *just right*.

"Let me show you what I mean."

J. P. takes Tyler's place on stage. He tosses T2 into the air and lowers her down so slowly it's like we're living in stop-motion. Kaitlin and I have taken up real estate onstage at the bar. That's not a typo; there's a bar as part of the set, and we are sitting there watching and shaking our heads at J. P.'s macho display, putting Tyler in his place. J. P. performed the role of the other, short, punky sailor in his time, so we are still surprised the tricky toss goes well . . . Wait, he's not going to do this kiss, is he? We practically stop breathing. *Is J. P. going to fucking kiss her?* It's like we are watching a car crash . . . *No, this can't be happening. Oh, it's happening.*

Perhaps it's the magic of the Robbins choreo that places him so realistically in this otherwise fantasy moment, but sure enough J. P. slowly kisses T2 right on the goddamn mouth. [Insert screeching brakes sound.] RED ALERT! Reason and logic have left the building! We are

---

* Fast-forward to 2020 and ballet masters are now referred to as "rehearsal directors." A change I fully support.

all in shock, and I instantly look toward the front of the stage where Deluz, T2's boyfriend (another macho man), is sitting during the rehearsal. Coincidently, he also dances the role of the shorter bruiser of a sailor. I see that he and Amar are laughing together, having missed this entire effed-up situation. An Animal Planet–style alpha-male contest situation has been avoided! Kaitlyn and I return our attention to the situation on the stage. Tyler begins talking about something else, trying to immediately move past the fuckery. T2 looks shaken, but she is also trying to hold on to any last thread of professionalism for the ten minutes we have left of this bananas stage rehearsal.

To this day, it is one of the most bonkers displays of toxic masculinity I've seen.

And while I know that he apologized to Tyler, Tiler, and Deluz, Kaitlyn and I are still awaiting our acknowledgment from the Patriarchy. Now, if this would have happened today, I would have reacted differently. I would have asked Tiler if she was okay. I would have spoken up about how offended I was by J. P.'s behavior. I am not proud of this, but I didn't take action. I didn't feel I had the power to speak up, and it wasn't the first time I kept silent about something I knew was shitty. When I was eighteen, I was riding in the elevator with an older male dancer. We were chatting, mindless elevator-ride banter, when I shared that it was my birthday.

"Oh, happy birthday!" If only it had stopped there. Apparently, this dancer felt that since it was my birthday, he would acknowledge my special day by cornering me in the elevator and sticking his tongue in my mouth. I walked out of that elevator feeling confused—and violated? I mean, there are worse things than being seen as the hot new piece of ass in the company by a powerful and connected principal dancer, right? But instead of lingering on how this bizarre encounter I definitely didn't solicit made me feel, I kept my mouth shut. I went to class and danced.

I warned you that things were going to get very, very ugly in the House of Balanchine. Let me save you a Google search. In 2017, Peter

Martins took a leave of absence after allegations of sexual misconduct, as well as allegations from five dancers that he had physically and verbally abused them. In 2018, Alexandra Waterbury took legal action against her ex-boyfriend, the principal dancer Chase Finlay, who shared sexually explicit photographs of her as well as a video of them having sex. Incredibly offensive and inappropriate text messages then took place between Finlay and two other dancers, Amar Ramasar and Zachary Catazaro, along with a young patron donor named Jared Longhitano. To make this long and terrible story short, Finlay resigned, Ramasar and Catazaro were fired (only to be reinstated. Some audience members actually cheered when Amar performed for the first time after all this came to light).

Our company was left reeling. This shit hurts, and there is much work and healing to be done, and sometimes it feels like these wounds will never fully close up. How can they, when we go to work and face a man who has been allowed to greatly disrespect the employees he works with?

I am not excusing any of this behavior, but I will say this. The intimacy of dancing with someone is very nebulous. And ballet has been very traditionally binary, with women in the physically submissive role while the male partner guides, carries, manipulates. A pas de deux requires real trust.* The general workplace etiquette is already warped when your job requires you to negotiate the placement of your lady business on a male coworker's clavicle during a lift. If a ballerina is doing a full penché (think the splits, but you're standing up), there sometimes is choreography—beautiful choreography, mind you—where a man's face will end up within intimate proximity to crotch. For instance, when executing the torch lift at the end of *Spring Waters*, there is a high likelihood of a finger in "the vagine." A torch lift is extremely difficult and high-risk; a man is holding me straight up in the air with one arm, balancing my whole person on his hand by way of my root chakra via

---

* Ballet is changing. A pas de deux could now include women partnering women or men partnering men.

my ass . . . carrying my body weight while running across the stage to exit in bravura flourish. My partner's hand is definitely all up in and around a very personal area. And I'm going to use the full space of that hand for balance because depending on the height of my partner, I'm six or eight feet up in the air. There is no spotter. If I fall, I get seriously hurt.

We often dance cheek to cheek, ass to ass, penis to vagina. There's a certain amount of consent given just by walking into the studio. It's not like acting a sex scene in a movie . . . a man can't carry a grown woman across the stage without actually touching her. However, one can feel the difference in the intention—when a partner grazes my breast bringing me down from a lift, I can tell if it's just his hand placement letting me down gently, or if it's something else.

So while we are really, really comfortable being in each other's personal space, sometimes those boundaries get blurred. Those boundaries were blurred for me for a long time. For many years, Amar used to "greet" me during company class by sidling up close, whispering, "You look fine today," eyes locked on my chest, and then he'd zero in on the goal at hand by—surprise!—tweaking my nipples. The first time it happened I was shocked and confused. We had tremendous chemistry as dance partners—but there was never anything else between us. But clearly this was a breach of trust, right? I can almost rationalize his thinking: He touched other parts of my body while dancing, so what's the big deal if he tweaks a nip? Our ideas of trust and intimacy warped wildly—he'd pinch my nipples, and rather than demanding he quit it, I'd respond by slapping his ass so hard that I'd leave a handprint. Of course, I was pissed that someone I was not romantically involved with assumed 24/7 access to my body. But I couldn't find the words to ask him to stop. Why? (I know, reader, you are screaming. Stay with me.)

I don't know.

Maybe because he chose to do this in a public and crowded place, in front of other straight men who laughed and egged him on in company class, I felt I couldn't win. Maybe I was just trying to focus on warming up my body for a day of rehearsal with Peter. But I do know for certain that my retaliation was swift and in the moment. The constant objectification I was subjected to began to take its toll on my psyche. I fought back while sparing them their egos. Amar, whom I started to dread seeing in class, would execute this nipple-tweak-drive-by, and I'd slap back so fast and so hard, sometimes my hand stung for minutes. But that's where the breakdown of communication occurred. I was growing more pissed at being taken advantage of, and he just looked forward to a little S and M between petit allegro combinations. It's taken me years to process what exactly had been happening. In that time of compartmentalization, I was just trying to survive, and in doing so, I was complicit in this behavior.

What recourse would I have had in that moment? Complain to Peter about Amar? HA. That seemed like complaining to Satan about his brother Hades. They both represented the same problem. They were dominators in a patriarchal environment. And while I'm clarifying why I was afraid to speak up, I'll point out something that is lost on no woman—on a basic level, men are physically stronger than women.

Although I know Amar would never hit me, as we had what I understood as friendship and a minimum of trust as dance partners, it also seemed to me that Amar idolized our boss. And Peter, on the other hand, had a widely attested history of violent episodes.

When I experienced Peter's anger, whether it was directed at me or not, the hairs on my arm would stand up out of fear.* It's an instinctual response that tells me I'd stand no chance in the wild if Peter was an actual predator.

*   *   *

In order to spare Amar and avoid confrontation with Peter about one of his favorites, I decided it was easier to devalue the respect I deserve as a woman and human. I am, as the reviewers have called me, a "uniquely

---

* Enough of Peter's anger has been directed squarely at me to last a lifetime.

attractive," "exotic," and "sloe-eyed" beauty. But beyond that I also have a very sensual demeanor. It's taken me years to embrace my right to present my authentic self to the world AND defend the idea that although those attributes attract a certain amount of attention, they do not equal a green light for any man to take advantage. Equally, I am not an outlet for other women to project their judgments either. It has taken so much work (and so much money) to get to the root of this key revelation. To understand and not hate, or solely blame myself for the things I have experienced as a result of embracing my magic. I have the right to establish boundaries, even in the very strange shades of grey that exist at City Ballet.

Why do I bring this up now? Because my experience as a mixed-race woman in a predominantly white, Eurocentric art form has been complicated, and I have been gaslit over many conversations and events, made to think I was crazy, greedy, or that I'd asked for it.

The hierarchy and power imbalance between men and women, artistic leadership and dancers, at City Ballet had gone unchecked for too long—and the behavior had spread. Peter was in charge of the company for thirty years. One gets a job at the age of seventeen, or in rare cases even younger, at NYCB. When you are so young and impressionable, it's easy to idolize a person as striking and charming as Peter could be. In my view, Peter is a complicated and deeply affected individual. Many would agree that he seems to have an anger always simmering under the surface, and in my observance, while he would also bully younger male dancers for being too weak, women seem to have taken the brunt of that anger when he can no longer prevent it from boiling over. When your work environment resembles an absolute monarchy, one person decides your fate as a dancer, so it's a big deal to be part of Peter's inner circle. When Peter was at the helm, he essentially had a fraternity of "bad boys" and a few select women who were allowed access into the periphery of affairs. It should come as no surprise that Amar, Chase, and Zach were scooped up into the fold when they were quite young, and they seem to have learned from Peter's example.

The dark truth is that Peter has had two DUIs and in the early 1990s was arrested for beating his wife (charges that were dropped after she refused to testify). I'm not making an argument that there should be no chance of redemption for humanity when it supremely fucks up; however, redemption is sort of hard to attain when one does not account for ANY harm done.

So it makes sense that when there was a complaint alleging that male dancers destroyed a hotel room on tour, reportedly providing drugs and alcohol to minors and causing $150,000 worth of damage, that the reprimand was simply: *They should try to confine such behavior to New York City.* It's also then no surprise that I was almost fired for being too curvy in the summer of 2002.

*   *   *

After J. P.'s bungled weight comment, I began to make my way from my dressing room on the second floor to the office where Peter camped out during our stay in Saratoga. It was an awkward path, full of twists and turns and dusty hallways. The walk felt like it was taking an unusually long time. The bowels of SPAC were battered AF. I made a split-second decision. I ducked into the house left wing and decided to walk across the empty open stage. I looked out at the seats and instantly felt a flutter of support. My home is on the stage, and I draw energy from it whether or not there is an audience in the seats.

As I made my way to the other side, I crossed paths with Ash. Aisha was the only Black woman dancer in the corps, and I secretly was an adoring fan of hers. She was another dancer poorly treated by the system. I think she sensed the crazy hurricane of my emotions.

"Hey, what's wrong, baby girl? None of that . . . I've seen you dance. You've got something extremely special. If he doesn't acknowledge that, he's a fool. You raise your head high and keep it high in there. We ALL know you've worked your ass off."

I was ashen, fighting back tears. I *knew* I had worked hard. I felt there was nothing more that I could have done. But the fat talk and thoughts of "not fitting in" were still circling around me. I soldiered on, rounding backstage left, past the practice studio, through the loading dock, through the admin office, and now up the stairs to Peter's makeshift lair. Everything about this place felt dark and claustrophobic, which is funny if you think about it, since I was actually in an open-air theater in beautiful upstate New York!

Rosemary motioned for me to come in and sit. Peter was already there. I didn't think I could feel any more agitated, but my stomach felt like it was about to drop. Akin to the moment before the roller coaster takes its plunge—you're not sure if it's going to be a thrill ride or it will end with you puking your guts out, the wind from the ride blowing it all right back into your face.

And back to that voice of Zeus: "Here we are."

Rosemary tried to cut the tension with, "You've worked hard since our talk back in January."

"Yes," Peter echoed, taking control of the narrative. His words and intonation gave no hint to what kind of news he was going to deliver. He paused, looking at me with steel eyes. "You are *so* different. Is this what you want?"

I respond immediately, "Yes, sir. Without doubt."

Another absurdly long pause, then finally, "Well, I've decided I'm going to give you a shot."

I got a shot! I was getting *a shot*? I wanted to cry—this time those tears would have been the result of happiness and relief, mixed with the lingering anger, and confusion. But no way was I going to let him see me cry.

"Oh! Thank you, Peter. I promise you won't regret it." I glanced at Rosie. She was smiling. He was smiling. I was awestruck.

"Now, Gina. The *real* work begins."

I got out of there like a bat out of hell and rushed to find a private space where I could process the information.

I didn't want to go back into the dressing room. Since my fat talk, a rumor had circulated that Peter was "on the fence" about me, and everyone was expecting news. But right then I didn't feel like I could face anyone. I rounded the corner and fell on my knees. After a few seconds I felt like someone was watching me. I opened my eyes, and there was Frog. Frog was a stagehand, and maybe even had a secret life as a country rock star. Long white hair, classic cowboy hat, big wire-framed glasses—Frog was the head carpenter for City Ballet, and he was great at his job. He had been an unexpected source of support for me that summer. Some of the dancers act like the stagehands do not exist, but for me, a quick chat with Frog was always a bright spot in my day.

"You okay? Did something happen? Wait, you didn't get your contract?" I told him I did, and he instinctively knew to help me up, not say a word, and give me a big welcome hug. "You are a strong one," he said. "Remember that." I thanked him and decided to go where the conductors hang out—you never see any other dancers there.

Once I was alone, I realized, technically, I had won. I wasn't being dismissed. I was now an official member of the corps de ballet. I was an honest-to-God professional ballerina. But it was confusing. Why didn't this *feel* like a well-deserved win? I had worked hard to get something— but it felt like it came with a caveat. I felt like I had been issued a warning. This is your shot! We've decided to give you this one shot! Don't fuck it up! I knew in that moment that this would never be easy for me. Nothing was to be handed over. Winning the Wein Award and dancing my ass off were not going to result in a "Congratulations, welcome to the New York City Ballet!" What this said to me was *we're not really sure about you, but we don't want anyone else to have you either . . . so we're going to give you one last chance to prove yourself to us.* My talent, work, and artistry weren't going to earn me an honest-to-God place in the heart of this company yet. I was just going to get a shot.

CHAPTER 10

Give Satan an Inch

Even today, with nearly twenty years of Saratoga under my belt, I still feel queasy as I drive along Interstate 87. By the time I hit exits 23–25, I have a tennis ball–sized pit in my stomach, even though so much good-natured frolicking and wicked bawdiness has occurred there. Sometimes our antics have been so outrageous that they've been elevated to legends among the locals. This is inevitably what happens when you import a hundred or so beautiful young professionals who are addicted to the immediate gratification and endless adventure of the big city to an otherwise sleepy town. Mayhem.

Roll call! While technically a tour, Saratoga is better classified as adult summer camp. A group of dancers sharing a house in Saratoga is like a huge coed sleepover. The vibe is a mix of classic '70s *SNL* wildness with musical theater camp influences (with a dash of *Lolita* flavor, as the age range of our company spans from sixteen to forty-five). The dancers would be spread out in various houses, rented in groups. We couldn't believe how far our per diem could go in Saratoga—more living space than any of us had ever experienced in the city—and that left us with plenty of money for booze and pigs. Whichever group had the biggest house would hold the weekend cookout, and in later years, as our grilling prowess matured, we graduated to the pig roast.

We've been known to engage in an epic battle of the houses. Best skit wins bragging rights for the year. During the week and in between rehearsals, we'd take turns going to the Price Chopper, aka *the Chop*. We'd load up on provisions for family dinner, eaten at a big table that would never fit in a typical New York City apartment. There was much drinking of wine and spirits, as per habit. These gatherings were loose in the chaperone department, and minors were usually invited in the spirit of inclusivity. But mix this with the awkward adjustment of having to drive oneself to and fro, rather than the usual city modes of walk-hail-ride, and I'll just say there have been a number of DUIs over the years, and one demolished mailbox.

We did not limit the party to private residences either. We'd hit the ole Parting Glass bar en masse, tinkering with the locals and paying homage to Hattie's glorious mint juleps and life-sustaining fried chicken. This restaurant was a popular choice should someone have a birthday or if a dancer was retiring. Pools were an essential when considering a house to rent. Diving contests (I am one hella graceful diver) and games of chicken would be played until the sun went down and it was time to retire around firepits. Trips to Lake George on the long weekends were a particular favorite. We still did our seven-show week. But because we performed two shows on Wednesday and two on Saturday, Sunday and Monday were days off. We got to experience the bliss that is normal life by enjoying TWO DAYS OFF IN A ROW! A huge ballerina rarity! A boat rental and a day on the lake made for a relaxing and restorative summer experience.

Occasionally we'd try our luck at the racetrack when the ballet and the races coincided. While fun in theory, we could be faced with a serious additional challenge if we didn't plan right. So. Much. Traffic. A ten-minute drive to SPAC could easily become forty if you didn't strategically plan a route via back roads. There's always an uptick in dancers who don't quite make our half-hour call time, nearly giving Tommy and Rosemary a goddamn coronary.

Dancing outside is a never-ending adventure in itself. We'd complain about dripping sweat, thick with makeup under the lights that added an additional 15 degrees to a temperature that was already on a par with hell. Then we'd complain just as much when the temperature dipped down to 40 degrees for curtain-up on the last ballet, ending at 10:30 p.m. And the mosquitoes. The constant, never-ending supply of mosquitoes. I'd be standing in formation in the corps, as a serene white swan, wondering why in the hell Odette wants to take this dumb bastard back, when I'd inevitably be bitten right on the goddamn forehead. To swat or not to swat, Gina?

These are beautiful memories.

Once, the show was delayed for two hours because of tornado warning–style weather. The orchestra pit was flooded. Generators were used to power the show for the extreme diehards who roughed it out. How were they thanked for their perseverance? Well, two people were struck by lightning. They survived, but seriously—pack it up at the first sign of lightning, people. It's just ballet!

Some memories fall into a category that I'd call "playfully sinister." Once, in a contemptuous contract-negotiation period when the dancers had been asked to endure a pay freeze right before an eleven-week layoff, a fired-up dancer showed Peter appreciation by keying his Bentley. Dancers would also pull parking pranks—stealing car keys while someone was onstage and reparking other dancers' cars in a distant parking lot that would take them ages to walk to. These lots are so far, and the hill leading up to the theater is so steep, that golf carts are ready preperformance to transport patrons who just aren't up to the task. Peter could never be bothered with this pain in the ass of a walk either; he'd park right next to the stage entrance. So trust me when I say there are few things more excruciating than finishing a triple bill and showering off the thick layer of summer-show sweat only to break out in a fresh new sweat while you huff and puff your tired ass zigzag-style up that hill.* ... *Surprise!* You've been punk'd.

The most infamous Saratoga story is also not exactly a shining moment for the ballet. A local cop spotted two of the male dancers "acting suspiciously" in a parked car in town, and when the cop approached, he saw one dancer (Peter's own son) trying to hide a small bag of cocaine. This stupidity resulted in a massive, widely reported scandal, ending with Peter's son taking the fall—driving a stake into the remains of a withering career—and leaving the other, Amar Ramasar, free to run amok and unchecked for many more years.

One summer, a local church we passed frequently had a welcome sign that read, "Give Satan an inch and he'll be a ruler." What exactly constituted giving Satan an inch? Skipping church? Underage drinking in a local bar? Being gay? Taking birth control? Capital murder? A group of principal male dancers looking for some extra adventure decided to "edit" the sign. The next time I was driving to the theater I noticed the sign now read, "Give Satan a bitch and he'll rule." This one admittedly cracked me up as I am all too familiar with the contradictions of the church, being raised a Catholic myself. Also, don't get me started on what that may or may not divulge about the mentality of the male dancers in this particular group. Looking back, the vandalism was taking things a bit far, but it was done in good fun, and the sign was really condescending.

* * *

Despite the laid-back atmosphere and the boat trips that heightened my summer vibe, Saratoga is clouded for me. It's haunted by the memory of how badly I needed Peter's approval; it's when I understood that

---

* Our physical therapists insist we walk up the hill this way as it is easier on already overworked calf muscles.

my career was going to live or die based on what Peter thought of me. I didn't *want* to want this approval—but without it, this power-hungry man wasn't going to hire me. I had to dim my light. I certainly got over the fact that my contract didn't come with cheers and whistles; no one was popping a bottle of Moët—but the strong grip of Peter's control, that was another story. Saratoga is where I became a full-fledged ballerina, and it's also where I learned that I would constantly have to be on the lookout. I needed to prove that bringing me into the family wasn't a lapse in judgment—a regrettable mistake. I got my shot and I took it.

This is how one should flaunt a "Jellicle Pussy." With Final Bow for Yellowface cofounder, Phil Chan.

"Hamilcat": when you dress as both a Cat and a cast member of *Hamilton* at an Andy Blankenbuehler–choreographed production.

A view the audience will never see: the house is behind me. Rehearsing Red Woman in *Russian Seasons* twenty-four hours before I tore my ACL.

[ABOVE] I had the night off, but that didn't stop me from making a dramatic appearance with fellow cat Tyler Hanes.

[RIGHT] I've been a cover girl exactly once.
Photo by Matt Karas.

[ABOVE] A con woman dripping in sass and diamonds. The great Carmen de Lavallade and her son, Leo Holder, were a dream to work with on American Dance Machine for the 21st Century.

Photo by Christopher Duggan.

I fell, but I had already lost that tooth.

Twinning with BFF Miranda Grove.

This photo with Tumey was taken right after she told me, "You are very talented. Very lazy, but very talented."

Summer 1995 & 1996
Gina Relay for life

[ABOVE] My mom has the caption game down here.

Official apprenticeship photo by Anna Drozdowski.

Photo evidence of my "not fitting in from here to there." Gawd, watch out . . . such a fatty!

Baby's first *Cage* (get your head out of the gutter—it's a ballet).

[ABOVE] *Western Symphony* babies. With beauty Ana Sophia Scheller. Yes, we are aware that our makeup does not match our skin.

[ABOVE] Talking to the little Angels during the filming of the *On Pointe* documentary.

Photo by Marty Prudenti.

America the beautiful.

Cats Class of 2016.

My *Cats* bow every single time. Photo by Krista Schlueter for the *New York Times*.

Dame Gillian Lynne teaching me the White Cat solo. Adam Murray in on the fun.

Leona Lewis and castmates.

Chita Rivera and me at the after-party of the awards show named in her honor. I DID NOT WIN for my nomination for *Cats*, but I did "win" in that I got to work with Chita on "Beale Street Blues" with ADM21.

Rogue Ballerina *Risky Business* homage.
Photo by Matt Karas.

Fancy Free, choreography by Jerome Robbins. Photo by Paul Kolnik.

A Midsummer Night's Dream, act 2. Choreography by George Balanchine.

Photo by Paul Kolnik.

Devastated by my injury but still inspired to move.

Photo by Nicola Majocchi.

Ocean's Kingdom (fun to play evil, but this highlights how often dancers of color are cast as the villains). Photo by Paul Kolnik.

[LEFT] Workshop performance, *Brahms-Schoenberg Quartet*. Photo by Paul Kolnik.

Tyler Hanes and I re-creating an iconic photo. *On the Town*.

Swan Dive #5

Sometimes your friends just aren't there for you.

It was another hot day in Saratoga, the temperature was passing 90. It was the last performance of *Opus Jazz*, a matinee in the hot butt crack of the day. I love *Opus Jazz*, but the costumes make it a real drag to perform in Hades-level temps. Black unitards for the ladies with white socks and sneakers—but the poor men, they were wearing ultrathick cowl-neck wool sweaters that looked straight out of a winter-themed L.L.Bean shoot.

At the end of *Opus Jazz* I get tossed off the stage. It's basically a cheer-leading maneuver. I'm launched up into the air, then thrown offstage into the wings. It's very dramatic and suggests infinity. By the end of the piece, there are usually three dancers who aren't onstage anymore who will safely catch me. But two out of these three guys had fled to the main rehearsal room to suck up some AC so their effing faces didn't melt off. This room is *adjacent* but not the most convenient dash from the wings of an ongoing performance . . . you can only *kind of* hear the music.

I can hear Church, the third dancer, whisper-shouting from the wing, "Gina! Gina! They're not here!"

The five guys who have just pseudo-gang-raped me on the stage (act-ing!) are wondering what to do. I blink at Justin, trying to signal . . . *Toss me.* Then, thinking better of it, I abort and try to signal . . . *Just a half toss. Church will catch me.* When the time comes to launch me in the air, I go flying, but they've also angled me so that I am being chucked into the curtains. I try to grab on to the fabric to slow down the speed of my body so Church has a better chance of catching me.

A stagehand has noticed what's going on and is standing behind Church to try to help break my fall. I make impact and whack Church awkwardly in the head with my body before sliding down his body toward the floor, landing as safely as I can on my butt.

Church is okay, but my tailbone is bruised. He helps me up, and we see two dancers rushing toward me with white faces.

"Oh my God! Paz! We are so sorry," they say as they run onto the stage during the blackout for the next movement. They missed catching me, but they did not miss their entrance! They seem very relieved I did not break my body in half.

"You fuckers owe me." I limp off to the rehearsal room. It is my turn to get some AC.

CHAPTER 11

Party on the West Side

Singing is not my chosen profession. Having had the pleasure of spending time with legit Broadway singers, I can tell you that while I can carry a tune, singing is not my primary gift of artistic expression. When you hear someone who has performed a leading role in a Broadway show nail the high E6 in an Andrew Lloyd Webber score like it's as easy as saying hello, you know when you should just stay in your own lane. When J. P. came up to me in the rehearsal room in Saratoga, I was bracing myself for a wild-card comment that was sure to be insulting despite good intentions. *What now? Do I look bloated from the summer humidity?* I was surprised when instead he said, "Hey, I'd like you to sing for Anita in *West Side Story*. Do you sing?"—all casual, like he was asking if rain was in the forecast and not if I wanted to try out for an iconic role in one of Jerome Robbins's most beloved creations.

West Side Story Suite is a New York City Ballet favorite. It features several popular songs from the Broadway musical choreographed by Jerome Robbins—"The Rumble," "Tonight," "The Dance at the Gym," and "America." The story goes that for years Peter had been asking Jerry (after decades at the ballet, I feel I have earned the right to refer to the great Jerome Robbins as Jerry) if he thought the ballet could perform a condensed version of the beloved musical, and would he create an abridged version. Jerry always answered no. The original choreography features jazz dancing, some ballet, and *singing*.

Eventually, because Peter gets what he wants, the first gang of dancers who could belt out a tune performed *West Side Story Suite* for the first time in 1995, albeit with a Broadway actress playing Anita. That I was now being considered for Anita was an honor. I had loved *West Side Story* since I was a kid—the story of falling in love and innocence lost was timeless. During this time in my career, I was losing some innocence myself, as I had started secretly dating and sneaking around with another dancer who was both older and married.

I had performed in *West Side Story Suite* once, as a wallflower at the gym, but as a Shark, of course, *because all of the dark-haired people were obviously cast as Sharks.* I never once imagined Anita was in the cards for me. But as the nonblonde, ambiguously ethnic, and perpetually sassy member of the company, I shouldn't have been completely surprised. The possibility of performing this role made me wildly excited but incredibly nervous. Singing? Sure, in the shower—and the occasional "Total Eclipse of the Heart" if I'm doing karaoke with friends. But onstage, in front of people? *Shit.*

J. P. was being very casual about the audition. "It's no big deal. You'll just, you know, sing a bit with the pianist, and then we'll see what you can do. Just relax! This doesn't mean anything. This does not mean you'll be called to even learn the role. I should be clear on that. Let's just take a few minutes and work with the pianist."

In typical City Ballet style, what "didn't mean anything" to them did, in fact, really mean something *to me.* I had only a few minutes until I was meeting J. P. and the pianist, so I ran to find Kurt Froman. Kurt was one of the only members of the company who had Broadway experience, and I knew he could sing. I found Kurt in the shoe room. We were performing *Swan Lake,* and all the shoes had just been dyed. The fumes were intense.

"Kurt, help me. I have to sing in two minutes. What do I do?"

Kurt turned to me. "You take the biggest breath you possibly can, then squeeze it out slowly from the diaphragm." We practiced some breathing exercises. "And that is your two-minute lesson on how you sing!" With that proclamation, Kurt walked out of the shoe room, kicking up dust and cobwebs into the chemical fog. I inhaled deeply.

Fortified with those words of wisdom and heady fumes, I booked it to the rehearsal studio where I was meeting J. P.

I do not have perfect pitch, but I can match pitch. I can't read music either, but the pianist gave me some tips, and I was able to follow along as she started to play "America." I was loosening up and I was starting to actually enjoy myself. "Okay, Gina—let's have you try it from over here." When J. P. spoke, it became clear to me how echoey the room was. I told myself to take a breath like I was diving for pearls. J. P.'s jaw dropped. He was awe-struck when I opened my mouth and belted out, "I LIKE THE ISLAND MANHATTAN," like I was channeling Rita Moreno, Ethel Merman, and Judy Garland all at once. "Oh, wow. I didn't know you could do that. Great! All done."

And so the next winter I debuted as Anita. I was backstage, my hair carefully stuffed into Anita's sexy short wig. I swallowed, but it was like I couldn't actually swallow. Jesus, no. I had the most intense case of cotton mouth. Just as I was wondering if I had time to get a sip of water— hell, I was so desperate I would have asked another dancer to just spit in my goddamn mouth—I heard those distinctive percussive beats—1, 2, 3, 1, 1—that sound right before Anita enters with her lady friends onto the stage. Get over yourself, girl, it's time to go out there and sing.

And at that exact moment, something changed about me as an artist. I felt truly and absolutely seen. It wasn't the first time I stepped into a major lead role, but the trifecta of singing, dancing, and telling a story was bliss. Just a few minutes ago I had been scared shitless, I had no idea how nerves can mess up your voice, and I had no idea how much time I spent not breathing when I danced. Not only was this experience supremely satisfying to me as an artist, but it was a huge lesson in how to be more efficient with my breath. Up until that moment I had not realized that voice lessons were teaching me how to breathe while moving. While it's not a good idea to hold one's breath while dancing, it happens. Obviously, it isn't physically possible to sing and dance without controlled, deliberate breathing. Learning to sing showed me how to breathe while dancing.

I absolutely adored it! I think the audience picked up on my joy, too—to this day, when I perform Anita, I feel a connection to the audience that is unlike anything I have ever felt.

Swan Dive #6

In 2004, I'd had my corps contract for about two years, but I was still one of the newest kids on the block. The two-week run of *The Sleeping Beauty* is brutal, especially for the corps. In the vision scene, the Prince thinks he sees Aurora, but no! It's just a bunch of ballerinas dressed in the same princess-style costumes! It's a pretty scene, very languid—fairy tale–esque. The Prince dances with his fantasy Aurora, and then there is a brisk finale movement that is carried on by the corps dancers in crowded groups of four. That's four tutus and eight legs trying to carry out some intricate and awkward Martins choreo.

It's tough to execute any movement in this formation; our tutus barely have room to pass by each other. Okay, one and two and three and four and relevé up and pas de bourrée and pas de chat . . . holy shit. I'm down!

I am on my ass, left adrift by my group of ballerinas as they ballonné off to stage right. My mind is spinning. I have to get up. Not only have I fallen, but I am so far detached from my group, there is no way to catch up to them. My mind is racing through choreo to determine the most subtle way to reattach. Tulle everywhere, large, fluffy moving targets. I am dizzy.

I have to walk for two counts to get back into place . . . two counts of destroying the ballerina magic. Think if you were at Disney World, and Snow White whipped a 40-ouncer out from beneath her skirt, threw it back, and burped loudly. That's basically what my pedestrian walking amounts to. I see an opportunity to try to jump back into formation, and I slip—AGAIN. This time with my back to the audience, so at least they can't see that I am about to laugh/cry with the absurdity of it all. I am stuck for another four centuries' worth of counts until I finally rejoin the tribe of my bouncing asshole colleagues, who are now all giggling.

When the fresh hell that was the vision scene was over, I had to rush to change costumes. I was miserable and embarrassed, but there was no time to think about it. Rosemary found me amid the brambles crowding backstage.

"Are you okay?" I could tell she was trying to be stern, but also about to crack. "Um, you really went down!"

As she walked away, I think I heard a laugh. *If a ballerina falls onstage and everyone who sees it laughs about it, will it keep her from getting fired?* Better polacca for my life in the third act.

CHAPTER 12

She Died Last Night

I was still sweating from the performance, waiting for my turn for the shower, when I received a most welcome message from Moira, my favorite waitress. "Hey. We have the stuffed peppers. Am I saving you some?" The mere thought of a beautiful pepper—stuffed with ground beef, rice, and the perfect amount of cheese to make it *just greasy enough*—revived me. I wouldn't be going straight home tonight. "Roger that! Incoming 20 mins!" I responded and then sent eight more texts rallying the troops to join me if they weren't already en route. Since joining the corps, I was experiencing a whole new level of exhaustion. But tonight, I'd be stopping by the Emerald Inn . . . stuffed peppers awaited me! Life in the corps opened my eyes to what real work was. Not that I hadn't been working hard—ballet *is hard*. But the continuous circle of class, rehearsal, performance was beyond anything I had experienced. Just the brain power it took to learn and commit to memory thirty or so ballets that were in rotation this season felt like a massive feat. But dancing in the corps meant that you were part of an ensemble. In addition to the physical demands, I had to learn to dance onstage in formation and in sync with as many as eight to twenty other women—and in rare cases the entire effing company. I was pushing my body hard, my brain harder, and my ego aside. And as with any office setting there is a variety of personalities one encounters while playing swan. With a bass-baritone order from Peter, I had gone from being a student—cared for, pampered a little bit even—to one of eighty-eight dancers in the corps, all of us left to our own devices. I was a "pro" now and I had to learn my place in the pack before I could even think about ascending within its ranks. My choices were: crumble under the pressure or take off flying. Most nights I went home, got in bed, and passed out faster than you could say Ambien. My body was always desperate for sleep, my muscles aching and needing to be recharged.* As tired as I was, I was also young and needed release from the massive pressure cooker that was my new life. Enter "Emerald"!

The Emerald Inn was a perfect example of a now nearly extinct New York City institution—the Local Dive Bar. During my patronage from 2002 to 2013, Emerald was a tiny little joint nestled into an old building on Columbus Avenue between Sixty-Ninth and Seventieth (alas, this space was taken over by a Kate Spade store, only to be taken over again by another store selling $50 T-shirts). A long mahogany bar gracefully stretched through the space; regulars and neighborhood peeps folded into the booths or at the bar side by side with the artists, dancers, and musicians alike of Lincoln Center. Emerald was a real *Cheers*-style spot for me. Charlie and John, the owner and bartender, knew us all by name, and Moira knew I loved those peppers so much that she'd take the time to call me and let me know when they were on the menu. I took my relationship with Emerald up another notch when I asked them to be the custodian of my spare set of keys. I knew I could count on Emerald should I ever lock myself out. Charlie always had our backs, whether it

---

* An unexpected bonus to this level of exhaustion is that to this day I am an expert napper. I can fall asleep almost anywhere.

was to turn a blind eye to our questionable age in the postshow drinks hour, or to let me into my apartment while I adjusted to life as a hybrid child/working adult.

Nights I decided to head home and hit the hay didn't always work out as I had planned either. The siren sound of Emerald was powerful, and my little studio apartment was right around the corner. Some nights I'd be deep in sleep, only to hear my name being called repeatedly, barely audible above the ever-buzzing sounds of Manhattan, like I was the object of affection in some sort of urban, ballet-themed romcom. Semiawake, I'd think, *Is some asshole leaning on my buzzer?* I'd stick my head under my pillow thinking, *I'm. So. Tired.* After twenty more seconds of incessant buzzer ringing, I'd drag myself out of bed and walk sleepily to the buzzer. "What?!" I'd respond, trying to sound both pissed off and threatening—like I was the kind of chick you did not mess with. Then I'd hear an unmistakable female cackle and a familiar male voice . . . "Your presence is requested. Emerald."

"Seriously, Loreen, Amar, FUCK OFF! NOW."

The buzzer continued wailing, threatening to wake up the whole building. Jostled awake, young, and in New York City, it seemed having a 2 a.m. cocktail was the most neighborly option and only reasonable choice. Just the week before, my new neighbors threatened to call the cops on me during a particularly raucous game of simultaneous double Twister at my housewarming (both mats took up nearly every inch of my tiny apartment). *The nerve.* I even invited them! They were doubly surprised when my cohort's husband, a cop himself, opened the door and flashed his badge before graciously extending an invitation to spin the wheel. Not my fault they declined!

On nights like this, depending on the weather, maybe I'd toss on a coat—but I never bothered to take off my pajamas. The Emerald was like an extension of my home. It was just a two-minute walk, and who are we kidding? It was the middle of the night and no one on the Upper West Side was awake other than my asshole friends and the folks hanging out at the Emerald. Those nights are a beautiful blur of memories—sing-alongs, drinking gimlets, life chats, dares, games, and late-night deliveries of Big Nick's Pizza. A rousing game of Fuck, Marry, Kill was often suggested when we were three gimlets in. Somogyi, a total wiseass, would get a certain gleam in her eye. "I'll go first." We'd all wait for her to list three names.

That night she announced: "Loreen: Pope John Paul the Second, Carrie Fisher, and *Amar.*" We are, not surprisingly, a competitive group. Everyone knew what was going down and was thinking about their own selections. Loreen swigged her vodka cran.

"That's easy. I'd fuck the Pope, marry Carrie Fisher, and I have to say I'd kill Amar."

The table guffawed at the blow to Amar's ego. While Amar was visibly upset that no one would want to sleep with him, he conceded, to his credit here, that he may have gone the same route. Loreen said to Andy, "Jeffrey Dahmer, George W. Bush, and Amar." Andy looked like he was thinking hard. "I guess I'd fuck Jeffrey Dahmer. I mean, he's not terrible looking, but I'm obviously not going to marry someone who will eventually kill me. Call me a money whore, but I'd marry George W. Bush, and that leaves . . . killing Amar." Cue more laughs. "Seriously? You'd fuck a serial killer?" Amar chided his close pal, who had caught on to the prank.

Then Andy said to me, "Dracula, me, Amar." I didn't even need to pause for a breath, "Fuck you, marry Dracula, and kill Amar." "Oh, come on!" Amar yelled over our laughter. His taking the joke way too seriously was only egging us on. He was one of us, but we all knew as well as he did that he was *that* guy. Amar is charming, good-looking, talented, and he uses this trifecta to manipulate the system. The game would go on (no one would want to fuck or marry Amar ever, no matter how hideous the other options. Don't worry; he got over it), more rounds would be bought—and eventually, very late in the night, pizza would be called for. A last-ditch attempt to suck up the alcohol before crashing for a few hours. We had class at 10 a.m., after all. I'd head home eventually, drinking a big glass of water before finally getting some sleep. I knew there was a good chance I'd feel like ass tomorrow. I'd be fighting my way through class with a headache and a bloated stomach. But I didn't care. I loved the Emerald like a favorite sweater. It was the only place I could slip into, the pressure instantly sliding off my shoulders, before I woke up to face it all again.

*   *   *

Company class is held every single day in the dance studio of the Rose Building, just north of Lincoln Center. The vibe in company class is not unlike your typical high school homeroom . . . if every single person in your high school wore tights and leos and could do a perfect grand jeté. People gather before class to catch up, spilling details of the latest dramas, late-night clubbing antics, and casting surprises. The Emerald crew would trickle in closer to the start of class and some a little bit later— all of us seemingly full of pep and vigor. *The first rule of Fight Club is that you don't talk about Fight Club.* No one needed to know that we were upping the level of prowess by spotting not one but three of our own reflections in the mirror. Pro tip: always spot the middle one. The play-it-cool game got harder if your sweat betrayed your poison. Vodka sweat, bourbon sweat . . . it's real and it's gross. You can sweat garlic, too, by the way. Be mindful before eating second helpings of pesto, people!

Company class is "optional." None of us *technically* have to go—but like most things with the ballet, it's not that simple. For one thing, company class is where you demonstrate your dedication to the craft. It's not just about perfecting your technique—it's an homage, a way to pay respect to the art form and to our bodies (regardless of choices made postcurtain). Although clearly not always the case, class has evolved into a form of meditation for me. Unlike a performance, it's all about my body and the music and keeping my instrument in tune.

Being present—and I mean this physically not philosophically, although that helps, too—at class is an expression of all that is holy in ballet, and dancers will go to crazy lengths to attend. Dancers (myself included) have shown up directly from the closing of a bar, wildly hungover, and, according to NYCB *and* ABT lore, once after basically rising from the dead.

The story goes that one particular morning, two male dancers were easing into their warm-up when dancer A asked dancer B (who referred to himself in the third-person feminine) what he did last night. Dancer B responded without losing a beat, "OHHH, GURL, SHE *DIED LAST NIGHT*." This wasn't an exaggeration. Apparently, Dancer B consumed so much cocaine that he had to be revived via defibrillator on the dance floor and was then hauled off to the hospital, where he was subjected to various emergency protocols. He was released at 4 a.m., leaving him just enough time to pop home for a nap, pull on some clean tights, et voilà! At company class by 10:30 a.m.! The dancer in question was generations before me, but his spirit looms large in the rehearsal studio. Searing menstrual cramps, broken toe, double pneumonia? *Mere child's play* and see your ass in class. You don't fucking miss class, even if you died on the dance floor of a nightclub.

Our unofficial motto is play hard, work harder. You want to go to a wild all-night sex party? Live your best life, as long as you can use those inner thighs to dance come 10:30 a.m. And for Lord's sake, don't trumpet your nasty moonlight life too loudly because a good portion of our coworkers are literally children.

By now I've been with the company for nearly twenty years, which is about a billion in ballerina years. While I'm still extremely dedicated to company class, I've earned the right to miss on occasion. To be clear, this doesn't mean I'm at home on the sofa pining over Mandy Patinkin (love him). I'm still going to class—just not the one at NYCB. There have been mornings where I get out of bed, walk my dog, make my eggs, pack my pointe shoes and various physical therapy implements into my bag, and jump on the subway to Lincoln Center. *Today I shall attend company class!*

But sometimes, something happens. When I emerge from the subway and my eyes fall on that iconic fountain, I have a physical reaction. It's almost like being horribly allergic to something lovely—like a flower. *Look at that! That's so pretty.* But moments later I'm sweating/nauseous/itching/sick and full of dread thinking about the cesspool of drama that's waiting inside for me. Some of it is typical coworker bullshit. Like Daniel busts out the inevitable massive sneeze every SINGLE day. Just one. I have never heard the man sneeze outside of class. The sound bursts out of him with such force that his lips quiver violently. His sneeze is so distinctive, so powerful that it's still very audible to me even on days when the men and women are split into separate classes. Like in any other work environment, some days you hear it and laugh. *Oh, there goes Daniel, consummate clown.* Others, his ridiculous eruption actually hurts my head. "WTF, D! Take a goddamn Zyrtec!"

Other annoyances range from Megan showing up in my purple velour leg warmers, the ones a dear friend made especially for me as a birthday gift—*with his hands.* I had loved them so hard and thought I had lost them forever.* A full season later they were revealed . . . Megan had torn them apart and refashioned them into a purple velour leotard. That leotard was unmistakably born from my leg warmers. Or a more practical reason: I busted my foot in the show on the previous night and needed a safe place to test it out without baiting the shark-infested water with a vulnerable, injured limb. If my emotional, spiritual, and physical state is precarious, I'll say, *Oh, hell no, not today!* And I get back on the subway and head up to Steps on Broadway, where I pay to take an open ballet class with a collection of random professional dancers,

---

* Ballerinas steal each other's shit. Kind of like a little sister "borrowing" your favorite top for the school dance but oops! She totally forgot to give it back, and now it lives in her closet.

elderly people, Broadway lovers, and a woman who uses a wheelchair.* I might not be at company class—but I'm still doing a class.

But no matter how senior you are, if you're performing in the evening, you take class that day. Period. Not only that, but you'll probably do a whole repeat of the barre as a warm-up later after a long rehearsal day.

* * *

I had a particular buzz going at the barre today, and it was not the result of any alcohol or other controlled substance (hard drugs were never my brand of fun). Tonight was gala night. And at risk of sounding like Eloise . . . I positively adore gala night! Gala night is guaranteed adrenaline. Performance not required for the dopamine effect! I display my preening, parading, and schmoozing skills unabashedly on and off the stage. But performing on gala night is the ultimate thrill. It usually means performing in a *world* premiere of a new ballet. It's an unveiling of all the work that's been put in during the past few weeks. Gala night is the apex of everything . . . Will the audience respond positively? Negatively? Do I know the steps? Have I re-downloaded that finale step that was changed only hours before? Will this designer's costume manage to hold up when my body is supercharged with adrenaline? Or will I experience a massive costume malfunction and end up topless like I did in the villagers' scene in *Swan Lake*? It happens, and it's not easy to correct a major costume issue when you're onstage dancing in front of 2,500 people with no exit offstage planned for the next twenty-eight minutes.

That ill-fated costume consisted of a peasant dress with a flowy chiffon skirt (in the ballet world, nothing says "villager" like chiffon!) in shades of puke and pea green topped off with a very, very sheer blouse. Curiously, the corset that was paired with this costume stopped imme-

---

* Bless her for her awesome dedication and love of dance (she's so keenly devoted she makes all of us look like assholes).

diately beneath my breasts. A nude leo underneath this creation was a necessity if I didn't want to look like I was dancing for tips.

Showtime.

I'm waltzing on stage . . . it's actually a beautiful waltz—it really builds. *Pas de bourrée* and pop . . . the clip on one side of my leo has come undone. Sticking through my sheer village lady blouse is an erect nipple. My fellow dancers and the first few rows of the audience have a full view of my boob for the next twelve minutes of this long-ass piece. I'm thinking about whether there's any point in the movement when I could quickly hook it back when *pop*: now both tetas have sprung free. Jiggling in the breeze, nipples as hard as buttons from adrenaline and an air-conditioned house.

My friend (and now current boss) Jon, who has been one of the more straitlaced colleagues, could not help but lose his shit. Jon is playing Prince Siegfried, and at this moment the Prince is brooding! It's his birthday, and his mother has ruined it by insisting he get married! He's sitting on his throne with his BFF Benno, when all of the lovely peasants come by to wish him a happy birthday. There I was, approaching the man who would eventually become my boss with my tits out. HAPPY BIRTHDAY FROM YOUR TOPLESS PEASANT, PRINCE SIEGFRIED! Jon's normally straight face is holding back laughter and is as red as a beet. I mouth them a *Screw you two idiots*, as I laugh and dance into another formation. At this point we are five minutes into the production, and the whole stage is cracking up. The word has begun to travel as dancers whisper as discreetly to one another as they can onstage . . . "Look at Gina; her tits fell out." That may have been the twelve longest minutes of my career. Clip-on leos are no longer part of my life.

* * *

While I always hope my costume can withstand the fervor of an adrenaline-fueled gala performance, I also have to brace myself to manage the logistics. Gala night can be complicated for me. We have rehearsal all day, the final tech of the premiere piece, then magically switch gears—being red-carpet ready and smiling for the cameras like you have no other business in the world than looking hot. Then off comes the red-carpet garb I've spent days curating but have only publicly worn for a few minutes because it's time to switch gears again and into our costumes. Over the years my gala-night costumes have ranged from a pair of jeans and a white button-down shirt (with all of my hair tucked into a pixie-style wig) to a gorgeous cape-wielding creation Stella McCartney made just for me, to . . . a horse costume. Imagine, if you will, equine S and M meets ballet. That little number consisted of a brown velour unitard, a custom-fitted saddle for my back, and the pièce de résistance . . . a whip-style tail that I could flail around however I pleased!

There was one element of that costume that I did flat-out refuse.

"So, Georgina. I'm thinking a face harness. I'll design a bit that you can hold in your mouth." It was one of the final fittings with Carlos Campos and Christopher Wheeldon. I channeled my inner Mr. Ed: *Oh, we are done here. You wanted a wild Argentinean filly, and I've been game for most of this bullshit, but I am not holding a bit in my teeth while I dance.*

I whipped the shit out of that tail in the performance, and I got a great review—no bit required. And by the way, I've got to take a sec to address some of my male colleagues—yeah you, you know who you are. I never was and will never be YOUR FARM ANIMAL.

Whatever I'm wearing, I'll dance my hardest, knowing full well it can be the inspiration for donors to open their wallets. The audience that night will be dressed to the nines; this is the elite of the elite of New York society and celebrity. After the applause and curtain calls, I dash back to my dressing room. Released of my fetish costuming, I'm primed for a stiff one (a DRINK! *Excuse you*). My hair and makeup are recalibrated back to red-carpet ready, my gown goes back on, and I head to the dinner to socialize, schmooze, and most importantly, partake in sustenance.

People have paid lots of money to have a real live ballerina at their table, and it's a role I'm conditioned to excel at. Although I will say that nowadays I've earned the right to be seated next to friends, so my schmoozing days are, thank God, mostly behind me.

But back in 2011, I'm the only dancer at a table of top-tier donors and a celebrity or two.

After salads and a dinner of some lightly poached fish that costs as much per plate as my rent, a donor approached from another table and leaned toward me.

"Hey, Gina. Dance with me?"

Michael Jackson is playing, so I'm game. I have been known to stop midsentence at a table and call, "Pause!" only to skid onto the dance floor to make a sixteen-bar refrain. As we walked to the dance floor, my gown swishing behind me, it quickly became clear that this guy had drunk his weight in cocktails. His offbeat swaying suggested more drunkenness than lack of rhythm. The dance floor was filling up. Dancers and various donors and socialites were swirling around on the mirrored dance floor. Shadowy images of all of us bounced around as the lights moved. I was finding my groove, feeling the joy in the music, when *wham bam thank you ma'am* I was flat on my back on the goddamn floor with a drunk donor splayed out on top of me.

The shit I do for work, man.

Fellow dancers Henry and Allen peeled the donor off me and discreetly escorted him back to the table. I was restored to my regular state of grace after exchanging a glance with Baryshnikov, and I will say, if being pummeled by a donor resulted in my being free at that precise moment to catch Misha's eye, it was worth it.

The rest of the evening I was dutifully chatty, charming, and fun. It's not an act either. I've developed genuine relationships with people I've met at galas. And really, sometimes it just feels good to be surrounded be hundreds of actual ballet-loving human beings.

As the donors started to pile into town cars, the catering staff began to pack up bottles of booze and wineglasses. Andy signaled to me: "You ready?" Gala night ends at the Emerald.

I wondered what it would have been like for the regulars on nights like this. Perched in their usual spot, a whiskey or beer in front of them. The dinginess of the bar suddenly lit up by a gaggle of young men and women stumbling through the door. Our tuxedos and gowns a stark contrast with the scuffed floor and the worn wood. We'd already be tipsy, having taken full advantage of the open bar at the gala. We'd dance and drink more until the exhaustion of the entire day settled on us like a weight.

I remember those nights at the Emerald with a fondness so genuine it nearly aches. We were bonded together, experiencing the almost sur-real fun of being in the city—pushing aside the pressure even if for just a few hours. Those were different times. They also were wondrous times. Now as a seasoned drinker, official New Yorker, and real grown-up, I wonder how the hell did we do it night after night *and* make it to work the next day? It wasn't just that we had a young person's metabolism and fierce dedication. It was something else—an energy and spontaneity we needed. So what if we were hungover in class? Maybe we knew that when trying to forge ahead in one of the most competitive environ-ments in the world, one doesn't always want complete clarity of mind.

CHAPTER 13

Fuck Your Brunch

It was a two-show day. There was a matinee and evening performance of various repertory pieces, but both programs ended with *The Firebird*. On a day like this, company class is held later, at 12:30 p.m.—Praise Jesus!—and there isn't a major rehearsal. This is the result of the union requiring overtime pay for rehearsing individuals who are already slated to dance two shows, so company class will be a sixty-minute affair, taking us right up to the half-hour call before curtain.

A half hour is not a long time to strap on, sew in, and costume up for those in the first ballet. That's why I was standing at the barre between dancers in varying degrees of readiness. For the overly nervous, it was always full stage makeup, hair coiffed with headpiece, performance tights already on. Some go to class with just half beat on the face. My personal go-to is full beat, minus eye lashes, hair down. However, there have also been days I've subjected myself to the company's giggles, taking class in a wig cap (no one's finest look). Any insecurity has long since been smudged out since my *Cats* run. If you've met me in real life, you know my mane has a life of its own. I leave the taming to the professionals—my dear friend Suzy Alvarez and Karla Elie, and before that, Stanley Tines in the makeup room. They have had my back and kept my secret that, even though I am a ballerina of twenty years, I have yet to master the perfect Balanchine bun.

I was sandwiched between dancers performing in the first show, who were using class to get warm and fight the inevitable preshow jitters—and I was feeling the slightest bit smug. I was not cast in today's programs, nor did I have rehearsal. So I was fantasizing about the gloriously free day ahead of me. During tendus . . . *Okay, so first I'm meeting Dean for brunch. We haven't seen each other in ages.* Dégagés . . . *He's gonna tell all about his latest brush with death doing stunt work on the new Jamie Foxx action movie, so drinks will be a must. Brunch with booze! How lush of thee!* Rond de jambe . . . *I should actually take him to the new Waxman restaurant downtown. Look at me leaving the Upper West Side! After brunch I'll take the foster pup Marco for a long-ass walk, and we can train a bit.* Frappés . . . *Then I should probably clean. I am all out of pink tights, and the house is a dust bunny graveyard.* Grands battements . . . *I could make osso buco for dinner! Oh, wait. No. Oh, wait. I have to meet Sam for a date.* Cue some Leonard Bernstein—*Anita's gonna have her kicks tonight . . .*

I'm reveling in thoughts of my beautiful freedom when my dancer senses are suddenly on full alert. And that's when I spot him in the mirror. Tommy. Yep. Tommy is standing at the back of the class—all anal attention, looking irritated as he scans the backs of the dancers, looking for his intended victim. *Hmm, maybe I should dip out of class now . . .* I take a breath, finish my combo, and bend down to grab my things. I see him skulking around, but he's skulking closer to me now. Taking note of the dancers to my immediate flank. *Well, Ashley is hurting, so maybe he's just checking on her?* There's a flurry of movement and chatter as we clear the barres for center. But I can still feel it. Sure enough, Tommy's stony stare is gliding across the room . . . His eyes pause briefly on each dancer like he's sizing us up. Now I'm the one who is irritated. He is totally destroying my feel-good chi.

Tommy's looming presence in class is never welcome, to me, at least. His appearance signals to everyone that something is amiss, whether a dancer forgot to sign in for the show or a last-minute casting change needs to happen. And as far as my relationship with Tommy goes— it's not chummy. I'm not like some of the other dancers in the room who sidle up to him, asking questions and trying to make themselves privy to the knowledge he holds. Tommy seems to love it when people kiss up to him, but I'd rather pluck my eyelashes than force a relationship with someone. For me he's a harbinger of upset in a fast-moving world where time is of the essence. If I had to describe his aura, I'd say it resembled a steel-grey storm cloud.* *That* storm is coming people! Take cover!

A few minutes went by, and the rain was yet to come down. Couldn't he just go ahead and do what he was sent here to do? Why the nerve-wracking delay, you ask? My theory is because at this exact moment, wandering around the rehearsal studio like Gollum, he has elevated status. This comes from his position as the messenger of the underworld: Peter's fourth-floor administration office, located directly beneath the large rehearsal studio.

The powers that be must have sent Tommy up from below to tag one of us to fill in for a dancer who is either sick or injured—and now it felt like he was dragging out the moment for full dramatic effect. He seems to get a sick twist from informing any dancer of their sudden change of fate. He usually manages to throw in some bonus comment, half-hearted humor presumably meant to lessen the sting, but when served with a side of objectification it makes you feel even shittier.

Something like, "Paz. We need you in the show. You'll have to wait until after *Firebird* to swallow." *Gross.* "Or you could just have him come to the show, Paz; you can give him a preview of the acrobatics, but *irregardless* you are on for Princesses."

---

* This usually indicates that something of immediate importance is going down.

In my experience at City Ballet, men of all sexual preferences have equally caused enough pain in their degradation of the female gender, intended or not. They say there are those who can only heal by paying the trauma and harm they've experienced forward, and that goes for everyone. I am well aware there are a lot of individuals affiliated with City Ballet (and perhaps in the broader world) who are going to sting reading that assertion, but I don't say it lightly or to overgeneralize. I say it because I think it's a cultural issue at the ballet that often gets a pass, and it shouldn't. For instance, in no circumstance is it appropriate for any person, colleague, ballet master, or patron to walk up to a ballerina who is standing in the back of the class, her arm protectively wrapped around her stomach, and make a joke, "What's the matter? Are you pregnant?" I can tell you from experience that *what's the matter* is that she's having a bad body day and confronting that day by staring at herself in a mirror. Applying corrections given on technique while comparing herself to the eighty other taller, thinner ballerinas in the room. Anyone with a beating heart can sometimes be a shitty human.

* * *

But coming back to Tommy. Pray tell, what is his job, you ask? What position does he hold that enables him to wield so much faux power with such verve? Tommy is in charge of the schedule. Scheduling ninety-plus dancers is a big endeavor; this I'll give him props for. We are a mass of people with constant and conflicting needs for rehearsal time and limited space to do it in. When you're in the corps, your relationship with Tommy is inconsequential for the most part. This is because you are generally participating in all of the larger rehearsals, and those get priority. These rehearsals will usually take place at the ideal time (right after class), in the best space (a room large enough for everyone), Rosie will be there (she is officially master of the corps, the fearless leader), and an actual pianist who will play along to marked places in the score. These are the crucial ingredients one needs to whip a ballet into performance shape.

But this gets more complicated for soloists and principals. Tommy controls who gets what rehearsal space, for how long, and when. He schedules the ballet masters and pianists, too.

This is how he can end up having a huge impact on our performances—not to mention our states of mind.

Say I'm cast in a debut ballet. Over the course of a few weeks, I'll learn it, rehearse it, work with a partner. While we are in the learning phase, that's one to two hours a day we'll be guaranteed a space with a coach and a pianist. But once that incubation period is up, it's up to me to *request* rehearsal times. I'm not paid for requests, mind you. Any rehearsal I feel I need to do my job is off the clock. Loophole in the overtime fine print. And whether or not I get them is up to Tommy. Hence, his outsized power.

For instance, just because you're rehearsing a role in *Diamonds* does not mean you will be cast in *Diamonds*! It doesn't matter if you've been rehearsing for the role and nailing it. You will have to wait until the official casting comes out to know for certain if you will be performing that role, and even then, shit can still go down. Anything can happen . . . a more prima ballerina objects to the casting, you've done something to fall out of favor, or someone gets injured, and the entire cast has to be rearranged (this, however, can also work in one's favor). Point is, the artistic director decides your casting. Tommy might just be privy to the casting before you are.

When a dancer doesn't get cast in a role they've devoted time and energy into rehearsing, they tend to feel pretty effing shitty and rejected. There's usually no discussion whatsoever that this has occurred. And if you dare ask, there are no good answers. So we are clear, the artistic director decides your fate, and it's that *one person* who does not want you to dance in the role.

Or perhaps that person does want you to dance, but the various politics of ballet masters got you bumped, and that person just doesn't want to advocate hard enough for you to get a shot! In any case, if you are rehearsing a role and you're getting shit slots on the schedule, this could be an indication that this is just a way for you to keep working. Soldier on! Because shit really does always go down at the ballet, I always say!

It's like getting ghosted after a long flirtation with a crush. It sucks, and it doesn't always make sense. *But I thought he liked me!* And this precious knowledge about casting is shared with us just two weeks before the performance. If you're cast in a role, learning about it just two weeks in advance can be intense. It's a lot to prepare for. However, it is possible for one to decode the schedule and get insight into casting decisions by paying attention to the minutiae embedded in the text.

How to Manipulate/Decode the Schedule at City Ballet

TACTIC #1: NOTE THE ORDER OF NAMES.

For soloist and principal parts, first, note the order of the names. If your name is listed first or second, you are probably in the first or second cast. If your name is third or fourth, you're likely a cover.

TACTIC #2: CREATE AN ALLIANCE.

If a dancer has played his cards right with Tommy, the dancer could request a space with the ballet master, and Tommy will set up the schedule so that the dancer can be coached. If a dancer has not successfully created an alliance with Tommy, this dancer and all of his requests for space, a ballet master, and a pianist will not take precedence. *Sorry not sorry!* It happens all the time. Tommy and his behind-the-scenes, Oz-like power can be used to manipulate the schedule in a manner that is advantageous to some and not to others. Tommy's power lies in his direct contact and influence with the people who cast the ballets, and the way he wields said power can be interpreted to be a bit biased in certain scenarios.

Tactic #3: Some ballets are held in higher esteem.

The schedule can also reveal which ballets the institution holds in higher esteem. The desperate grab for rehearsal space is not limited to the dancers. The ballet masters must also request rehearsals for the ballets they are in charge of. Sneaker and contemporary ballets tend to get the late shift, the unpleasant 5:30–7:30 p.m. slot, regardless of where they fall in the order of a season grid. Why? I have no idea, and you'd have to ask Tommy. One theory holds that these ballets must be easier on the bod because they don't require pointe shoes or classical technique. I can tell you from firsthand experience: this is a myth.

Tactic #4: Search for what is missing.

What is not there holds just as much meaning as what is there. Hypothetical situation! Say you hoped to get a shot at the *Raymonda Variations*. You've been taught the part. You are hungry for it and want to rehearse the shit out of it so you'll be ready, ready, ready for your glorious moment debuting in this role! But alas, your requests for rehearsal time are not being granted. Instead of the prime times, you're being scheduled a week after you've made a request, on a Saturday night from 6:30 to 7 p.m. And by the way—no ballet masters are available to coach you, and yeah, all the pianists need a break, so just go ahead and use the tape machine. This situation clearly indicates that oh, honey, you are so not getting a show. Your shitty rehearsal schedule was Tommy and the institution throwing you a bone to gnaw on and keep you hopeful. And while you continue to dance in the back line of the Garland waltz, you should keep your head down.

And there you have it. This is my asshole take on what is happening with the schedule at the New York City Ballet. Truth is, there's really no way to do this right. Someone always gets fucked.

* * *

I wasn't making eye contact on purpose, but I felt the burn of Tommy's laserlike eyes on my backside. I was putting on my pointe shoes for center when he finally spit it out, staring down at me on the floor.

"Paz, we need you to do Princesses."

Motherfucker-fucking-fuck. And just like that it's goodbye brunch and the leisurely walk in the park, and Anita is so not getting any tonight except an ice bucket and sore calves. Princess treatment indeed.

When I was new in the corps, I wanted to be chosen last-minute; it was an unexpected and extra opportunity to shine! And yes, I always love performing. I will love performing tonight. It's just that when one survives long enough to reach senior corps status, you want that ounce of respect you've worked so hard for to matter. You are given a very small window of opportunity to experience the simple joy that is living the life I have scheduled for myself on a day off. In the end we are a company. We are there for each other. And you never know when you're going to be the dancer who screws up brunch/dates/bridal showers/hair cut appointments/sleep for everyone else. I can't let myself forget. I too have been *that* dancer.

* * *

Some ballets are woven together like a fine tapestry. Remove a single strand, and suddenly you've got a very big mess. One dancer goes down, and the rest of the ballet follows. I had once requested a "feel out the stage" and a "get puffed"* rehearsal on a Sunday and was blessed with the miracle that is the immediately postclass rehearsal with a pianist. I'd get to run through everything prior to my 3 p.m. show. The ballet was Eliot

---

* "Feel out the stage": get on the physical stage and acclimate to floor space; just the sheer size of the stage can be an adjustment to the system. We have rehearsal rooms that mimic the stage, but nothing is as big.

  "Get puffed": work myself out and get my heart rate going to the point that I am panting. Out of breath after sex? That's puffed. Run to catch the train and out of breath? That's puffed. The first puff of the day is always the hardest.

Feld's *The Unanswered Question.* It is an acid trip of a ballet in which I had a crazy-insane solo (literally insane in this case). My role was to embody mania in the form of a woman in movement.

The stakes were high for me, as it was my first shot stepping out of the corps to dance a soloist role. I wore one red pointe shoe and one black (because nothing says crazy like different colored pointe shoes!). And then there was my costume, designed by the famous Willa Kim. It managed to be both avant-garde and weirdly sexual, and it is in this getup that my character has a complete breakdown onstage. *Drama.*

Later in the ballet, things get even weirder. I reappear onstage, take a sousaphone* from another dancer, place it on top of my head, and disappear through the secret trapdoor in the stage.

I can see how one would be tempted to assume that said secret trapdoor would let out into an easy passage to the wings. *Because that would make sense.* Should you ever attend a performance at Lincoln Center and see a dancer disappear through the trapdoor, know that it leads into the orchestra pit. That dancer is now awkwardly crouched down among the musicians, trying not to get bowed in the face. This is the ballet I was rehearsing when I became the reason for a complete change of program, ruining the plans of a few senior corps ladies.

I am on the stage, going through my moves. The choreography includes an abrupt scoot backward in arabesque. To achieve said scoot effect, I take nearly all of my weight off the foot I am sliding back on. Think of taking a pen to a piece of paper so lightly that it doesn't make a mark. That's what I'm trying to do with my foot—it's a powerful maneuver that takes a delicate balance of force and finesse. We're talking the graze of a hummingbird's wings here. Ballerinas are masters of physics when it comes to our own bodies; we have to trust our weight. But this time, as luck would have it, I hit a slick spot on the marley, and

---

* Yes, the sousaphone is part of the tuba family, and it's enormous. Your average sousaphone weighs thirty to thirty-five pounds. That is the approximate weight of your average four-year-old.

suddenly I don't have enough weight on my scooting foot. Instead of an exciting but calculated scoot, the velocity is amped up to full liftoff from the floor. Now I am flying horizontally backward through the air in Superwoman position. This takes just seconds, mind you.

I am still able to calculate in my head that I am not going to fly off the stage (huge plus), but I have to break my fall with a) my hands or b) my face. I chose the former, and smack. I feel the pain right away, and I know something is wrong. I stay down for a second to process. Okay, well. Maybe I can just walk this off? I try to continue, making a sad attempt to try some floor work that comes later in the variation.

I probably should have picked up on the tunnel vision closing in from the shock of it all. I am trying to work through it, but it feels like my left hand is dangling with the weight of a five-hundred-pound lifeless tuna. *Shit*. I drag myself upright, holding on to my tuna-hand with my regular hand.

Do I stop? Oh no . . . instead I stubbornly (and stupidly) try to execute a turn while holding on to the casualty that is my dead-fish hand. Then came the searing pain. I dismiss Elaine the pianist, trying to act casual and like I had wrapped up my rehearsal early. No problem, all good, nothing to see here!

I headed for the elevator, as part of me actually believed this was a problem that could be fixed in the PT room. I got in the elevator and pressed five. I didn't even notice another dancer was riding with me until I heard her speak.

"Babe. Are you okay? You're as white as a sheet."

It was at that moment that I stopped denying what had happened.

Haltingly, I muttered, "I think I broke it."

Now I was in full-blown shock. I arrived in the doorway of the PT room and managed to spit out something along the lines of I-think-it's-bad-but-oh-my-God-maybe-you-can-fix-it shit. A flurry of activity unfolded. The dancers instinctively moved away from the table; they know an injury takes precedence over their scheduled appointments.

The doctor on call was summoned, but it was Sunday, and he was in Westchester. The word had gotten around—*a dancer is down!*—and it had been exactly three minutes since I entered the room.

That's when Tommy appeared, flanked by a concerned Rosie, "What's going on?" The PT was icing my now one-thousand-pound wrist as it continued to swell.

"We're waiting for the doctor, but it looks like Georgina broke her wrist."

Rosemary asked, "Who else knows her part?"

Everyone looked around. It was the last performance of this ballet. I was already the replacement for the principal dancer originally slated for the part, who was out on extended sick leave. There was no one who could be inserted into the intricate role. It would also require an emergency rehearsal with Local 1, as the trapdoor was used—and on a Sunday, this would cost a fortune. In addition to the pain and the fear that comes with any injury when you have a physical job, I just felt like shit. They'd have to pull it. I *ruined* the ballet.* Rosie left to assess what other piece in the current repertory was about the same length and could be inserted instead.

"Paz. Can't you just man up and pull through?" Tommy asked. "Sally Leland performed Dew Drop with a broken foot. This is a moment that can make a career."

The physical therapist started to respond, "Tommy, I wouldn't suggest that; she's in total shock—" But before she could finish the sentence, a thick French accent filled the room.

"What the fuck, Tommy?"

Marco, a principal dancer, had been sitting silently in the PT room, taking in all the drama. I had barely noticed him and was glad I hadn't because Marco was so handsome, and being aware of him would have

---

* As a young corps member, we were often warned by many in authority en masse not to "ruin the ballet." This is the one time that I did, in fact, "ruin the ballet."

only made my situation more embarrassing. It's hard to look fetching when you're seething in pain and your limb has doubled in size.

I had barely heard Marco speak, ever. And here he was yelling at Tommy with full-on fury.

"That's fucking ridiculous. How is she supposed to carry the damn sousaphone with one hand? Too far, Tommy. She's scared. Show some fucking compassion!"

All of this is coming out with a thick French accent, and I was practically swooning through my delirium. Marco's veins were pumped, and I found myself thinking about the meanings behind certain tattoos. He had a teardrop tattoo just under his left eye . . . *Did I read somewhere that those are symbolic tattoos people get after they've killed someone? Or was it after they lost someone? Hmmmmmm.*

He was killing me softly right now, in fact. Tommy gave up and walked away to call in dancers. It was determined that the most logical and reasonable course of action was to put on *Concerto Barroco* instead. It has a corps of eight, two principal women and one principal man. It's about twenty minutes in length and was just performed last night.

I was still sitting there, waiting to be taken to the hospital, when I heard the senior corps girls bitching about missing brunch (thanks to me). Oh, how the grass is greener on the other side. Tommy walked by the PT room. "It's a shame, Paz. You were really dancing great this season." He had a look I couldn't place on his face as he walked off. His attempt at a kind comment still felt like a dig. He seemed to understand the gravity of the situation: I'd had momentum, but now I was out of the game thanks to a freak accident—and out of sight means out of mind at City Ballet. Getting hurt would hurt my career, and Peter could think this was an example of how I couldn't handle the pressure.

The pain in my wrist was growing, and now my anxiety was, too. Then Allen, my sweet roommate, came in. It was time to take me to the hospital. I hoped *Concerto Barrocco* went well that afternoon.

Swan Dive #7

The first time I danced the Woman in Red, I had about an hour to learn the role, so there was no time to be nervous. Another dancer was injured, and I was being thrown on for the role in *Russian Seasons*. I've always admired this role, so full of passion and fury.

I had made such an impression with this unexpected save-the-day that I was entered into the cast rotation of the part, getting promoted from my featured ensemble role to this lead part in the ballet.

I was seasoned enough to know the possible pitfalls of the demanding role. The first solo is over two minutes long, if you survive that, you get to leave the stage in a crazy-wild flurry of movement. This is so much more satisfying than landing a perfect finale pose.

I start the variation just fine, building the tension. This Woman in Red is experiencing an internal struggle . . . moody chaînés, triple pirouette, which I nail.

Huzzah, okay, stage feels good. Gina, let's rev up the engine on these grands jetés backward. One, two . . . they look like reversed panther strides, low, powerful split jumps that glide just off the ground backward. And then just as I attempt the last in the combination, I catch the tip of my pointe shoe on the slippery tape on the stage, and WHAP, I go down, *hard*.

Hard enough that there is a collective and loud gasp from the audience.

It is the kind of sound you make if you shock yourself running into someone turning a corner. I am on the stage, on my belly with my face to the side. Since my costume is an ankle-length, empire-waisted skirt, and I am wearing a low bun, I am aware that from the perspective of the audience, especially in the fourth ring, I look like a pile of fabric right now.

I will myself to GET UP, assessing the damage as time warps into slow-mo. *Damn, Gina, did you hurt yourself?* I am still moving at normal speed; my body seems to be in order—but there is just one problem. I can't breathe. I knocked the wind out of myself like the time I took a face-plant off the swings as a kid. My entire diaphragm is locked up, spasmed in one big contraction. I am literally gulping for breath like a goldfish who's been taken out of its bowl by a curious toddler. Just let me have one breath before I perish!

I am growing anxious, as it is hard to do the big expansive next movement even while breathing. *Tendu fourth, pirouette, pirouette, pirouette . . . , huh. Holy shit—this is unexpected, I'm still going!*

My muscles are so contracted, I am pulled up beautifully. *Is this really happening? Am I about to do a quadruple pirouette onstage?* And bam, ladies and gentlemen—we have a quadruple pirouette. *Huzzah.* It is incredibly rare for a woman to hit four pirouettes en pointe during a performance—even for ballerinas who are turners. It is like the ballet equivalent of Boitano landing a triple axel. I am at that moment being blessed by the dance gods as I am mustering the courage to double down on the last half of the variation.

The ballet master had flown to the wings from her seat in the first ring in the house when she saw the fall—everyone was wondering if I was hurt. Ice was waiting; PT had been summoned! I can't yet breathe normally, but I seem to be charging toward the finish line. There is the wing. Scene. Major claps from the audience. Nothing gets them in your corner like a wipeout. The first person I see backstage is Tyler Angle.

"Damn. Girlfriend got her ass handed to her . . . but four pirouettes, though. Oh. My. God."

CHAPTER 14

Dressing Room #19

My dressing room at the New York City Ballet is like a womb. It's a comfy, safe space I can crawl into—a reprieve from all the stress and pressure. It's not just the place where we get ready for shows and put on our makeup. My dressing-room mates are my peeps. We decompress, get ready for dates, cry over bad news, drink cocktails, perform foot surgery, and cuddle with dogs. Savannah and Liko would often be hovered over MCAT study guides, still in tights and leos, their hair in buns, wisely planning for an entirely new, postballet career.* The dressing rooms for female corps members are on the fourth floor, and soloists are housed on the second floor of the theater. We are not assigned dressing rooms at the New York City Ballet, but there's a clear understanding about who goes where. Dressing room #17 is for fresh blood, #18 for seasoned professionals. Others are reserved for principals and those who deem themselves queens of the ballet. It's kind of like a looser ver-

---

* Until not long ago, preparing for a "second career" would have been considered a blatant example of noncommitment to the ballet, rather than shrewd planning for survival for when your dance career inevitably ends.

sion of the Greek system, where women band together based on mutual interests and needs—such as your comfort level with public nakedness or your affection for dogs.

So, circa 2014, when I was asked to join dressing room #19 as a senior corps member, I couldn't have been more thrilled. I had been accepted into an exclusive sorority with open arms and promises of postshow tequila (and my beloved dog Jett was allowed to join a bit later). While the inhabitants have shifted over the years as ballerinas come and go, the staples of dressing room #19 have included Savannah Lowery, Amanda Hankes, Sophie Flack, Saskia Beskow, Ellen Bar, Ellen Ostrom, Dara Johnson, Katie Bergstrom, Megan LeCrone, and Rachel Rutherford. The newer generation includes ride-or-dies Gretchen Smith, Lauren King, Emily Kikta, Meaghan Dutton-O'Hara, Likolani Brown, Jenelle Manzi, and the incomparable Marika Anderson. These women are characterized by their dedication, talent, friendliness, and humor—and we all agree that no dressing room is complete without a fully stocked bar. For me, at least, pot has its place as well.

For example, if you were in the audience when I was dancing the role of Scala in *Ocean's Kingdom,* you'd have no idea that between movements, one of my partners in crime from dressing room 19 and I were having a heated argument about what to do with the huge bag of pot we'd just found backstage. She wanted to turn it in or give it to the stagehands, while I was like, "Girl, please. Let's smoke this shit."

Number 19 has gone through many iterations, but the spirit has always remained the same: Leave your ballet-drama, eating disorders, and supercompetitive natures at the door. Man-drama, however, is always welcome.

Our barracks are simple but comfortable. There are two thin beds in the dressing room. Sometimes we need to just pass out from exhaustion or catch a quick nap. But indeed, over the years there have been some less savory uses of the various twin beds scattered about the dressing rooms of the theater.

For a while, it appeared that one of the more frugal ladies of our flock was always last to leave and first to arrive. This pattern continued long enough for us to grow suspicious. Was she living at the ballet to save on rent? To this day we have no answer, and honestly, I don't blame her. The rent in New York is too damn high, and our City Ballet paychecks too damn lean.

A dancer who shall not be named once admitted to spending the night because he lost his keys clubbing. And one day we discovered a used condom in the back hallway that led to the "Jersey" dressing rooms that were located way, way back by the two unmade, abandoned twin beds. We screamed like 1950s housewives who had spotted a mouse.

These were not considered unforgivable offenses. The only time a dancer was ever exiled from dressing room #19 was not due to dancer-drama or man-drama—but dog-drama. Dog-drama proves to be the most contentious of all. I'll say now that dressing room #19 is very pro-dog. I bring my black lab, Jett, to work with me nearly every day. I'm by no means the only one. Number 17 has Luna and Pippen. In 18 you've got Freddie, Quincy, and Carmen; 20 belongs to Shallot and Duncan.

The dogs I've just listed belong to my fellow ladies here at City Ballet. There are more to be found—I didn't even touch on the dogs living with the menfolk. If you were to pop into a company class, you might think you've stumbled upon some bizarre dance studio for superprivileged urban pups.

Furry cuteness is great for cutting the tension bred by the competitive environment of the rehearsal room.* But if your overbearing dog

---

* I believe it helps that the ballet masters are reminded that we are not just bodies, incapable of executing their awkward corrections—we are actual humans, and we are dog moms to boot.

proceeds to shit and piss all over the dressing room . . . then sister, we have a problem.

While we are grown women, it could be argued that our dressing room somewhat resembles a bedroom shared by messy tween girls. We aren't total slobs, but space is extremely limited. It is a stressful job, and there just isn't brain space left for organizing makeup or folding our warm-up clothes à la Marie Kondo. As a result, the room is strewn with tights, leos, pointe shoes, ribbons, needles and thread, makeup, hair implements, and other random stuff. While on the surface, it is shared interests and values that draw dressing-room mates together, deep down it's probably really about a shared ability to function in mayhem.*

One midwinter-season afternoon, I got dressed in regular New York lady clothes because I had plans to have lunch out in the world with Lauren. I wasn't going to just whip on some leg warmers and an oversized sweatshirt atop my sweat-slicked skin. This isn't *Flashdance*. We enjoyed a civilized lunch of Cobb salad with shrimp and a glass of Grüner each. I admit to eating all of the rolls in the breadbasket.

"Um, sorry. Did you want one?" I managed to mutter, my mouth full of bread (luckily, she didn't). We walked out together practically humming and into the stage door.

A lovely day, a lovely lunch. I made my way up to #19, knowing I had just a couple of hours of rehearsal left before I got to call it a day. I hung up my coat, set my bag down, and started to peel off my street clothes when I heard King's shout, "Oh, hell no!" It was then that I did detect a whiff of pee. "Dickinson† peed in my fucking boots!" He doesn't even live with us, how the hell did he get in there?

I noticed that Dickinson was sitting sheepishly in the open door of the dressing room, looking at us like, Yeah, I peed in your La Canadienne

---

* It has been noted that the messier a dancer's dressing room spot is, the more OCD they are about their home. Curious.

† Some of the dogs' names have been changed. As a dog lover myself, I would never throw a dog under the bus by revealing its true identity.

boots, and I do not give a damn about it either. Lauren and I exchanged a look that suggested shit was about to get serious. This was not the first time a dog had caused drama. It had been a while, but Savannah once called me at home sobbing, "Shit, Gina. Alfie peed on Ellen's pointe shoes. The ribbons are soaked with pee. She already hates Alfie!"

The anxiety in Savannah's voice was growing. I knew I had to remain calm. "Savannah. Listen to me. Where exactly did the dog pee? Is it like both shoes, one shoe? Details matter, Savannah!"

Savannah muffled a cry. "Okay. Well, let's see. Actually, it's the ribbons. The ribbons are soaked in pee." This was welcome news. "Great. Wash the ribbons in the sink and dry them with the blow dryer! What Ellen doesn't know can't hurt her." Ellen never found out.

Unfortunately, Lauren's La Canadienne boots, which will set a woman back at least $400, did not recover.

But the most outrageous drama I have witnessed to this day involved Pebbles, one of those yappy types—owned by one of the impossibly naïve and self-involved rising talents at the time. We were transitioning from *The Nutcracker* right into winter season. In other words, we were dancing our asses off doing five ballets a week, but with the delightful bonus of being able to eat whatever we wanted. What was getting the ladies of #19 through a grueling four to seven hours of class/rehearsal/performance was a cheesecake. A beautiful homemade cheesecake lovingly made by Hankes's mother and delivered to her at work. After we got offstage, we flew up to the dressing room like a pack of savage Golden Girls—we wanted cheesecake, and nothing would stop us! We entered 19 en masse to discover that the cheesecake had been massacred, smeared remains surrounding an upside-down pie tin. A travesty. All two pounds of cream cheese deliciousness had been eaten by Pebbles, who was sitting in the corner bloated AF and looking not so happy. Hankes lost it.

"Pebbles, you asshole! You do not fuck with a hungry ballerina's food!"

Like my colleagues, I was disappointed and angry. But I did not understand how a dog weighing two pounds—four, tops—had just consumed nearly its entire body weight in cream cheese. How was Pebbles even alive? Shouldn't he go to the vet? He looked like he might explode. Much to my amazement, that dog never so much as belched. Needless to say, after the cheesecake incident, Pebbles was wagging his tail on some dangerously thin ice.

That situation came to a head a few nights later. Following a tough two-show day of five ballets combined, I dragged myself into the elevator and pressed four. I was next-level exhausted, and all I could think about was washing this show off me in the shower—and going home for a bourbon before crashing. I was first in line for the shower, God bless. I turned on the water to let it warm up and walked into the stall, the steam already relaxing my tired muscles. I washed my face and then reached over for my loofah, but it wasn't there.

"Holy shit!" I screamed. My loofah was lying on the floor of the shower. Perched on top of it were two perfectly round turds. Pebbles had left some rocks on my loofah.

I whipped the curtain open and stomped out naked and wet.

"Look at this! Just look at it!" I shouted to the other ballerinas waiting for their turn in the shower.

I was about to carry the poop-loofah over to the toilet to flush the turds away when I thought twice. It was not actually the dog's fault. He was still a little dick, but you know who was responsible for this . . .

"I'm done with her. Her dog is out of line, and if she wants to be a pet owner, she needs to house-train her animal." Everyone huzzahed like I was speaking at a pep rally. We were in total agreement that a line had been crossed. Hankes tossed me a towel, and I wrapped myself in it. We looked at each other, then at the turd-studded loofah. I took the loofah, turds intact, and gently placed it at Pebbles's mother's dressing room spot.

"Amanda. It can stay here. It's her dog; she can clean up after it for once. This bullshit has got to end." I dig out a piece of paper and a pen among a pile of lipsticks, tampons, and bobby pins, and I write, "CLEANING CREW: PLEASE DO NOT TOUCH THIS. DO NOT TOUCH THE LOOFAH. LEAVE IT, THANK YOU!"

That loofah remained there and acted as a wonderful "top o' the morning to ya, madam" for Pebbles's mom. We knew she found it because we heard the gossip at barre the next day that she was superoffended and pissed. "What kind of person does that?!" she whined. Well, bitch, collective reasoning says that when dealing with insanity, you checkmate that crazy and shut that shit down. Toward the end of the season, Pebbles and her owner moved into a different dressing room. One crazy down, one crazy memory, and a photo that still occasionally pops into my DMs as cheeky reminder of how far we've come.

Onstage, we're graceful and as ethereal as mist, but once the pointe shoes and tutus come off, it's a different story. Ballerinas can be gross. If you've seen Darren Aronofsky's ridiculous movie *Black Swan*, you already know we're disgusting because of that overdramatized scene where a bloody toenail pops off poor little Natalie Portman's foot. Yeah, I've lost toenails (and a certain dog has allegedly been caught eating the toenails of a ballerina who clips them into the carpet). But do you want to know what really fucking hurts? Carving out a space in your pointe shoe (they're made of paste and cardboard btw) for your swollen, mangled toe, and then covering it with flesh-colored tape so you can still dance, albeit in a pain-induced high. When you do something so intensely physical for a living, some barriers go down.

There is no separation between our bodies and our art form. I have never worked in an office, but I'm fairly sure that if you walked in on a naked coworker with her leg extended, her foot stretched up to her face (rendering her lady business 100 percent visible) in order for her to get a better look at the foot corn she's cutting out, it would be considered inappropriate. A preshow shaving of the cooch is not out of the ordinary either. God forbid you have to wear a white leo, and the audience sees a single pube—no shadows of humanity allowed! Ballerinas are pure class—the very definition of grace. But our grossness bonds us as much as our love of dance does, and in dressing room #19, we've buoyed each other's spirits for years, through fat talks, breakups, serious injuries, and professional disappointments.

We processed the massive change that was Peter's removal in 2017 and years earlier we cried together when he laid off half of dressing room #19 in 2009. We shed collective tears of sadness/joy when a beloved member of #19 retired from the ballet to pursue an entirely new career. And we rejoiced when our darling Liko got a full ride to NYU medical school after studying for the MCAT between rehearsals and performances. If the entire company is my extended family, the ladies of dressing room #19 are my sisters (and my therapists, and my dance-off support team). I wouldn't have made it this far without them.

Swan Dive #8

It's highly unusual to have a night off timed with that of a fellow ballet buddy. So when it was discovered that Hankes and I had a matching free night, we were pleased to discover we could actually do happy hour *at happy hour*. We had some catching up to do. We had both gotten our real estate licenses (just in case), and Hankes was transitioning out of dressing room #19. She was getting ready to leave City Ballet. After three margaritas, the bartender sent another.

"Amanda, it's crazy; seriously, I am not feeling this alcohol at all."

I started to tell Amanda about a recent adventure, and I was getting rather animated in my storytelling. I threw my head back in laughter, apparently too far—because the next thing I knew I was flying through the air and then lying on the floor of the bar.

"Jesus, Gina." Hankes looked down, unfazed—we've known each other a long time. "Are you okay?"

I clambered back up to my seat. The bartender looked concerned, like maybe he shouldn't have given me that last margarita.

"My ego may be obliterated, but I'm fine, everyone! Thank you for your concern." Happy hour between two ballerinas with a matching night off went on.

CHAPTER 15

Thigh Master

Throughout the years, I've built up a solid shield against the relentless body shaming that occurs on company time.

"Gina, you're just not looking your best. I've seen you look better." I knew by now that comments like "You're not looking your best" did not mean "You look tired; are you getting enough sleep?" This was not an inquiry into the balance of my chakras.

It was a euphemism for *Watch out, tubby; looks like you've lost your focus on what's important.*

I was in the senior corps, and because I had graduated out of many of the ball-busting, heavy-lifting corps parts, I had a slow start to the season. Everyone else had been dancing two or three ballets for the first week and a half, but my ballets that season hadn't been in rotation yet. So, while I was like, *Seriously? Give me a minute because we all know that dancing six ballets in two days drops the weight right quick.* If only my mind stopped right there. I had also been trained to look at myself and see everything that was wrong, and eventually, if you always only search out the ugliness, you start to see a monster. Years later, I could still see

Peter drawing that imaginary line from my knee to my butt. When he said my thighs kept me from "fitting in," it was cemented in my head that my body was flawed and that flaw would stand between me and the roles I wanted to dance.

I had been working out and taking extra classes, but I was at a breaking point. I knew in my heart these actions weren't going to make a difference. Drastic measures were going to be required if I finally wanted to fit in. I picked up the phone and called Dr. Bergman, who seemed to know what he was doing based on the scads of glowing reviews online from what I assumed to be women with newly trim thighs and full breasts. I set up a consultation. When I went to his office in Midtown, I put on a hat and sunglasses like I was a starlet who didn't want to be tailed by the paparazzi on her way to rehab. I was ashamed that the only way I could see to solve this problem was surgery.

When the doctor called me in, he kindly asked, "What are you interested in? You're perfect!"

"It's for my job."

I saw a look flash across his face, and if I had to guess, he was thinking, "Ohhh. Breasts! She's a stripper!"

I explained what I needed in great detail; that I can always work on my turnout and presentation, but while I've tried everything under the sun, I couldn't shrink my thighs. I told him about the "nutritionist" and his packets of chalk, the swimming, the extra classes and workouts. I was desperate, and this represented the last-ditch effort for me. The doctor did an examination.

"There is some fat I can take out of your legs, but I can't guarantee this will help a lot." The price tag for this maybe of a solution was huge: $10,000. I had a two-week break in March, and while most people don't have to stand around half naked with their leg next to their face such a short time after going under the knife, the doctor thought I'd have enough time to recover.

I didn't tell anyone about this decision but my dad. His immediate response was, "You don't have to do this." It was my dad being a dad, but I knew I had to go through with it. I was going down a slippery slope, and I needed a way out of hating myself and a way past the barrier currently blocking the road to getting taken seriously at City Ballet.

My dad knew me enough to know that it was already said and done. I was committed and had already forked over the hefty down payment. He agreed to be my lipo buddy and drive me out to Long Island, where the procedure was going to take place. I was conflicted. I was waffling back and forth between feeling empowered because I was taking control and thinking I was insane . . . *What are you thinking giving up $10,000 for this? You don't have that kind of money!*

As I was being prepared for surgery, I was given an anti-nausea pill that ironically made me more nauseous than I had ever felt in my life. I started to panic. What am I doing—couldn't this go wrong? Jesus, take the wheel! Am I going to die?

But then the Propofol hit, and I was out. I woke up in a hospital bed, the sounds of *The Young and the Restless* playing on a TV in the background. A short while later I was able to prove I could hold down crackers and apple juice, and I was released to the care of my dad.

He brought me back the next day for a follow-up appointment.

"I got five hundred ccs out. That's like a two-liter bottle of coke—I was really surprised!" Dr. Bergman told me. "This is going to make a huge difference. It would have been nearly impossible to lose fat from that spot. You're going to see much more definition in your legs." After a brief lecture about the importance of compression pants, I was sent off to recover.

When I went back to work two weeks later, I wore sweats over my compression pants, and no one suspected a thing. For the most part I was pain-free, and on days I did feel anything, a simple Tylenol covered my needs. A week and a half later, the company went on tour to D.C. Peter walked onstage for a complete of *Concerto Barocco*—when the boss is present (especially Peter), it was the unspoken rule that everyone should strip down. Leg warmers, sweatshirts—all those go so our boss can see our bodies in this final rehearsal if we aren't in full costume. *Barocco* is one of Ballanchine's ballets that is danced in just a simple leo with a skirt, so we don't need to rehearse in them prior to the show. When I revealed my new legs, people noticed something was different, even if it was subtle.

"Wow, Gina! Your legs look really long in those tights. Who makes those?!" Dr. Thigh Magic had achieved just the right result I was looking for.

But the first time I saw my sister, she knew what I did.

"Your inner thighs don't touch anymore, Gina. So, are you happy?" she said it with a side dose of snark.

The answer was yes. I don't really want to say that. I'm mortified by the idea of little girls hearing this, *but I was*. After years of being told I didn't have the right body type, my confidence was boosted, and it wasn't because I was starving myself. I have pushed my body to the brink for this art form. There were so many years I didn't even eat my own birthday cake. Now I eat my birthday cake. Years of therapy have taught me to learn to fuel my body. I need to eat a lot to do what I do! I need meat! I cook most of my own meals and mostly eat clean foods, but never again, *never*, will I walk away from my own goddamn birthday cake.

But listen, really, it makes me sick to write this. I think it's important to be honest about what I did, and the kinds of choices we think about in this career, but it doesn't mean I want young dancers to think it's a good idea. It's not—there are risks, it's expensive, and what you need to know is that however you look right now, you are perfection. My path to being comfortable in my own skin is far from the only one.

You are perfect and you should eat your birthday cake. Go back for seconds.

CHAPTER 16

Sloppy Seconds

"Y ou're not looking your best, Gina, and Peter's not sure you should do Hippolyta."

I knew what was really going on. Peter had promoted another dancer and had a new soloist he wanted to play with, much like a toddler with a new toy.

I was the more senior soloist and I had been rehearsing the role. Instead of telling me like it was, why not just toss out a casual body-shaming comment to pass the blame for my not getting cast directly onto me?

"Rosemary, I hear you loud and clear. I'll make it so good he won't be able to not cast me."

Turns out he gave me ONE show. This is annoying for some dancers. All the rehearsal and stress for one show? But to me it was just another chess move, and I took it because I had this role in my pocket. I had always wanted to dance this role in *A Midsummer Night's Dream*—and it's definitely not everyone's favorite. A lot of dancers downright dislike it for several reasons:

1. You have to dance with a prop (a giant bow and arrow), which is hard, especially when it comes to balance. I nail props!

2. The role requires wearing a cape. Again, a cape can provide a challenge, but to me they are child's play! I danced the shit out of my role in *Ocean's Kingdom* in a cape!

3. You're dancing around in dry ice. Dramatic, but not easy to see where the hell you're going.

4. The cornucopia hat—it's like a big foam golden turd, and it really has some weight to it.

I understand why other dancers would not relish this role. I really do. If you think about the physics of executing a fouetté turn in low lighting (thanks to all that fog), while holding a bow and wearing a cape and a one-pound cornucopia on top of your head, shit can really go wrong. But there's something about this wickedly challenging combination that I love . . . It's very *Xena: Warrior Princess*. And did I mention Hippolyta is Queen of the Hounds? I would get my very own set of hounds! So, needless to say, I was very excited to debut this role. There were going to be seven performances, and I would get to do it just once—but even still, I was willing to happily accept this "one and done."

Even though it was my debut, I wasn't going to get a full cast complete (that's a proper dress rehearsal most likely with orchestra, a full run of dry ice, and in full costume with props and scenery), which due to the complications stated above seemed crucial to my success. Like I said, shit can really go wrong when you add props and effects to ballet. I felt like everything was stacked against me. The best I was going to get was a chance to go through the choreography while wearing the costume—and this is where I knew things were going to get very messy.

When it comes to costumes, the ballet is frugal. Classic nonprofit attitude, but annoying-because-we-have-a-big-endowment type of frugal. There are not multiple costumes for big roles, and there's no never-ending costume room with Mother Goose skirts in multiple sizes. *We share*, and that's where things get awkward or in some cases just wrong. Once, when Savannah got seriously injured during a performance of *Stars and Stripes*, the costume was literally ripped off her body the second she was off-stage. Not only was she probably terrified about the state of her career (any injury can equal the end) and in a lot of pain, she had to suffer the humili-ation of being stripped to her bare breasts while she was lying on the floor so another dancer could step into her role and finish the ballet.

Ashly, another soloist who was also performing Hippolyta, was getting her "full complete." She'd get to rehearse with the costume in a proper sequence of events with the rest of her cast.

There was a short Hippolyta costume and a tall Hippolyta costume—since we were both on the petite side, guess what? We'd get to share. That meant the second she was finished, she'd have to pull off the costume at breakneck speed so I could stuff myself into her sweaty, sloppy seconds and get back onstage to do my run-through.

I admit I was not in the best of moods. I was frustrated I couldn't get a proper run-through. I explained my situation to Grace, my dresser. She dug out an old (but clean!) pair of Hippolyta tights for me to wear. They were last worn by Savannah, who is tall, and this meant they reached all the way up to my neck.

"I'm calling it now. I give it a two-minute wait time before Peter starts to lose his temper."

I knew Peter would be anxious to get my run-through over with. I mean, he barely wanted me to do the role, let alone watch me dance it or coach me in it. He would not have the patience to wait for me to pull on a sweat-drenched costume while he's anxiously looking forward to his lunch break like everyone else.

Nothing ever seems quick enough for Peter. Ashly didn't want to wear the cornucopia hat—so thankfully it was already affixed to my head, and I had on the tights, my pointe shoes were on, and I was ready to go. I felt like I was running a goddamn relay race, not getting ready to dance.

Hippa 1 was done, and the rest of the act was finishing up. *Fucking hell.* I had somehow forgotten that it's Hippa who closes the entire act, so she has to be onstage up to the very last second.

Ashly gets off the stage, and the work lights are already on; everyone is anxious for their lunch break. She scurries to the dressing room and begins to pull off the harness skirt/cape and sweat-soaked body suit. By the time it is off, thirty seconds have passed. The dressers are helping me shimmy into a damp, clingy leo and corset (not unlike putting on a soaking-wet bathing suit—except it's not wet from the pool, people!). At about forty-five seconds we are really hustling, and I hear:

"GINA! WHERE IS GINA?"

"I'm here! I'm coming, Peter!" I can tell he is agitated, but I need to rehearse this role *with the costume.* Peter is yelling over and over, "Gina! Where are you?"—singing it like I am off playing hide-and-seek. *Do you really think I'm crouched backstage hiding for fun, asshole?*

Rosemary and the ballet masters stand by. I am nearly dressed, but I don't have my bow yet. Grace, my dresser, goes out to try to calm things down.

"There is only one costume! She's nearly ready," she shouts and comes back with an honest-to-God "Gina, you really called this."

When I settle into the grossness of the wet costume, an inner rage starts to flicker, directed toward Peter. I am really trying to get dressed as fast as humanly possible.

"GINA! GINA! COME OUT, COME OUT, WHEREVER YOU ARE!"

But now Peter has stomped backstage, following his own rage and looking for me. He bumps right into Craig Hall, another soloist (and as it happened, another dancer whom Peter never really had the time for).

"Craig, have you seen Gina?"

"Yes, Peter, she's putting on the costume; she's coming." Peter looks angry with Craig, as if he has anything whatsoever to do with this situation. At that moment, I finally get all the shit on and bound out of the dressing room.

"Hi," I say, beaming with cheer. "I have to share a costume. I'm just going to get some rosin so I—"

"Okay!"

Peter takes this as a cue that the pianist should start. Never mind that I am still on the wrong side of stage and haven't found the prop bow yet. But the music is already playing. *Well, forget rosin, here we go.*

I sprint past Craig muttering, "Are you fucking kidding me? He couldn't wait twenty more seconds?"

Now Debbie, Peter's assistant, and a few other ballet masters have come down to watch the "show." I only see them because I am running across the front of the open stage to the other side to make my entrance.

"Oh, there's the bow!" I grab it off the prop table as I make my final turn into the fourth wing. I am fired up as hell and manage to enter on time for my cue. I am pissed, but I use every bit of this adrenaline in my performance. I feel like the audience who has gathered, including Peter, is expecting to see me fail.

Huzzah, ASSHOLES. Watch all five feet, five inches of me eat this stage. First entrance down. Piece of cake. I make it back to the wing on stage right, where only a minute ago I was trying to put on rosin.

"Fuck. That. Dick!"

Second entrance. Sail through. One of the ballet masters is in the front stage, left wing when I exit.

"You are doing great!" she sings with an expressionless grin on her face.

"Yeah, I like this role, glad you came to 'support' . . . Excuse me now."

After a quick thirty-two-count catch of the breath is the next entrance—my favorite entrance. The fouettés.

I burst out onto the stage with another gigantic leap fueled by vindication, and I proceed to do the most solid and on-the-spot turns I could ever have hoped for. At this point, Miranda, who was moving to Italy with her new husband and had snuck in to watch the dress rehearsal since she'd miss the show, audibly hoots and claps from the audience.

ALL of them—Peter, Rosemary, J. P.—turn around to see who this is. I start to laugh as I saut de chat triumphantly right over Peter's head (he's sitting right there on the stage) into the wing. One final entrance to go, and I feel amazing. *Why don't you light my bow on fire while you're at it? Go ahead—I can take it!* I float through the final set of grand allegro jumps and end my dance without much to do. Miranda is still going wild in the empty house.

I take a second to collect myself. What a rush! And I casually strut out onto the stage. Rosemary can't help it. She is beaming.

I am still slightly puffed, but I manage to say, "Do you have any 'tickets'"—meaning corrections—"for me?"

Peter stands up slowly. I'm sure it was painful for him, but he says it. "It's really very good." As he starts to walk away, he turns back. "Start the fouettés farther back on the stage just in case."

"Sure thing, Peter, I can do that."

CHECKMATE.

* * *

I was excited to be working my classical chops on the Fairy of Courage variation, and I really wanted to keep this momentum flowing. I thought a next appropriate step would be to learn the role of Princess Florine in the Bluebird pas de deux, which takes place in the third act of *Sleeping Beauty*. I currently only danced divertissements in the first act.

If I could just break the ice, it would be a great opportunity for me to demonstrate my classical ballet technique. I asked principal ballet master Susie Hendl (yes, the same Susie who gave me my first scholarship to SAB back in Pittsburgh) what she thought.

"Sure, come to rehearsal!"

Some of my close colleagues didn't understand why I shouldn't just discuss my wish to do this role with Peter. *Just talk to him!*

I set up a meeting, feeling that my wanting to learn the role made sense, and I wasn't asking for anything beyond my skills. It wasn't like I was asking to learn Princess Aurora out of the blue.

It turns out that my meeting with Peter fell on a day when he was having back-to-back meetings with corps members—fat talks, you're-not-dedicated-enough talks. The ugly talks. He was fired up and angry before I even walked into the room. I sat down on the absurdly low sofa while he towered over me in his chair. I was trying to approach him in a respectful way, while also sharing my need to grow as an artist. He listened to me explain why I wanted to be in the rehearsal room for Bluebird. He stared at me.

"You know, I just don't ever see you in that role. I don't know why you see yourself in that role."

I shouldn't have been surprised by his immediate shutdown.

"Because I'm a very good classical dancer. I'm in the senior corps, healthy, carrying my workload, and excelling at my soloist and principal role opportunities consistently. Every outside choreographer who comes here wants to work with me. I want a chance to show you I can also do these roles because they're an important part of our rep."

"Georgina." A huge exhale. "The roles you can do, no one else can touch you in them."

I cringed because this basically meant, to me, slut roles, the goofy character roles. "Strong woman" roles that are satisfying to dance but don't always require classical prowess. I knew where this was going. I was about to be dumped in the dreaded pigeonhole, categorized as one type of dancer forever. Then he opened fire.

"It would be a waste of resources to have you learn Bluebird."

I was a waste of resources . . . for wanting to learn? Train? Expand as an artist? HUH. This upset me.

"Well, I can certainly understand—"

"You're not listening to me, Georgina."

But I heard him loud and clear. I just wanted to know if he'd come right out and SAY IT. Our conversation escalated from there. I made another valid point, that Susie was more than happy to work with me on the role. She just needed clearance from Peter so I could be officially put on the schedule to rehearse with her.

He stood over me, literally waving his fist in my face.

"You're not listening to me!" His temper unleashed in a way that was actually starting to alarm me. And as I sat there—a strong woman confronting an angry man—it occurred to me that he might hit me. It would not be the first time he'd laid hands on someone before—and he supposedly *loved her*. I was staring up at him. He looked like a giant and he was furious. I clocked that his fist was clenched even tighter now and felt a pang of fear.

I decided not to poke the bear because once he was set off, there was no turning back. For either of us.

"Okay, Peter, okay, let's just . . ."—I pointed to his clenched, pumped hands—"take it down a notch. I'm just lost. I'm trying to understand what your plan is for me here as an artist. I need some attention and guidance, and you have all the power."

"I want you to stop wanting to be something you are not."

"How do you know I'm not anything? You haven't seen me dance it yet. I can show you if you let me." I said this as calmly as I could, holding back condensed rage.

"You don't take no for an answer. You do not listen."

I made one last stand.

"I hear you. You want me to cease and desist on trying to be anything other than what YOU want me to be."

He had my entire career in his hands, and he expected a thank-you for it. Meanwhile, I thought I kinda made my own career with hard work and dedication. This conversation was over. My career here was over.

I looked at my watch. "Are we done here?"

I had rehearsal in fifteen minutes, and I needed to compose myself.

He was silent and seething. I was seething right back at him. The moment was thick with tension.

"I hear you. I just don't agree with your lack of consideration for me, beyond what I easily contribute already. I'm an artist. I need to grow, so I need food."

"We are finished here. Go to rehearsal."

I left his office sulking. There was no future for me here. I'd have to get used to the fact that I'd never be seen beyond his forged-in-steel opinion of me. I should have left him a long time ago to pursue a career in film. Earlier in my career, Peter used to love to say, "I'm just waiting for you to leave me to go star in movies." A backhanded compliment that was easier to drop at my feet rather than having a real conversation about the trajectory of my career.

This man would never ever see me as a princess or a queen. He clearly thought that was beyond me. What I didn't understand then was that my face is not the face of a queen or princess *for him*.

Suddenly, the despair and rage bubbled over. I was barely out of the admin offices and walking down the long hall toward the dressing rooms when I let loose the biggest scream I had and shouted, "I want a divorce!"

I had been with the company for nearly fourteen years. What else did I need to do? I'd had the fat sucked out of my thighs! I felt he wanted to break me; he wanted me in a cage, to be okay with his idea of what a dancer who looks like me should be. I went home and made a call to San Francisco Ballet. Maybe they would appreciate what I had to offer. In the meantime, I doubled down. I was working on classical variations. I put all of my energy into playing a mean Carabosse.

He had seen me dance classically as the Fairy of Courage and nail it every time for the full week prior, and he continued to watch me in the role for the coming week after that fight. But I put my head down and avoided seeing him at all costs. If my performances at City Ballet were numbered, I might as well give it my all. No drama, no distractions.

It was two weeks later that I rode downtown, convinced I was facing my final performance. Instead I got promoted. And we know how that convo went.

Was a fight of epic proportions the only way to get something through his head? Or had Peter simply, shockingly, opened his eyes and seen the kind of dancer I could be? I'll never know, but promotion aside, I also knew I'd never be Bluebird.

CHAPTER 17

The Slap Heard
Around the World

In 2007, I played a role that I have tried to erase from my memory. It was filmed for public television for all to see, but I have never watched it and I never will.

I was cast as the nurse in Peter's production of *Romeo + Juliet*. I should have felt grateful. I was in the spotlight. But being cast as a caricature made me question how I was viewed in this company. I wouldn't be doing any dancing at all. Instead, I was to play the ignorant servant.

As Bonnie, the costume mistress, was hiking up the straps of my cheap-ass, skinny-strapped, Victoria's Secret bra as high as they could go—in a futile attempt to make my chicken-cutlet breasts look like actual *cleavage*—I was gritting my teeth. I took a breath, the straps of my bra digging deeply into my shoulders. It was time for me to waddle out onstage like a baboon.

The nurse's first appearance featured me fanning my sweaty armpits and then crudely grabbing a stool, sitting on it only to realize, Oops! I forgot to close my legs! I was to cover my mouth and make a cutesy embarrassed face. The indignities didn't stop there—while it's well known that in the original play Juliet's nurse provides comic relief, Peter's MILF version would take that to new heights. In a scene where the nurse helps Juliet get ready to go to the ball, oops! She falls down a flight of stairs! Every night, I had to hurl my body with as much slapstick as I could conjure. Maybe Peter's thought process was that the audience would think a highly trained ballerina violently falling downstairs is hilarious.

Sterling (who was Juliet) and I were close friends, and the chemistry we had onstage could be felt all the way from the fifth ring—there was no reason that scene needed to be a Muppet spill. The fall had nothing to do with the narrative—it served no purpose other than for Peter's real-life wife (who played Lady Capulet) to come over and shake her finger at me. *Shame on you, bad lady nurse, for fucking up the party.*

Even worse, as much as I tapped into my inner Lucille Ball, the stunt fell flat every time. The audience never laughed.

I did occasionally get a laugh during a scene in the town square. The nurse is bringing a note from Juliet to Romeo, and naturally it is carried in her nonexistent bosom. Mercutio and Benvolio want to intercept the note. They pick me up, legs splayed open, and spin me around. The audience would have had a perfect view of my crotch if my low-cut peasant dress wasn't full-length. They boldly try to retrieve the note from my bosom, sticking their hands down my dress, but I keep pushing them off. More spins, more legs open, more embarrassment for me. My character was supposed to be so crass that no man would ever be legitimately interested, so I'm supposed to be over the moon that these two assholes are chasing me. The nurse is finally like *Fuck this shit*, when she takes the note out of her dress dead center stage so they won't touch my boobs.

Spoiler alert: they do it anyway.

I hated it. I also hated that the only time I ever got a laugh was in this scene. I get it. I played it off. I'm charming. The nurse was supposed to enjoy it! But Georgina hated the role that was created just for her, by Peter, that featured choreography that required my colleagues to reach down my costume, onstage in front of thousands of people as well as on television for millions to see. I didn't want to do this, nor was I thrilled about using my time and energy to vamp it up in this otherwise serious and essential role. But I knew voicing my displeasure about being harassed onstage would be viewed as ungrateful. Someone else would surely be slipped into the role, and I'd be reminded later that when given a shot—I'd turned it down.

I still don't like to think about this production. I know that after every single performance I felt spent. I was emotionally spent by the heartbreaking story, and the effort it took to infuse any seriousness into this whackadoodle character Peter created for me. The sharp bra straps cutting my skin were like a punishment, and the cherry on top of this bullshit sundae was . . . *This is how your boss sees you.* You're a clown with cleavage.

It's hard not to see this production for the insights it offers into who Peter is. I believe in making art; he believes in making *this*. He was right; we don't see eye to eye. Peter's version of Romeo and Juliet just didn't feel right. It wasn't just the nurse's role that he adapted. This production took the darkness of the story to a new and utterly unnecessary level.

When Juliet (who has already married Romeo) refuses to heed her parents' wishes that she marry Paris, Lord Capulet slaps her—knocks her to the ground. The audience would gasp at the violence of it. There is no slap in Shakespeare's *Romeo and Juliet*, nor to my knowledge is there a slap in any other production. Standing onstage, as Sterling is slapped to the ground, only to be comforted by the arms of Darci Kistler as Lady Capulet, seemed an especially strange choice. As I mentioned, Darci is Peter's wife, and in 1992, Peter had been arrested on charges of assaulting her. How could that piece of recent history not run through all our minds onstage? And the minds of any audience members who were aware of the story, too?

When PBS recorded the show for television, Peter was interviewed by Leslie Stahl backstage after the first act. Various dancers could be seen in the background getting ready for the next act. She asked Peter about the ages of the cast members and why he wanted to work with dancers who are so young.

Peter responded, "I don't want people to act the role. I want them to just be."

When pressed further—"What did you gain by making that choice?"—Peter responded simply, "I gained everything."

This was hard for me to hear. He used this production as a vessel to promote most of the cast (alas, not *moi*). I had not been promoted for my contributions, and all I was left with was a bruised ego and this mess of trauma I'm still trying to work through. I had my legs splayed and breasts fondled onstage by my colleagues. I threw my body down the stairs repeatedly. I had my anatomy once again shamed, *this time* for not being curvy enough.

If I had to find a minor positive, the role was so incredibly mind-numbing that while sitting in the wings I was able to do my taxes. I didn't get promoted, but I did get my taxes done.

If the Fates Allow

CHAPTER 18

The World's Most Successful Flop

The success of *The Nutcracker* as a revered holiday tradition in the United States is baffling to those ballet historians in the know and yours truly. The US is the only country that regularly performs a ballet that everyone else in the world considers unwatchable. It was a flop from the start. Tchaikovsky's *The Nutcracker* first premiered in December 1892 in Saint Petersburg, Russia. Words used to describe the debut performance included: "lopsided," "amateurish," and "insipid."

OUCH.

It didn't help that the original grand pas de deux, one of the most exciting parts of the production (that shit is seriously hard to dance, let me tell you) didn't happen until *midnight*. Tchaikovsky's decision to debut his new opera AND *The Nutcracker*, one after the other on the same night, was highly questionable. There's only so much culture people can take in one sitting!

Fast-forward to New York City, 1954, and Balanchine's much-improved, fantastically lavish production of *The Nutcracker* bowled audiences over with its dramatic sets, dazzling costumes, and a massive, forty-one-foot Christmas tree that slowly emerged from the stage to dizzying heights (and set the company back $80,000). *The Nutcracker* has been performed in New York City every year since—eight shows per week for six weeks, step, spin, repeat. And if you don't live in the tristate area, fear not! There are over 120 different productions of *The Nutcracker* nationwide. Whether you live in Alaska or rural Oklahoma, chances are *someone* is putting on a production. Even people who would never normally attend the ballet have been dragged to a performance at some point.

It is, undeniably, an audience-friendly ballet. Tchaikovsky's score is beautiful and classic, there are dancing animals, twinkling snowflakes falling from the sky, glittery tutus and tiaras, adorable children miraculously popping out of an old lady's skirt. Even I will admit there is much to adore about the show. Like many dancers, it represented my first onstage performance. I still remember how thrilling it was to be dancing for the first time onstage—even with the scratchy, sweaty costume and the canned music.

Just in case you are one of the five people in America who have never seen *The Nutcracker*, allow me to quickly recap: Drosselmeyer (a zany character to be sure) shows up at a party and gives his goddaughter Marie a gigantic nutcracker for Christmas. What could a young lass possibly want more than a device for cracking open pecans? At the stroke of midnight, her nutcracker comes alive, grows to life-sized proportions, and engages in battle with a magical mouse of equal stature with his crew of gingerbread soldiers. Marie, in an effort to save her Nutcracker Prince, renders a devastating blow to the Mouse King's ego by nailing him in the head with her slipper. At that point, the Nutcracker takes advantage of the moment to kill the rodent and then, bathed in gloriousness of victory, transforms into a handsome young prince. The prince escorts Marie into a magical forest, neither of the lovestruck littles alarmed at all by the impending snowstorm. A living, breathing, dancing flock of snowflakes will guide them into the second act. Act 2 finds the pair in the "land of sweets," where sweet treats from around the world, including Spanish chocolate, Arabian coffee, and Chinese tea perform for them while they sit on a throne made of candy.

Um, what?

One of the times I've laughed hardest in my life was watching the absurdity of the brilliant dancer Jared Angle, one of the world's best dance *partners* to boot, putting on a gigantic mouse head like he had a side gig at Chuck E. Cheese. While I guess I understand America's enchantment with this ballet, dancing around the stage dressed as coffee just doesn't light me up inside the same way dancing Alexei Ratmansky's Woman in Red or Anita from *West Side Story Suite* does. I have never once been leaping through the air in *Russian Seasons* and thought, *Huh. What should I have for dinner? Hmm, tacos? Wait, no. I don't have the right ingredients. Maybe pasta?* I admit that I have had these very thoughts during many a *Nutcracker* performance, while standing in the corps dressed as a flower, waiting for two counts of eight while Dew Drop does her solo.

But the first time I had my mind totally blown by the ballet was when I was nine years old. It was my first-ever trip to New York City, and I was taken to City Center to see *The Cage* by Jerome Robbins, performed by the San Francisco Ballet. *The Cage* is performed to Stravinsky's Concerto in D, and it features the story of a group of female insects who prey on the males of their species (ballet is not all princesses and sugar plums, readers!). The ensemble of women dancers called "the Group" brutally murder not one but two of the male insects. The second sacrifice taught the Novice the natural law of their world—that postcoitus there is nothing more needed of the males but the sacrifice of their bodies for food.

Oh my. I *loved* the visceral theatricality. If you happen to be attracted to women, please read the footnote.* I'd never seen the female form

---

* I'd like to say that ultimately in relationships, we should not tear each other apart physically or emotionally. I am a huge fan of endeavoring to live in partnership.

look so powerful and so beautiful. The play on female empowerment expressed through movement amazed me. I've never forgotten how I felt that day, watching this remarkable insectile drama unfold on stage. I understood then that ballerinas are more than dancers—we have the extraordinary power to make you feel things. We can embody music in our movements, but also story, emotion, and the very rhythms of life.

While *The Nutcracker* features magic in abundance, it doesn't elicit those down-deep feelings the way *The Cage* did for me when I was a kid. The pas de deux at the end of *The Nutcracker* is spectacular to watch and requires tremendous skill, but the cavalier escorting his Sugar Plum delivers a different message. It doesn't pack quite the same punch as the theatricality of Jerome Robbins's alternate universe where women banded together in strength and power.

And yet, *The Nutcracker* admittedly does have many charms (and there's no denying *The Nutcracker* is the bread and butter of our ticket sales). All dancers have some good *Nutcracker* memories, too, but no one strives to get into the New York City Ballet to play a maid or a mouse in the fucking *Nutcracker*. Most of us dream of playing the Firebird or Juliet—or originating a new, gravity-defying role choreographed just for us and our own unique gifts.

Although there are many who love dancing the *Nut*, I have done it for the last twenty years because it's my job. *The Nutcracker* represents the tradition of paying your dues and proving how tough, how compliant, and how impervious to exhaustion you really are. Each new corps member and apprentice is expected to perform in every performance. Every. Single. One. The first *Nutcracker* season is the ultimate rite of passage for a new dancer, and only the strongest survive. Over the course of the season, the theater itself becomes a cesspool of injury and sickness. Our ties with friends and family are pushed to the limit—and our undying devotion to the ballet often comes into question. This is why I affectionately call it the NUTBUSTER.

"Has anyone seen Paz?"

There was an urgency to Rosemary's voice—a tone we are all familiar with. She meant business; stop fooling around and answer me now,
young lady. It was the third week of the Nutbuster season, and everyone
in my dressing room (I was still practically a baby and in #18 at this
point) was struggling to keep their energy up. We were fighting colds,
fighting with boyfriends, and for the newbs, with parents who couldn't
understand why we couldn't return their calls about when we would be
home for the holidays. (Never. The answer is never!)

The other dancers were sitting on stools in front of their individual mirrors, applying makeup and tucking up their hair. A few were
giggling, others side-glancing toward the wall I was crouched behind,
stark naked, hiding from Rosemary, who would not be pleased with my
childish behavior (to be fair, technically I *was* a child). Until Rosemary
walked in, I had been running around the dressing room like a maniac,
as nude as a plucked chicken, using my most operatic voice to sing, "Two
turtle doves and a partridge in a pear tree"—both to the amusement and
annoyance of my dressing-room mates. We were all Christmas-crazy
and *Nutcracker*-exhausted, and I was trying desperately to keep all of
our spirits up.

"Girls. Come on. I need to know where she is." Rosemary walked
toward the mirrors, dangerously close to encountering my nakedness
but more concerning, my foolishness. I had already learned that you
didn't mess with Rosemary.

I'd seen her make grown men twice her size cry. To avoid her, I
quickly dashed across the dressing room, hiding behind the other wall.
It was like an episode of *Scooby-Doo*, me darting around corners just
before she got there. Standing flat-faced against the wall, I felt my hair
against my bare back and thought, *Why am I naked in front of all of my
coworkers and running from my boss? This is not normal workplace behavior. Seriously, what is wrong with me?*

The charade continued for several moments until she gave up,
shouting out a message about an important last-minute casting switch

in a manner that suggested she was aware of my presence and knew I was acting like an asshole. I answered with, "Roger that. Uh, thank you, Rosemary."

Spontaneous laughter erupted from the girls.

"At least you're warm . . . ," Rosie chided.

The casting schedule for the Nutbuster is intense, to put it very mildly. First of all, this is a huge production with countless moving parts—and it requires a ton of people to see it through. There's the A cast and the B cast, each one consisting of parents, mice, flowers, snowflakes, actual commodities like coffee and chocolate, soldiers, and over two dozen tiny kids who can't be let loose to roam the theater. The children require supervision! Then there's the principal roles and soloists. When you are managing roles for this many people, for so many shows (endless shows), the actual, ever-shifting schedule resembles the scribbles of a raging madman.* Figuring out what the schedule actually says is like putting together a giant puzzle with pieces made out of parents, lots of snow, coffee, tea, flowers, tons of kids, and weird uncles.

Even though the schedule is nearly impossible to read, it's preferable to the call-in of years past. Before the birth of email, Rosie or Tommy would read the entire schedule into an answering machine. I'd call up, waiting, waiting, waiting to hear my name so I'd know when to show up for rehearsal. Sometimes I'd be sitting there for five minutes, filing my nails like a 1950s secretary while listening to the entire company's names being read before I'd finally hear PAZCEWWWWGIN.†

We all play multiple roles, and for years one of them is snow. Snow is nonnegotiable.‡ There is no escaping the snow. It's beautiful, just like the first snowfall of the year; then it becomes a real pain in the ass, and you

---

* You know how I feel about Tommy, but in this case I'll give him credit. His job is hard and essentially impossible.

† Nothing makes a girl feel more loved than her employer mispronouncing her last name.

‡ Now that I'm nearing my second decade in the company, I've finally been released from snow duty.

want to be done with it already. Sure, the audience loves it. It's snowing! How gloriously Christmassy! But that snow sticks like nothing else. The snow is recycled from show to show, and I am not being hyperbolic when I say the same snow has been used for about three decades. After that scene, a stagehand sweeps it up with a big dirty broom and shoves it back in the barrel so it can be dumped upon the heads of some of the world's most elite dancers once again. When I have pointed out the snow to guests who have visited me backstage over the years, the reaction is always the same:

"Seriously? But it's greige!" or "They dump that shit on you guys? That is disgusting."

I don't know what the lighting people do to make that snow shine, but obviously they are lighting geniuses. I genuinely wonder how many strains of influenza the snow contains. This plague-pox time-capsule snow inevitably slips down my throat while I'm dancing. I've gotten it stuck in my eye and have snorted it up my nose. While the stagehands are generally excellent at sifting out any foreign objects when recycling the snow, occasionally something gets missed. Snow will be drifting upon you and then clunk—a nail nearly misses pegging you in the head. Months later, I will pull a shoe out of my closet and discover a tiny pile of leftover germ-ridden snow nestled right inside, taunting me from Nutbusters past.

It's a true testament to the cast, crew, and administration that *The Nutcracker* is pulled off every year—considering all the kids, the multifold injuries, and the disease-laden snow. As Nutbuster season progresses, the schedule looks ever crazier, as if colored over by a frustrated toddler armed with a red marker. Injuries happen, dancers are shifted into different roles, children lose their shit, and accommodations are made for dancers who are contracted out (I'm going to get to that; stick with me here). But the real Christmas miracle is that there aren't more mishaps due to scheduling madness. When this does happen, *it is spectacular.*

I'm relatively new to the corps, and I'm dancing boy doll in the party scene. There are three life-sized prop boxes onstage, decorated as big presents that we pop out of. As girl doll and I crawl through the slit in the scenery on our hands and knees to take our positions in our boxes, I notice right away that something is off. I look to girl doll and shrug and quietly say, "Where the hell is the soldier?" in the middle of a performance. Normally, the three of us would take our hiding places to position ourselves for our dance at about the same time. Very soon in the party scene, Drosselmeyer (played by the incomparable Robbie La Fosse) will open a box, and a toy soldier will pop out to do a brief but bravura-filled solo. The music for the soldier dance begins, as girl doll and I are crawling back into our boxes after finishing our dance. As I'm crawling back in, my suspicions are confirmed when I don't see the telltale soldier feet that I have to step over to get off the stage. I crawl out faster because, quite frankly, I can't wait to see what's going to happen next.

Drosselmeyer opens the toy soldiers' box, and holy shit, it's empty—no toy soldier here! La Fosse is onstage, in front of a full house, with no toy soldier. I'm now in the wings watching with great anticipation—Robbie is so theatrical. The show must go on, and I knew that whatever La Fosse was going to do would be sheer gold. I see Robbie jump into action. Robbie La Fosse begins performing a quasi-soft-shoe-meets-ballet number (think a ballet-infused jig). It gets better and better as he settles into the music. More cast members are gathering in the wings to watch, holding back hysterical laughter. Robbie's improvised solo is amazing—a full testament to his theatrical background. Imagine a Dickensian Sherlock Holmes character dancing on the stage with a giant monocle doing random movements. The music is building and building, and Robbie gets more and more dramatic. I can barely hold it together when Robbie pulls out his pocket watch and starts whipping it around dramatically; *that's innovation, people.* He continues his dance, complete in salt-and-pepper beard and an eye patch. Just as we think it can't get any better, he ends in a piqué manège on the HEEL of his character shoe, eventually landing on his knee. It was fantastic.

After *a lot* of serious scolding, we were informed that from now on, and until further notice, we would present ourselves *in person* to sign in for the show with stage management a half hour before heading up to the dressing room. It turns out that the dancer who was supposed to be inside the box got confused by the schedule and was sitting at home watching football or out at the movies or something, thinking he wasn't on that day. He had been signed in by a well-meaning coworker who saw him at rehearsal and assumed he was present. Thanks to the quick thinking on the part of Robbie La Fosse, the show was saved. He also gave the gift of hysterical laughter to the rest of us. No present could have been better.

And this is especially generous because when you're a ballerina, your celebration of the blessed holiday is abbreviated at best.

CHAPTER 19

Home for the Holidays
for Five Minutes

I imagine for most people, the holidays are a delicious cocktail of warm drinks, cozy memories, and hurried shopping excursions. Amazon packages are ordered in abundance, children are taken to see Santa so they can feel all warm and snuggly and *accomplished* as the first snowflake of the season flutters past the window. I, too, have fond Christmas memories—the excitement of Christmas Eve when I'd fall asleep in my parents' bed watching *A Claymation Christmas Special* with special guest stars the California Raisins, waking up with my five siblings to the enormous pile of presents under our tree.

But that was then. Now, by the time actual Christmas Day rolls around, my Christmas cheer is a cup of chaos with an extra shot of insanity. In the months leading up to December 25, after a few weeks of rehearsal, we will perform a whopping six weeks of shows for the glittering denizens of New York City and their antsy, rebellious children. When they bring out the cocoa this year, I'll take mine with an extra shot of bourbon.

Ever since my first year in the corps, I've hitched a ride home to Altoona as soon as it was possible with my brothers from another mother, dancers Tyler and Jared Angle. Luckily for me, they're also from Altoona, and we've performed together since we were kids. We'd hop in our rental car as soon as the Christmas Eve show was over, sit in the hell traffic that is the Holland Tunnel, drive all night, and get home in the wee hours of the morning. After a couple hours of sleep in our child-hood bedrooms, we'd spend the day with our families—our relatives all commenting on how thin we looked, "Don't they feed you in New York City?" Dancing eight shows a week will drop pounds fast.

After an early dinner, I'd drive back to New York City with my dancer friends, blowing off steam and secure in the knowledge that at least we were in the final stretch. As of 10 p.m. on New Year's Eve, we'd be Nutbuster-free! When I first left home to move to New York, I would deeply long for more time with my family at Thanksgiving and Christmas. I'd be stuffed into the back seat of the car, surrounded by Christmas bounty, when a light but persistent layer of loneliness would sweep over me. I'd imagine the scene I'd just left continuing on without me. My sisters and grandmother, nieces and nephews, playing cards and watching movies in their pajamas—right now it feels like those simple activities would lift my spirit higher than any *Nutcracker* performance ever could. Back then, if Santa offered to grant me one wish, it would be for a few more hours to eat cookies with my fam and give my body a break. But when you are new to the corps, asking for time off over the holidays is out of the question, even if you are so young that you basically just learned Santa isn't real. Under the helm of Peter, wanting time off during the ballet's busiest time was a clear indication that you weren't dedicated. You just didn't ask for a few days off to fly back to California to enjoy some holiday cheer with your family.

Now that I'm heading into my nineteenth year of the Nutbuster, I remind myself to be grateful. Even being able to spend a few hours with them has been a gift. Dancers who live farther from home aren't so lucky. They usually rely on an invite from a stranger, or they spend the day at home, FaceTiming their families. I also remind myself that Broadway shows are running, too, so no Christmas for folks on the Great White Way either. My wham-bam-thank-you-ma'am Christmas is much more than most dancers get, and I know now to be grateful.

Swan Dive #9

Nutcracker season hurts . . . literally. The sheer amount of dancing I'm doing means I often can't even bear to walk down the steps to go to the subway at night. In the pre-Uber, pre-Lyft days, hailing a taxi was the only option. Postshow, with the entire audience unleashed onto Broadway, it's a mad rush for a taxi, especially if there's rain, snow, or in this case, slush. One evening after a 2014 Nutbuster performance, I saw a Christmas miracle. A free taxi. I waved my hand and hurled myself into the street before a family in their nice coats and fancy shoes could grab it. As I was gaining on the taxi, I was sliding . . . and down.

No, to be more clear, *I was underneath the fucking taxi.*

The driver saw me fall. He came rushing out of the taxi, holding a Gatorade bottle. And I discovered I had caught him in the middle of an emergency pee break.*

"Are you okay? Do you need help?"

I noted the nearly full pee bottle. "No, thanks. I got this. I just need you to take me to the Upper West Side."

I shimmied my now soaking-wet body out from underneath the taxi, took a minute to collect myself while he presumably took a minute to deal with the pee. In the end, I was granted safe passage home, where I enjoyed a well-deserved postshow shot of tequila.

---

* Before you judge, know it is nearly impossible for a taxi driver to pull over and park and go to the bathroom. Going to the bathroom in New York City is a lot harder than you would think.

CHAPTER 20

Holiday Bonus

While the Nutbuster is the most exhausting of all ballets, it's also an opportunity for ballerinas to earn a modest amount of extra cash. New York City is insanely expensive, and most of us wouldn't survive if we couldn't earn some extra green on top of our meager ballerina salaries. And so the top ballerinas get contracts to perform in productions all over the country. I can tell you from personal experience that Ballet Etudes at the Westport Country Playhouse in Connecticut puts on lovely productions! And sometimes you get to dance a role you've not yet performed in New York City, which is always fun. There's one caveat. New York City Ballet is SO not letting you borrow a costume, and whomever you're performing for expects you to show up with one, preferably something spectacular. You can rent a piece-of-shit tutu that looks like it's graced the body of one too many dying swans for a few hundred bucks, but this is not going to make you feel like a queen in the land of sweets.

The *Nutcracker* costumes we keep at the theater were, up until a recent revamp, among the oldest, most worn, and grossest costumes we have. It was only last year that I went in for a fitting for my very own coffee skirt—did I mention I'm about to hit my twentieth season of *The Nutcracker*? This isn't out of disrespect, but it's luck o' the draw budget-wise. It is the opportunity to earn some extra cash that persuaded me, like many other dancers, to invest in having my very own tutu made. It set me back $3,500* and is one of my most prized possessions. It's a vision in shimmery gold (pink is not my thing), made of the finest tulle. Any contract I get in another city, that tutu comes along with me, and I'm ready to go. Other than my studio apartment, it's one of the smartest investments I've ever made. I've worn it to dance in *Sleeping Beauty* and *Raymonda* as well as many, many *Nutcracker*s.

Last season I wore it when I picked up this crazy Sugar Plum gig on Long Island. As one of the few resident people of color (and a very strong personality onstage), I don't see such roles very often. I'm Anita. I'm Coffee. I'm the MILF nurse. In 2015, I, at long last, had my debut in the role of Dew Drop and it felt so right.† I was truly in my element that night, drawing up the energy from my supportive colleagues in the wings and feeling the love from the audience. It was a triumphant moment in my career, and I know I'd make an awesome Sugar Plum if only City Ballet would embrace the idea of a colorful sugarplum.

There are as many versions of *The Nutcracker* as there are recipes for Christmas sugar cookies. However, a balletgoer can only experience Balanchine's own special recipe at the City Ballet.‡ But it's not unusual for regional productions to hire NYCB dancers to perform just the roles of Sugar Plum Fairy and Cavalier. In these cases, we are

---

* That might sound crazy, but owning a custom tutu is crucial to my craft, and that comes at a cost. I also spent a small fortune on my bed—it's worth it for the things I put my body through.

† It always tickles me that administration is shocked when I dance something classical well. I'm like, no shit, Sherlock, I am a ballerina, have been a ballerina, and continue to be a ballerina. Thanks for putting on your glasses tonight, though . . . happy you've seen the light.

‡ Okay, fine, actually, newish development: you can see the Balanchine version at Miami City Ballet and Pacific Northwest Ballet. But that's it!

literally cutting and pasting ten minutes of the Balanchine version and inserting it into the regional production. Allowing other productions to use a piece of Balanchine's choreography is like a magical Christmas gift from the Balanchine himself (he decreed this!). It is the only time Balanchine's choreography can be used without expressly seeking permission from Balanchine's trust and paying a fee. Merry Christmas, America!

I did it for the Benjamins. In addition to providing us with a nice chunk of change, performing in other *Nutcrackers* gives dancers an opportunity to perform roles we may not have performed at City Ballet. I have yet to debut Sugar Plum Fairy officially at NYCB, and I'm the only female soloist who hasn't done it. "There's not enough shows, Georgina. Not everyone can do it." Seriously? Your optics are murky at best on this decision. If the actual math works out to get all of the soloists and principals onstage, and you say it's not my weight or my technique that's the reason for not casting me, what *exactly* is the problem?

Even though the NYCB audience has yet to see my Sugar Plum, I have danced this role many times. The Westport Country Playhouse contracted me to dance Sugar Plum for two weekends; the only thing was, I had to bring along my own partner for the pas de deux. The dancer I performed with during weekend one was not available for weekend two, but that's fine because my backup was on a plane from North Carolina.

It didn't go unnoticed by me that the snowflakes (the actual outdoor kind!) that were fluttering around in the early evening were really kicking up speed.

When my phone rang at 11 p.m. at night, it felt like a harbinger of things to come. "Gina. It's Gonzalo. The blizzard is really kicking up here. My flight is canceled."

Shit. I can't exactly do the pas de deux by myself. I jump into action calling and texting any dancer I can think of who might be available. It's like a ballet version of a booty call. "Hey, what are you doing? I need to you to spin me and lift me up in the air in about twelve hours. Whaddya think? Feeling sexy enough to sweat all over each other to Tchaikovsky?" My hopes are briefly raised at about 1:30 a.m. when Russell texts me back.

"Sure, I'd love to dance with you, but it's been a long time since I've put on white tights. Do you know which Russell you're texting btw?"

UMMMMM EEK and WHOOOPS! Turns out I didn't text my friend Russell Janzen, I ballet-booty-texted Russell Kaiser, my former ballet master who now works in Boston, at nearly 2 a.m., while he was sleeping next to his wife of many years, former principal ballet dancer Margaret Tracey. *Awkward . . .*

And so I had yet to solve my problem.

I'd used up all my resources when I heard from Gonzo.

"Gina. They're getting me on a flight to Newark. I'll land at 10:30 a.m."

That is cutting it seriously close, as our asses need to be on the stage by about 1 p.m. I quickly hatch a plan:

1. Rent four-wheel-drive vehicle.
2. Do full makeup and hair before leaving. Including crown.
3. Fetch Gonzo's late ass at Newark airport.
4. Drive like a bat out of hell to Connecticut.

I drove on 78 West toward Newark in near-whiteout conditions, the car practically sliding up to the curb. I adjusted my crown as I waited for Gonzo, who eventually landed in the passenger seat looking exhausted and out of breath. We had less than two hours to drive to Connecticut in a fucking blizzard.

"Oh my God, you made it! Buckle up and get your makeup on."

As we eventually hit the Merritt Parkway, I was congratulating myself for renting the four-wheel drive, and we flew along the highway like this was nothing but a light spring rain. We pulled up to the theater and flew out of the car, and I had no idea if it was parked legally. I found the nearest bathroom, put my tutu on, and straightened up my crown again, all while doing a few pliés and tendus to warm up. In a mere ten minutes from arrival, Gonzo and I were on the stage, smiling our sweetest *Nutcracker* smiles. We made it.

This drama wasn't quite over. We had to get back to the city, and I was attending a wedding that night at the New York Public Library.* Since we took the highway to Connecticut and arrived alive, it seemed logical to travel home the same way. The storm had kicked things up, and I couldn't see more than a few feet in front of the windshield. I was seeing cars flying off the highway, and I was driving this Volkswagen Touareg thinking, *I cannot kill Gonzo. Jett is in the back seat. I can't kill Jett! Drive, Gina, drive,* and *Seriously, is this shit worth it?*

After the two-hour ride (made four hours of driving 15 mph with hazard lights and jaw clenched tighter than a top-notch face-lift), I made it back to my apartment. As a dancer I was accustomed to the quick costume change. I threw on my gown, put pretty suede heels on my feet, and stomped out into the storm to catch a taxi. Dear reader, should five raindrops fall in New York City, getting a taxi becomes nearly impossible. In a blizzard? Laughable. A cab appeared on Columbus Avenue like a pre-Christmas miracle . . . the bonus version. Forty minutes later, I exited the taxi and step into about twelve inches of slush. My feet instantly went numb. Why didn't I wear boots and bring my heels like any sensible New Yorker? I gathered up my gown and waded over toward the imposing iron doors of the library. I made my way up the icy stone stairs—once again feeling like I could do anything.

I was shivering, and I felt the wardrobe-judgment of Lady Astor and Lord Lenox, the imposing massive stone lions perched in front of the library, knowing I looked like Rizzo the Rat from the Muppets with a side dose of Miss Havisham.

---

* For any of you not familiar with the landmarks of New York City, the library is one of the most glorious. This was going to be my dear friend Monique's seriously classy wedding, and I was not going to miss it.

The iron doors of NYPL are epic—something you would expect at the Taj Mahal, not your friendly neighborhood library. I felt so small in comparison, but right now these doors are the only thing standing between myself and a bourbon. My half-frozen paw reached for the door and pulled—nothing budged. *I know you've been up since 2 a.m., Gina, and driven a through Donner Party–level snowstorm, but you've got to get past the door.* I kept frantically pulling but that door was locked. I started pounding on the door, which was totally absurd as the wind was howling, and there was no way anyone could hear my pleading on the other side of what is essentially a bank vault. I actually thought for a second, *If I could only locate a battering ram.* It quickly became clear that no one was going to save me. I would die here. Shit, what if I got frostbite? I could not risk losing a toe.

Fueled by desperation, I picked up my now soaking-wet gown and trudged around the side of the building, shivering and crying-screaming to myself. As I approached Forty-Third Street, I saw a halo of light— evidence of live human beings! I walked up to a totally regular-looking door, pushed it open, and dramatically stumbled into the building. I heard the sounds of a wedding: laughing, clinking of glasses, "Celebration" by Kool and the Gang.

Tyler comes rushing over. "Jesus, Gina, are you okay?"

"I don't know. I think I almost died like three times today, and I just really wanted to make it to this wedding."

He takes me by the arm and leads me toward the hallway. "Honey. You need to get cleaned up. You look like the joker."

I stood in front of the bathroom mirror, my actual ice-crusted dress feeling heavier than any costume I'd ever worn. But I would fix the smeared mascara, adjust my hair, throw back a double bourbon, and dance my friend into wedded bliss.

CHAPTER 21

B Cast Forever

"*Geoorginnahhhh*. Hey, gurl! You ready to get up on that stage with your ethnic family?"

One of the senior corps members and one fine-ass Black man, Henry, called out jokingly before we got on stage, doing his best to conjure up the voice of an old-timey Southern man. I laughed it off, preparing myself mentally and physically to do my job. I was a raven-haired apprentice newbie, cast as a maid in my first City Ballet *Nutcracker* because I was new. But it was clear I'd made B cast for a very different reason: my race. The older dancers joked about the B cast all the time—B cast = POC. A cast = lighter-skinned folk.*

It didn't take long for it to sink in that there was an actual, visible division in the casting of the New York City Ballet under Peter Martin's direction. It wasn't always as blatant and painfully obvious as

---

* I'm talking about the race of the adults in the party scene. I'm not referring to the nine million children it takes to pull off a production of *The Nutcracker*. The cast of POC adults was a weird and consistent phenomenon for years until dancers finally spoke up and it was finally addressed. Hallelujah for A and B cast integration!

it was with the B cast *Nutcracker*—we were virtually all people of color. But generally, if you were a member of the New York City ballet and you had black hair, you could enjoy a career of dancing in the B cast or as an evil villain. *Romeo + Juliet*? Montagues were the blonds, Capulets were the dark-haired people. The villain was played by Albert or some other available Black dude. Every. Single. Time. Need an ambiguously ethnic, badass female? It's Paz to the rescue! It is shameful that it has taken the ballet thirty years to figure out that these casting divisions are deleterious to audience and cultural perceptions and shouldn't be the norm.

Frankly, I felt awkward when I looked around and realized the entire B cast was made up of biracial folks (myself included), and that I'd likely be typecast my entire career. The ballet is finally waking up, but it doesn't change the fact that thousands of *Nutcracker* performances still featured a B cast of color. The dancers are determined to change the landscape. Come next *Nutcracker* season, I assure you things are going to look different. Balanchine himself was said to refer to dancers as being flowers of all colors. We are committed to making that happen, now. Even if it seems at times that I personally have to hold people accountable. Old habits die hard.

Yes, casting minorities for the B cast and Eurocentric races for the A cast was blatantly racist and wrong. But at least every member of the B cast had a helluva lot of fun working together. There is something about the monotony of Nutbuster that usually leads to a prankish atmosphere. In the corps, most of us are playing introductory roles—maids, parents, flowers, mice—and after, say, thirty performances, it starts to feel like the movie *Groundhog Day*, a replica of the night before. If we aren't careful, monotony will completely take over, numbing our bodies, minds, and souls, so we take measures to jazz things up a bit. During *The Nutcracker*, we are all still attending company class as well as rehearsing for the winter season. Come New Year's Eve, *The Nutcracker* will be almost instantaneously replaced with another series of ballets, and we all need to be on our game and ready to perform.

All work and no play make for dull ballerinas. So we loosen things up a bit and let our guards down. If you've attended *The Nutcracker* at Lincoln Center, chances are your eyes were following those adorable little children (every season, one of those darlings gets so nervous she pees right there onstage, God bless her), and you weren't watching the adults. Because if you were paying attention, you would have observed some crazy shit. You would have seen men who are now principal dancers in the classiest of ballet companies walking with their eyes closed and arms out, stumbling and nearly falling out the window. You would have seen mice voguing—pretending to eat the cheese, tossing it around . . . Cheese tossing was not part of Jerome Robbins's original battle scene choreography.

Eventually these antics reached a fever pitch, and New Year's Eve became the performance where we all joked around on purpose. Can you blame us? New Year's represents the last of a long string of ruthless, repetitive performances, and if we were lucky, we'd have enough energy left to have one or two drinks at someone's house party—only to head home shortly after midnight and crash, *hard*. New Year's Day is always a day off, and most of us put it to very good use . . . sleeping like the dead.

One year, Stephanie, my partner in the Chinese Tea number, and I were chastised by Rosemary for acting up onstage. It's honestly not too taxing of a dance. We were exaggerating all the movements and ginormous piqués, balancing, and piking contests. We thought we were being terrifically entertaining and hilarious, and judging by the miniaudience we had amassed in the wings every night—we were getting the Siskel & Ebert two-thumbs-up review.

"Ladies, you're so over the top no one is paying any attention to the principal dancer." Which was hard not to do because he was the most atrocious trope, dressed as a coolie—garish in his rice paddy hat, Fu Manchu mustache, and slanty-eye yellowface makeup, while doing split jumps. And to make it all worse the principal dancer is emasculated by being stuffed into a box and wheeled out by Stephanie and me—and out he pops out of the "tea box." *Oh, really? Tea comes in a box? You don't say?* Truly intended to be a charming moment perceived horribly wrong by a major part of the audience.

"You've got to dial it down!"

For us to steal the focus in such a scene was a feat in itself. Upon reflection, I suspect my raucous portrayal was born out of a feeling of extreme discomfort. My morality was being challenged. The Chinese Tea dance is, in my opinion, over-the-top offensive, and every night I was forced to go onstage to make a mockery of Asian heritage (including my own). The number, and ballet in general, still features some of the worst Asian stereotypes ever conceived—pointed hats, yellow-tinted face paint, slanted-eye makeup—the audience sees, but do they care?

If that doesn't make you queasy, the choreography consists of pointing fingers in a "chop chop" motion and shuffling feet, multiple head nods and bows—so Asiatic! The icing on this racist cake is a stereotypical geisha wig—wrong culture, pro tip, but let's just lump all of us together, shall we? No nuance needed. Just caricatured orientalism.

Despite my gleeful rebellion, once Rosemary called us out on our behavior, we agreed to knock it off. Apparently, we weren't the only members of the company who were itching from *Nutcracker* fever, and messing around, because soon there was an announcement from Peter himself that this New Year's Eve there would be "no antics whatsoever." Fair enough, we are professionals. I wasn't going to cross Rosemary, much less Peter. I wanted to live to see the new year. But not everyone was so happy to fall in line.

Steph and I were ready to go out for the finale—we were in our costumes complete with wigs and makeup. And yes, we were on our absolute best behavior. I leaped out onstage, twirling around Steph, doing the dance as intended. As per the choreography, I whipped my head forward and lifted it back up. Chop chop! But I noticed something immediately—my head felt wrong. Too light. I realized instantly that my horrible, racist wig had fallen off and landed directly in the path of principal Tea dancer Antonio Carmena. *Fucking hell.* There I was, standing onstage decked out in yellowface with just a black wig cap.

The audience found this hilarious—her wig fell off! They all began laughing, loudly.

There's an unspoken rule that if you drop something onstage—a wig, a shoe, a hat—you find a way to discreetly pick it up and remove it from the stage during your exit. But something about the way we were all positioned made me unable to get to where the wig had landed.

Out bounded Dew Drop, played with supreme grace by principal dancer Alexandra Ansanelli, who swept down and grabbed the wig and finished her finale step, dead center stage, with a series of relevé in passe arabesque turns—alternating the wig between her hands with each turn. While I'm on the side of the stage in my bald cap trying not to pee myself with laughter but also thinking, *Welp. I'm going to get fired.*

The crowd went wild! My coworkers who were actually onstage were also dying with laughter. Dew Drop spun and spun, basking in the moment, then saut de chat'd triumphantly off the stage. We were all dead—yet I feared I'd become a huge unintentional joke.

When Peter came up to me after, I was trembling.

"GINA! Did you do that on purpose?! Did you not pin it?"

My wig, the pesky culprit, now looked like a dead bird resting in my hand. I responded that *Of course I pinned my wig. It came off due to the fervor of my dancing!* I was upset, scared. I didn't know what the repercussions would be. He placed his huge hands on my shoulders, a gesture many of us had experienced with differing reactions. In this case his attempt at a simple physical connection felt like a signal of power. But then a chuckle broke from his otherwise stone-cold face.

"Pretty funny, though." He walked away, and thank all the muses of ballet that I didn't get in trouble—but I was still mortified. My boss was laughing at me, too. They made a rule from that performance on that the costume department now attaches all wigs, and I was thankfully moved out of the Chinese cast the next season, leaving other, less fortunate ballerinas to perform yellowface onstage.

I never felt comfortable with this depiction of Asian culture. There I was onstage, a biracial woman with Asian Filipino heritage, improperly representing Chinese culture with an outdated caricature. It never felt right to me. As a young member of the company at that time, I was not in a position to announce, "I'm uncomfortable doing this. This is racist." I couldn't turn around to my colleagues and shout, "Are you all really okay with this?" Allen, whose mother is Japanese, was one of the only other Asian dancers in the company with me at that time. The depiction of the culture was wrong, and so was the culture that permeated City Ballet. I believe had I expressed my feelings, I would have been pushed aside, my role given to another dancer who would be happy to step into the role. *Shut up and dance* was the sentiment.

It wasn't until 2017 and joining the new state-mandated diversity committee that I was able to make use of these memories and get to the root of why I couldn't take this seriously. I also know now that I tend to default to humor when I feel awkward. I could not do the dance seriously because it felt so wrong to be making fun of Asian heritage. To be standing onstage, a biracial Asian American woman in yellowface makeup. There was no way I could approach this dance the way I approach *Jewels*, or other ballets I love performing in. I know my treatment of the Chinese dance was wrapped in disrespect; this was my own form of rebellion. *The Nutcracker* is literally a peek around the world, and I believe we can do better when it comes to depicting different cultures. My dear friend and personal dance historian, Phil Chan, and I are determined to do better. We started the Final Bow for Yellowface pledge, urging dance companies around the world to eliminate Asian stereotypes from ballet. We're now a globally recognized initiative, and changes are happening. In 2019, the NYCB's Marie was a biracial

Trinidadian Filipino girl. I like to think Final Bow for Yellowface's work paved the way for that to happen. All of this piping "hot Tea" makes the "We don't have enough shows for you to debut Sugar Plum, Gina" look a bit more nefarious, doesn't it now?

* * *

It's usually sometime in mid to late fall that I'll be walking my dog out of Central Park, when I notice a sign on a bus stop—"New York City Ballet presents *The Nutcracker*, November 23rd through December 30th." Here we go. So much has changed at the ballet over the past year at the time of this writing. I think about the abuse we have faced as a company under Peter's reign. How it's left many of us wounded but recovering. Our resilience will be put to the test again as the Nutbuster season comes rushing upon us. But soon we will be stepping back into that rehearsal studio, scratching our heads over the indecipherable chicken scratch of a schedule, hoping not to get peed on, knowing we'll be ordering Christmas presents during rehearsal breaks, declining invites to holiday parties (if anyone bothers to invite us), and dumping gallons of fake snow out of pointe shoes. While I can't exactly say I'm excited to hear the famous opening notes to Tchaikovsky's score, as I write this, I find myself for once feeling a bit hopeful. There are fewer of us now, but we are strong, optimistic, and hella determined. It might be a new start—a time to bond as we work together through the craziness of all these shows. Maybe this year, when that snow falls—it will be like a beginning. I walk into my apartment, and Jett goes to lie in her bed. I sit down to check my email. If I had any doubts at all that the mayhem was about to begin in earnest, it's gone. There it is, sitting in my in-box—it's the official first forwarding of the link to "It's Decorative Gourd Season, Motherfuckers." The classic fall essay by Colin Nissan really speaks to me, especially when he says, "Felonies and gourds have one very important commonality: they're both extremely fucking real." Oh, they are, and you know what else is real? Constant rehearsals with ballerinas on the verge of cutting someone, dancing with a sinus infection you caught when some skanky biohazard snow lodged right up there in your nasal passages, sliding your pretty pink pointe shoe through *piss*. Merry Christmas, everyone! Shit is about to get real.

Swan Dive #10

There was a time in my life when I was young and selfish, and my morals clashed with my emotions. I fell in love with a fellow company member. While he made himself available to me, he was legally married to someone else. My choices hurt people, and it's something I will always be sorry about. I do not suggest following this path, even if your heart is screaming for you to follow it wherever it wants you to go. I would never do it again.

One *Nutcracker* season, the story of this affair broke publicly, and whether I liked it or not, my private life was splashed on the pages of the papers. It was so mortifying to have my personal relationship (and my bad mistakes) on display. I was getting concerned calls from my family, the *Sun* was calling my relatives and asking for "Georgina." Thankfully, since I am rarely called by my given name around family, my sister-in-law was like, "Wait, who? I don't know anyone named Georgina."

I came into work, completely embarrassed. The whore was out of the bag. I had to call and warn the company that the press was likely to reach out to them about this. All of my colleagues knew. I was too embarrassed to go to class, and I kept as low a profile as I could until half-hour call, before I was dancing lead Spanish. I put on my headphones and was doing relevés and tendus backstage. Rosemary was on the opposite side of the barre. She gestured to me to take off my headphones.

"Hey, I'm just checking on you. Are you okay?"

I replied with a quick "Yep! I'm fine!" I actually let myself believe she was asking about my body, if after a long haul in the *Nutcracker* everything was in order.

She tried again, "No, but are you really okay?"

I read her actions as someone trying to affect girl talk, but I was so embarrassed, and I was trying to hold on to any semblance of innocence I had left. I was thrown off by her being supportive rather than stern.

"Let me know if you need to talk." I nodded as she walked off.

The Spanish Dance. I was partnering with Daniel Applebaum. The thing about dancing Spanish is that the costume weighs a good ten pounds. That's a lot of extra weight, especially around the hips.

And the dance starts out with a bang, like I'm shot out of a cannon. That night, somehow in running toward the end of the stage, my foot comes around too fast and knocks my other foot out of place. I am lying flat on the ground, my arms reaching up toward Daniel, who is desperately trying to get me up because I can't seem to muster the energy to get up myself. It is like a slap in the face from the gods of ballet.

Poor Daniel looks like he is trying to start a lawn mower in his futile attempt to get me off the ground, but as soon as I hit the ground, the emotional floodgates opened, and I am close to hysterically laughing. I am desperately holding it in, not looking the other corps members in the eye because I'm going to lose it. I can't even look at Daniel, who is dying as well. When the dance is finally over, I bow and beeline off-stage, and Rosemary is standing right there.

"Are *you* okay?! Something like that was bound to happen. I knew it. I knew something was going to happen."

And if I ever forget what that time in my life was like, I can watch this fall over and over because it's immortalized on film. My moral swan dive was featured in Page Six, but my falling-on-my-ass-as-a-result swan dive is featured in a reel of *Nutcracker* bloopers, available online for your viewing pleasure and to haunt me forever.

Flying Solo

CHAPTER 22

Single-Room Status

When I came to, I was lying on the floor of the bar. Luminescent pendulum lights still swinging above my aching head like a strand of pearls. *Shit, am I alive?* The loud bass beat of 1990s dance music mixed with my friend Loreen's cackle confirmed it.

"Nice try, Gina. But I think he won."

My fellow company members were gathered around me, and they helped me back on my feet. Standing across from me, looking concerned as hell, was the French ballet dancer who had just defeated me in our impromptu off-hours dance-off. It had started out as innocent fun—a night out in France drinking with our company members after a performance. The dancers from the Ballet nationale de Marseille were there, too. We all wanted to blow off some steam. We could barely speak to each other, a mash-up of rudimentary French/English respectively, but it didn't matter. Dance bridged the gap where language failed us. We had pushed the tables aside, creating our own, albeit very small, dance floor. When the Euro techno music was replaced with "Wanna

Be Startin' Somethin'," *it was on.* Michael Jackson was all mine, and my colleagues knew to back off and let me do my thing.

A small but powerfully built Asian dancer from Marseille beckoned to me on the floor. I started out by doing eight counts of a move—a seriously hot one, daring him to repeat and add on. He did, adding his own special flair that both fueled me and put a huge smile on my face. He was *so* good. As we danced, the fierceness of the moves escalated fast. Suddenly, he was crawling on his knees—advancing toward me with a serpentine dance move so great and achingly original, I wouldn't have believed it if I hadn't seen it. He was undulating as if suspended in water. It was so graceful—so sexy. So skillful and beautiful. He was Ursula in the goddamn *Little Mermaid*, and I would have happily turned over my voice if he asked. *Okay, sexy man, I see you. Watch this!* I got onto my knees and bent myself backward in order to propel myself forward like he did. Instead of creating the effect that I was floating peacefully in magical waters, I fell backward, cracking my head on the floor and knocking myself out in front of the entire bar. And there remained my flattened ego and my sex appeal probably for the rest of the night.

I have a pretty intense wanderlust and I love exploring, so I'm incredibly fortunate that my job takes me to places far beyond the inner belly of the theater. My fellow dancers and I have had adventures onstage and offstage that have created some very memorable travel experiences. I've always thought there is something wildly sexy about transient living. I think of secret agents, swooping into an exotic or maybe dangerous foreign land, ready to face whatever the new mission requires. It's glamorous (in idea, anyway). Add the adrenaline of a powerful performance, lots of good-looking people (other dancers or just hot locals), a per diem, and BINGO! You have all the necessary ingredients for a cocktail of wild fun. Our travel antics have even inspired a motto, "No sleep on tour," and the other diehards and I live by this. Depending on our repertoire and locale, this motto may take on various iterations, but if you're imagining secret affairs, mistaken identities, and drugs, topped off with an occasional Michelin three-star restaurant—you, reader, are correct. All of these things fit in beautifully with our simple take-life-by-the-hair motto.

One thing we should clarify first. There are two distinctly different types of tours, which bring with them entirely different experiences. There's official New York City Ballet company tours, and then there's small gigs or pickup tours that require far fewer people and have much more intimacy. When the New York City Ballet travels overseas, massive dramatics ensue. The mere logistics of it all are impressive. We are about ninety-seven dancers, and that's just the dancers. Added to the mix will be the ballet masters, a select group of musicians, hair and makeup crew, and stage managers—we can basically take over the majority of the plane. All of these people play a crucial role when NYCB takes it all on the move. Each dancer is assigned their own theater case—think big, old-fashioned, heavy—an awkward-to-carry-yourself kind of suitcase. We can stuff it with whatever we want, but in the mix will be essentials like our stage makeup and accompanying brushes, performance tights, rehearsal tights, clothes, vitamins, weird physical therapy tools, and *snacks*. Who wants to be wandering around the streets in a foreign city in search of ProBar Bolt organic energy chews? It's different than looking for some basic chips or roasted almonds. You need a specific pre-show nosh? Pro tip: pack that shit. One thing I will give America, we've got a solid snack game. But gotta say it, Japan has snacks and beer in public twenty-four-hour-access vending machines (they also have vending machines offering women's used underwear, but this is solely mentioned in observation; I'm not judging anyone's kink game).

When traveling abroad, our theater case becomes a clutch tour luxury, especially in light of all the bullshit of airline travel today. And bonus, they are big enough to accommodate any treats you might stumble upon in foreign cities. The best use of my theater case was, hands down, on a trip to the spa town Baden-Baden. It had been an intense trip, notably due to a ghostly encounter at the hotel (the ghost had also visited another dancer, so I know I wasn't imagining it), but I had fallen head over heels in love with a scrumptious white wine unique to the Black Forest region. In a fit of passion, I purchased a case of what might as well have been bottled moonlight (it was positively otherworldly) but realized it would cost a ridiculous amount of money to ship my love juice back home. *But wait!* I proceeded to empty my travel case of essentials—forget makeup, which can be replaced—and wrapped each precious bottle lovingly in my dance clothes. Voilà! Shipped home as freight and free of any customs nightmare, courtesy of City Ballet.

Japan: SCREW WITH A VIEW—Sexiest place to get down and
dirty while looking out at masses of unknowing but highly orga-
nized pedestrians of Shibuya from your massive twenty-fourth-
floor, floor-to-ceiling windows.

I love Japan. The beauty, the appreciation of nature, the food. Out of all our travels it's Japan that has captured my heart. We were all exhausted from an epic travel day (IN COACH) and grueling performances, but the reward to me was the city itself. We were in *Tokyo*, for Christ's sake. Being in Tokyo (Shibuya, specifically) is like being inside a decorated Christmas tree. Especially when your vantage point has you perched above the streets. There are lights everywhere, ornamental ads twinkling in nearly every direction you look. It's sensory overload in the most delightful way. It's fascinating that amid all the craziness, it's the sea of people—millions of them—who create organization in the landscape. In Shibuya's center, people cross in the crosswalks en masse, people split the stairs in uniformity. One side for up, one side for down (take note, New Yorkers!). The mass transit system is easy and reliable, and the nightlife is lit. The audiences in Japan are demure but appreciative, and despite a formidable language barrier, dance unifies once again.

Dining in Japan is a treat as long as you don't have a gluten sensitivity or aversion to textures. It's always an adventure. For starters, no one bats an eye of judgment when you sidle up to a Kaiten-sushi joint for a solo meal. The conveyor belt sushi bars of Japan are really convenient and provide delicious eats on the go. The pricing is by the color of the plate, and you just watch selections go by until something strikes your fancy. There was only one time I bit off more than I could chew, *literally*. I ventured to eat the octopus. The nerve endings on the suckers had yet to get the message that the octopus was freshly deceased and gripped onto the roof of my mouth. I realized, nope, this is a texture I do not prefer at all. One night when we had off, a group of us followed up on a local insider tip and went to some crazy place under a railroad track. In addition to getting to experience the debauchery of Japanese businessmen (and some women letting loose), we had another reason for seeking the place out. It was the highly recommended specialty of the house. What was that specialty? Cod sperm. It was presented with all the innuendo to the table, and I as well as a few other brave souls ate it with no reservations. To be brutally honest, I've had better. What helped wash it down was that we accidentally ordered a $700 bottle of sake. Our per diem is not enough to cover boutique top-shelf sake on that level. After some negotiation and a few displays of ballet dancer agility, we worked out a compromise with management.

Perhaps energized by the sperm, we found a karaoke bar and sang until the wee hours. But we weren't done yet! Next, we found another bar near an empty club and enjoyed a dance party ending with impromptu lifts in the somehow-empty Shibuya crossing, lit by ads that made Times Square look dull by comparison. When it finally occurred to one of us to note the time, we realized it was 4 a.m., but we were happily drunk and still going strong. Circadian rhythm be damned! We made the brilliant decision to make our way to Tsukiji Sushi market, the largest fish market in the world, to beat the crowds (I am proud to say we did this before Anthony Bourdain made it a thing and before its closure). Eating sashimi right off the boat and stepping into Japanese history was an otherworldly experience both sobering and magical at the same time. We saw firsthand the discipline and skill of those fisher-men. Filled with sushi, we made our way back home to the hotel, took a catnap, and in a nod to our own discipline, made it to company class a few hours later, too.

Tokyo is just a gateway drug of Japan; Harajuku, Kyoto, Osaka, and Nara are all magical places to visit as well. I love the sacred deer, tra-ditional tea ceremonies, fashion, tranquil shrines, and bonsai gardens. From the underground music scenes to the street-food culture, Japan is the kind of place that seduces. There's something about it that makes you want to say, "Let's risk everything."

Dancers at City Ballet are bonded by our altered childhoods; nearly all of us entered into the professional world long before we were old enough to vote—some before we were old enough to drive. Our odd alternate reality of an upbringing connects us, and sometimes on tour it feels like we're making up for the missed experience of a carefree youth. We view the world through the lens of curiosity; we acknowledge the rare opportunity to explore while doing what we love—all while under the watchful eye of a "parent" and a per diem. On our third tour of Japan, the ride-or-dies decided fugu or bust. After taking the high-speed train from Tokyo to Osaka, we made a reservation at a restaurant that has a licensed fugu chef on the premises. We technically knew eat-ing blowfish could kill you. One blowfish contains enough poison to kill thirty people. The skin and liver are just flowing with the deadly poison—but it's the ovaries that are the most lethal. *Fascinating.* But who wants to miss out on the chance to eat a thrilling Japanese delicacy? Even if the thrill is directly related to life, or death by a particularly grue-some combination of paralysis, shitting, and throwing up all over your-self, culminating in death by respiratory distress when your diaphragm stops working? Who wants to miss that? Our fugu dinner was accom-panied by a lot of sake, but we all left the restaurant alive and well and at a somewhat reasonable hour. I was performing *West Side Story* the next day, and I needed to get some sleep.

I think it's fair to say I was drooling, jet-lagged zonked when the hotel phone rang. It was 2 a.m. and it was Gwyneth.

"Gina, I think I'm having trouble breathing. Are you having any trouble breathing?"

"Ummm, no, I'm not, G Star. As far as I can tell I'm fine. I'm just really tired. By the way, you're speaking completely normally. A sign of decent respiratory function." I hung up, and just as my head hits the freshly flipped, non-drooled-on side of the pillow, the phone rings again.

"G!!!! Don't hang up. Faye is freaking; she says she can't feel her feet. Should we go to the hospital? My toes are tingling; are your toes tingling? This is serious; are we gonna die?!" I think to myself, *Another perk of single-room status: no roommates to work you into a psychosomatic frenzy.*

"You guys do what you gotta do . . . the only thing I'm serious about is if you wake me up again, I'm gonna kick your ass." I'm sure if I'd been awake enough to think about it, I could have found some part of my body that was slightly numb. We dance for a living, we'd been traveling; this shit hurts, for Lord's sake. I fell back asleep; the morning came. All of us lived to see it.

Copenhagen: I like the size of your sausage. (In other words, your rød pølse.) I'll take a puff of your KUSH.

Long live the hygge lifestyle. Denmark is the birthplace of dance heavyweights Hübbe and Martins, but it is also the home of Tivoli Gardens, the world's second-oldest amusement park (the oldest, Bakken, is located north of Copenhagen and opened in 1583. The Danes were obviously way ahead of the game when it came to amusement parks). Apparently, Hans Christian Andersen was so taken with Tivoli that he was inspired to write "The Nightingale," a story about the emperor of China becoming obsessed with a mechanical, bejeweled bird. In addition to the typical range of roller coasters and rides, Tivoli features *world-class* culture. Pantomime, classical music, and ballet. City Ballet was doing a run of *Serenade*—in the middle of an amusement park, and we couldn't be happier about it. After a pretty rigorous rehearsal as the Russian Girls (I was still in the corps this trip), we tossed on our warm-up clothes and ran out the door with our ride tickets to get in the VIP queue for the Rutschebanen. The Rutschebanen is an ancient wooden roller coaster. It is so old, and so steep, that you are putting your very life in the hands of the guy who operates the brake to slow the thing down after the big drop. Between performing and the Rutschebanen, it was like having a weeklong adrenaline orgasm. *It was thrilling.*

On more recent trips, we upgraded to perform in the new opera house, the most state-of-the-art theater I've ever set foot in. Most theaters are vintage, and so dry and dusty you can feel the moisture being sucked out of your pores. This place had *humidifiers*—I didn't feel like a husk of a person, and I belted out "America" in *West Side Story Suite* like nobody's business. After rehearsals and performances, we'd take the water taxi back to the city and eat at the only joint that remained open: McDonald's. I didn't mind the near-daily dose of royale with cheese and a side of fries. My per diem was long gone. That's because when we found out we were coming back to Copenhagen, nearly a year prior, we'd decided to book a table at the best restaurant in the world, Noma.

Getting a reservation at René Redzepi's Noma was like getting *Hamilton* tickets in 2018. They open up reservations three times per year, months and months in advance. One of our group bravely volunteered to make the reservation, getting up essentially in the middle of the night hoping to score a table. When you eat at Noma, you're also forking out all the money for a luxury experience. For a group our size, we were paying literally thousands of dollars: about $750 per person, including wine pairing, to eat a twenty-course meal focused on foraged Nordic foods.* It's a theatrical, almost otherworldly experience. One course was a beau-

---

* Foods served at Noma have been known to include potted plants, mold, ants, and dried moss. It's some crazy shit.

tiful little nest cradling a perfect, tiny egg and a doughnut-encased fermented fish. Then I was presented with a plate of carrots that had been slow roasted for four days. I can't begin to explain the short ribs; the words simply do not exist. There were wine pairings, a kitchen tour, and memories made with my colleagues that I truly cherish. In fact, Noma's location on the island of Christiania made indulging in a postdinner recap on a high a different sort of appropriate. Good luck to the reader who wants to try that now, though. It's still puff at your own risk.

Heidelberg: Charming AF. I can only imagine Christmas here.

Baden-Baden: Haunted AF, but the spas are on point.

Paris: Place most likely to get your per diem snatched out of your pocket.

Lyon: Better than Paris (terrific food).

London: Epic pub crawls.

Moscow: Mind the holes in the sheets.

Spain: Guitar and flamenco. *Me encanta.*

Madrid: The energy of the people is infectious, and the paella delicious.

Barcelona: The party town.

Costa Brava: Romantic AF.

Bilbao: The Guggenheim.

Chile: Place where you're most likely to be robbed of your phone in a taxi at gunpoint.

Italy: Be still, my heart.

Taormina: Seafood, A+. Likelihood of us seeing the sagging ball sacks of naked German sunbathing tourists, 100 percent. WOW, low-hanging fruit.

Bassano del Grappa: Best place to fake horseback riding skills in order to view the Alps from the mountainside. Also, what's good enough for Hemingway is good enough for me. Pro tip: Grappa contains 35–60 percent alcohol by volume. It's my preferred digestif.

Florence: Museum mecca.

Venice: Watch out, single ladies, the gondola man will ask you to
    marry him.

One of my earliest trips to Italy was with a pickup company. We
shall henceforth refer to them as gigs. It wasn't an official New York
City Ballet tour, so I got my very own hotel room. At NYCB at that
time, I had yet to pass through the ranks of the corps up to soloist,
where we are contractually and blissfully granted "single-room status." I
had been living on my own since I left the dorms at the School of American Ballet when I was just seventeen. I was young but already had years
of experience buying my own tampons and almond milk, paying bills,
washing countless pairs of tights and leos, and dancing for the sophis-
ticated, discerning, ballet-loving crowds of New York City. However,
none of these adultish activities mattered when traveling en masse with
the New York City Ballet. If you danced in the corps, you had a roommate. That's how it worked. After being folded like a pretzel in my seat
because ballerinas only fly coach, I'd land in Italy, France, or Japan, only
to be ushered into a tiny hotel room with aching muscles and a multi-
hour time difference WITH A ROOMMATE.

"Single-room status" was a contract perk reserved for principal
dancers and soloists. Until I hit that level, I could look forward to my
roommate's tights dangling in my face while I showered and pooping in
small bathrooms with another ballerina a mere few feet away. This tour
was different. Even though I was one of the younger members, a room
was booked for me as a gesture of kindness. A *massive* kindness.

My excitement about having my own room took a free fall as soon
as I opened the door. I'd already had my doubts, especially when navigating my wheelie suitcase around the "prostituta" who was uncon-
scious, nearly spread-eagle in the middle of the lobby. But I'm the kind
of person who likes to maintain a positive outlook; it's just my nature.

Then I was certain. I had been booked a room, albeit my *own* room, in a total shithole. It was like a cross between a prison cell and a nun's chambers. Dark and dirty but spruced up with a single threadbare blanket, a Bible, and a worn picture of the holy mother. It smelled like decades of cigarette smoke, fish heads, and despair. I heard loud shouting and sinister laughter from down the hall. I didn't understand a word of Italian, but I know the sound of a threat when I hear one. This place was shady AF. I was exhausted after a long flight and wanted nothing but a shower and to go to sleep, but there was no way I was doing either in Venice's own Ostello California. While my Italian guidebook contained helpful phrases such as "Di notte chiudete il portone?" (Do you lock the door at night?) and "La doccia non funziona" (the shower *didn't* work, I checked!), there was nothing remotely close to "This shady joint is vile. Where is the nearest hotel where I won't be violated in my sleep?" I had only a few hours until I had to be at the theater to warm up for the role of jumping girl in the Balanchine ballet *Who Cares?* (yes, that's actually what it's called).

My hostel/hell hovel was right across the street from where the rest of the company was staying—at a grande dame of a Venetian hotel, dripping in opulence, romance, and red velvet. Just the façade of the place conjured up images of gondola rides and under-bridge kisses with dreamy Italian men. The glowing lights of the good hotel beckoned me with promises of hot water and amenities, free red wine, decent water pressure. I felt an actual ache in my heart, and I longed for my family— not the one I had back in Altoona, but the ones I had said goodbye to on the street just moments ago. I was so excited to have my own room that I didn't stick around to discuss plans for post-nap late-night pasta and negronis. I lugged my bag back across the street and walked into the lobby. Its opulence was outrageous, so much so that I thought to myself, *Dracula would love this shit.* I knew my friend Megan had probably just slipped into bed, hoping to give her body a rest. I didn't want to wake her, but I was desperate, scared, and really wanted to be alive for our next performance. So, after an awkward and fraught conversation with the front desk clerk, I convinced him to dial Megan's room. I heard a ring. Before I could even speak, she said, "Yes, Gina. Come up, you can stay with me." Single-room status was overrated.

Swan Dive #11

I was probably still flying high from something—the ballet, roller-coaster adrenaline, or just actual drugs—when Gretchen suggested a bike ride and I said yes. I can execute thirty-two fouettés, but put me on a bicycle and I will lose all of that coordination.

Riding a bike in Denmark is a very Denmark thing to do. However, because everyone in the entire country is so pro-bicycle, it means there is actual bicycle traffic. I started out okay—I made forward motion. But then I turned the wheel too hard, like car driving, and was headed right toward the curb.

I thought, *Oh, I know, I'll just jump the curb like a badass. Wait, no. Too scary. Abort!*

I hit the curb and fell off the bike, but instead of flying into nearby traffic, I slid off the seat, falling straight down—hard—wedging my lady parts on the bar with my feet landing on the road, bringing me to a full stop. I hate to think what would have happened had I not stopped the bike with my vagina.

CHAPTER 23

Dancing Machine

Ⓘt is a truth universally acknowledged that a single woman reaching her thirtieth year will feel compelled to make some sort of massive change. I did not wake up on my thirtieth birthday and think, *Wow, I should have a massive party with a frozen margarita fountain to recognize this milestone* or *Huh, I'd like to be pregnant with twins.* But as I went through my day, walking my dog, going to company class, I did feel an urge to make a change—and what I wanted as I entered a new decade was artistic fuel. I wanted to try new things. I'm an explorer at heart, and I'm not saying this because I've eaten cod sperm and potentially deadly fish ovaries in Japan. It's that I've always been a naturally curious person. Between seasons at the ballet (if I don't have a gig booked), I definitely stay occupied. It's during these breaks that I have procured a real estate license (I'm essentially a practical Midwestern woman), taken butchery classes with LA's finest sustainable butcher (Need thick-cut bacon? I can take apart a pig for you no problem; just stand back, please), and gotten certified to scuba dive. I like to keep life fresh, and it was about high time to do that with dance.

I got a brief but delicious taste of what dance was like outside of City Ballet when I stepped into the role of Ivy Smith in the 2014 Broadway revival of the *On the Town*. I loved everything about this experience. I played the role after one Ivy left, but before another was slated to step in. Those two weeks were like an amuse-bouche. It was a small sampling, but I was very excited about what might follow. It ignited my appetite, and I wanted more, more, and more.

Enter American Dance Machine for the 21st Century. This is a reboot of a downtown dance company that focuses on restaging lost Broadway musical dance numbers. If you look at the "book" from a Broadway musical, you'll find all of the music and the script, but where a dance number comes in, it will just say "dance break." The choreography is nowhere to be found unless someone recorded it, which didn't start happening with any regularity until the late '60s. Imagine your favorite production number from a Broadway musical—now think about what it would be like to re-create that number with only written notes. It would be like someone shoving a set of Ikea furniture instructions in your hand and saying—go forth and build me a house! It's nearly impossible. That's why dance masters play such a crucial role in my world (especially before the era of recording); they are passing down firsthand knowledge. They danced with Balanchine and know they are passing on that knowledge to the next generation of dancers. American Dance Machine's goal was to preserve all that amazing choreography by connecting dancers directly with the people who were closest to the source, and *this is even better than a recording*. Working with the original Anita, Chita Rivera, was mind-blowing—but what made that encounter extra important is that Chita worked with Jack Cole, who is the founder of what jazz dance is in America. She was able to give me the inside scoop on all the crucial elements about what made his dance special—the secret, intimate details that aren't written down anywhere. It's the difference between making your grandmother's meatball recipe by yourself in your studio apartment, the instructions lovingly written down in her hard-to-read cursive on a

yellowed recipe card, and standing next to Grandma* in her kitchen, the smell of her perfume dangling in the air, the sun streaming through her faded curtains as she guides you through the process. *Roll them gently! Don't squash them! And dear God, why are you making them so big! They're meatballs, not baseballs. Smaller! Smaller!* The artistry is passed down with love.

Think of it like a living museum of Broadway dance. American Dance Machine was like a full-on buffet of musical theater awesomeness.

I had the opportunity to work directly with Chita to perform her role in Jack Cole's "Beale Street Blues." She is a woman I truly admire, and it was refreshing to be coached by someone with such wisdom and generosity. She is also iconically cool. She'd show up in a black turtleneck that looked beautiful with her sassy haircut, and she's not afraid of a statement necklace. When coaching me, she'd kind of scat along with the movements . . . and at one point her note to me was *Make it cooooool*, the word drawn out in a manner that suggested it had meanings that mere mortals such as myself cannot begin to understand. *Coooool* like maybe beatniks playing jazz and snapping their fingers in some secret cellar bar in Greenwich Village back when the Village itself was still actually cool.

It was at American Dance Machine that I was approached by the choreographer Margo Sappington to perform a pas de deux from one of the most controversial theater productions of all time. In the early '70s Margo was asked to assist Michael Bennett, who was doing the choreography for a show called *Oh! Calcutta!* She was his assistant at the time, and he needed help. His request had an interesting PS, though—everyone in the cast was performing naked. Bennett eventually decided he wasn't going to do the show, and the producers asked Margo to take over when she was just twenty-one.

Oh! Calcutta! was one of those hypocritical theatrical productions, panned by critics—"It's indecent!"—but everyone (from movie stars to

---

* To be clear, I am not calling Chita my grandmother. *She's my queen.*

police officers) showed up to see it. It ran for years. The idea of an all-naked show was so crazy in 1969 (oh my God, HELLO, 1969), when it was first performed, that the theaters on Broadway wanted nothing to do with it. It opened downtown in a former pornographic movie house instead.

And this ballerina had been pegged by Margo Sappington to re-create the iconic and naked pas de deux she had made iconic herself. The dance has full-frontal naked contact, but it's also incredibly beautiful. Margo wisely suggested I think about a partner whom I could fully trust (for the most obvious of reasons), and I knew one of the only people I could do this with was Craig. Craig Hall was a colleague of mine from City Ballet, a fellow soloist who has always been one of the best partners in the company. The juxtaposition of his stoicism onstage and happy-go-luckiness in life made him a good choice for this because it's not every day you ask someone to dance butt-ass naked with you if you don't want to fuck them.

Margo had an interesting rule. All of our rehearsals would require Craig and me to be fully nude. In addition to the rehearsals being naked, they also had to be scheduled around our rehearsals at City Ballet. Our first rehearsal was in a large space at Pearl Studios at night. We had to insist that the shades be drawn. We were in the middle of Midtown Manhattan—windows of other buildings just a few feet away. We weren't putting on a free show for anyone. At our first rehearsal Craig and I entered the room wearing rehearsal clothes. Old habits die hard? We had not gotten to donning the robes yet. Robes were actually a big deal in the original production. Apparently, the producers decided that there was to be "no casual nakedness"—so if an actor wasn't involved in a scene, they had to don a gold robe especially made for everyone in the production. Daily sensitivity exercises took place, too. There would be an announcement, "Robes off," and the cast would throw themselves into some sort of naked exercise.* Craig and I didn't have to be naked in front of a throng of other cast members; it was just the two of us, and Margo

---

* https://www.nytimes.com/2019/06/17/theater/oh-calcutta-at-50.html

our wise guide. The first night of rehearsal we took off our rehearsal clothes like it was the start of a new ritual. We were calm; we were ready to work. But then the door to the studio opened, and a janitor with a mop and bucket entered, looked at us, and immediately retreated. Then he opened the door again like he had landed in some '70s sitcom and couldn't believe his eyes and had to double-check. Indeed, there was a fully clothed older woman and two stark naked people. At that point I screamed, covered myself with my hands, and ran the length of the big room seeking cover that did not exist. Ultimately, I'm sure I put on more of a show by dashing across the space than if I had just stood there with my hands cupped over my vag.

We'd soon see there was a method to Margo's madness of the naked rehearsal. Bodies are bodies, and friction is friction, and what I'm saying here is that boners happen. When Margo performed this role in the original production, her partner was straight—regular breaks were taken for the sake of composure. Physical reactions were had with Craig and me, too, and rehearsing naked meant we could learn to adapt to this. Whenever necessary, we had a pact that we take a "dick in a box" break. Safe space. I got aroused at times, too, but it's not like I was dripping onto the floor. It was one of those instances where having a vagina just seems so much more reasonable than dealing with a penis. The naked rehearsals also taught us to account for other issues that would not have occurred had we been clothed—sweat making our bodies slippery or sticky. Eventually we got so comfortable with each other that the nakedness was barely noticeable. We got to a point where we could easily show up, drop our clothes, and bound around the studio if we felt like it. Dancing this way took everything to the bare bones—literally— but also it was so freeing. Sometimes I'd go to work at City Ballet after another naked rehearsal and be immediately faced with some typical ballet bullshit, and I'd think, *Fuck you, City Ballet, I've done some seriously scary shit already today. I danced naked for nearly two hours. This bullshit you're throwing at me, Pete-meister? It's nothing.*

The Joyce, in the Chelsea neighborhood of Manhattan, is a pretty intimate theater. When you are doing a nude pas de deux, it would honestly be less frightening to perform at Madison Square Garden. Small in this case equals close-up—*Here is my vagina! Take a look, everyone! And don't forget about my breasts, because they're out here too for all four hundred of you to see.* I don't know what Craig was feeling, but if it was anything like what I was feeling, it was intense. Phones, however, were confiscated prior to the performance. No way was this ending up on YouTube. At some point during the rehearsal process, we had "Kiki" and "Mo" embroidered on our robes. This was it; it was time to remove Kiki and Mo and get out there. It was exhilarating, the dance was beautiful— and I will never forget the experience. Neither have the stagehands, who know I've performed at that special show and think of me as a female version of Jagger (I've got the moves AND I've got the body). Here I was, newly thirty, dancing nude with one of my best friends in front of an entire audience *full-on full monty.* I was scared, but I did it. This was the change I wanted to start off my next decade. Margarita fountains and twins would have to wait. American Dance Machine for the 21st Century was just what I needed. The Broadway divas I had the privilege to work with there have been so overwhelmingly generous of spirit. That's a rare experience at the ballet; that level of openness and generosity of spirit free from competition simply does not exist at Lincoln Center. These women got more gratification from sharing their experience so that another, younger dancer can feel the magic. They weren't holding on to all the magic for themselves. Chita Rivera, Donna McKechnie, Dame Gillian Lynne, and Carmen de Lavallade. Creatures of true grace and talent. Thank you to each of these ladies. I could cry right this moment; these experiences have been so meaningful to me.

↩

CHAPTER 24

Cats:
It's Not for Pussies

There was one other extraordinary diva I would meet at American Dance Machine for the 21st Century: the great Gillian Lynne, former ballerina with the Royal Ballet who would go on to choreograph the original productions *Cats* and *The Phantom of the Opera*. Gilly (as I was allowed to call her), by the way, was Dame Commander of the Most Excellent Order of the British Empire. Not bad for a girl who'd been so hyper and fidgety that her mom took her to the doctor to figure out what was wrong with her. Thankfully for all of mankind, the doctor prescribed dance.

And most thankfully for me, because I got to work with Gilly on the role of Victoria, the young, naïve white cat—also played by Gillian in the London and Broadway productions of *Cats*.

The first thing I noticed about Gilly was that her aura was bigger than her body. She exuded so much energy, but if you really, really looked, you'd see how small she was. Once again, rehearsals were sandwiched into my ballet schedule. Gilly would greet me with "It's an ungodly hour. Let's get to it, shall we?" The time was 8:30 a.m.; who knows what she does at night? She knew exactly how to communicate to me, and she was so in tune with the connection between the movements and her body.

"This move comes straight from the nipples, Georgina!" she'd say. Every word that came out of this eighty-nine-year-old woman's mouth was dripping with sensuality. There is a coccyx balance that Victoria does in *Cats*, and it's one helluva "negotiation," if you will. The assistant choreographer Adam Murray and I were both trying and failing to execute it. Gilly, technically a senior citizen, just plops herself on the ground and does it like it's as easy as using your arm to fork food into your mouth. No big deal . . .

When I was performing in *On the Town* there had been whisperings backstage that *Cats* was coming back to Broadway. People were urging me to audition. In my head I was like, *Well that would go over great with Peter.* I put any thoughts of it out of my mind. In the beginning of the midwinter season, I got a call from Tara Rubin Casting. "Gina, your name has been tossed around in the mix for *Cats*. Would you be interested in auditioning?" I was flattered as hell, as this was a thought my witchy side had tossed out into the universe in an effort to be proactive. Peter's comment when he promoted me that we "would never see eye to eye" forced me to think about second acts for myself. Could Broadway really be one of them? At that time, I didn't know which cat I was being considered for, and it did not escape me that I am 100 percent a dog person. I was generally pro–*Cats* the musical—but I wasn't a die-hard fan.* *Cats* is polarizing—people love it or hate it. Yet while I considered myself very fond of *Cats*, I wasn't exactly sitting around memorizing T. S. Eliot.

As fate would have it, I was auditioning for a different movie project helmed by Andy Blankenbuehler that required some dancers. Blanken-

---

* I had no idea how die-hard *Cats* fans could be. People would show up dressed as cats or with cat toys to dangle in front of us, and once, a woman actually dressed up like Hamilton, but as a cat. A hybrid Blankenbuehler show cat.

buehler is most notably the choreographer of *Hamilton*, among other great Broadway shows, and was tapped to join the revival of *Cats*.

"Georgina. It's a pleasure to meet you. As preceded by the buzz, you are quite a beautiful dancer. Coming next week to the audition for *Cats*?"

Wait, did this man just say I have buzz?

"Enchanté, Mr. Blankenbuehler. This afternoon was the most fun I've had in a while. Uh, no, I don't believe I received any info about a *Cats* audition."

He responded immediately, "You should audition for *Cats*."

Well then, that gave me a lot to ponder on the ride back down to NYCB, where I rehearsed for another four long hours. I went to bed with my thoughts still racing. I was excited by the idea of testing out my merit in a different medium. But I'd have to be really discreet about this. It would all have to happen when I wasn't under Peter's watch. It was almost like I was flirting with the idea of an affair.

Sure enough, the next day I received an official request to audition—to clarify, I was part of a very large invited call. It seemed like every dancer east of the Mississippi River was at that audition. It was nerve-racking, and I was suddenly aware of what a cushy gig I had at the ballet. We don't audition; someone else chooses. If we aren't chosen, we still technically have a job; we still get paid. Here everything and anything was up for grabs. That is where my utmost respect for Broadway dancers and actors was cast in stone.

When my two weeks with *On the Town* were over, I went back to my job. Shortly after that, the show announced it was closing. That those insanely talented men and women audition over and over—not knowing when the next job and paycheck will be coming—is extraordinary. A Broadway show can close after one performance, people! All of that work, all of those hopes and dreams squashed. Next! And then it's back to auditioning and finding that next role. I have an immense privilege being in the company of the City Ballet, and I want to make this clear. I am one lucky lady. Luck also favored me in that I had more than a few friends among the throngs of dancers at that huge audition, and this took the edge off my anxiety. And it's a testament to Andy (and the entire creative team) that the vibe in the room was so positive during this audition. I felt like I was at a massive dance party hosted by Blankenbuehler. *It was ridiculously fun.* The differences between Broadway and the ballet were always so stark.

The audition process took what felt like ages. Before getting the role, I had auditioned at least five times. All of these auditions were secret, taking place before company class. I had been gaining traction at the ballet, too, and it was a wildly busy time. I'd do my *Cats* audition in the morning, and then run uptown for my rehearsal, and then perform a lead role in Justin Peck's *Paz de la Jolla.*

Time would pass, and I'd tell myself it was over—*Be happy you have the ballet!* Then I'd get called back. Two weeks passed, and I was on tour in D.C. with City Ballet when I got word, again, that I was being called back.

"Georgina, we need you to come in again. Andy will be there." That was a lot easier said than done.

"Oh. Well . . . I'm in D.C. Can I tape it?" I didn't know what to think. This had been going on for so long. Do I kill myself trying to get there? Was there any chance this was going to happen?

"Sorry, no. We need you to be here tomorrow."

I made the call and snuck myself out of the theater and on the earliest train back to New York, spent a good portion of my paycheck on the ticket, and made it to the audition. When I walked into the room, I was confronted with a brand-new set of people. *Where the hell were other potential cats I had been seeing throughout this entire process? Are they starting over? Will I be too old to perform the role by the time a decision is made? I just can't guarantee I'll be able to execute a flawless coccyx balance when I'm eighty-nine like Gilly.*

I didn't have much time to think about this because my ass had to be back on the Acela to D.C. to make curtain for the one show I had slated the entire D.C. tour, which of course fell on the same night. Soloist purgatory is real.

That was the first week of March. A few more weeks passed—then my agent called.

"Get out your white unitard. You're going to be Victoria in the *Cats* revival."

Holy shit! It's happening. I'm thrilled—but then it hits me.

I'm going to have to talk to Peter about this.

Accepting the role meant taking an official leave from the ballet, and that was (to put it mildly) a difficult conversation. Moving my life just a few subway stops down to the Theater District would be viewed as a betrayal. When I went into Peter's office to discuss my plans, I felt physically sick. This was also the man who jump-started my career when he chose me out of seventy other dancers in the SAB winter program and gave me an apprenticeship. Now, twelve years later, I had countless performances under my belt—but with just one look from him, I was an awkward teen fresh off the turnpike from Altoona, PA. Unsure of herself, not completely in control.

I hated that Peter's validation still meant something to me. His power impacted my professional life as well as my mental well-being, and there were a million ways he could punish me if he chose to. But this role was something I really wanted. *Cats* is effing iconic! I had to force myself to focus on what I needed to say. I walked into his office calmly and sat down.

"I've been offered a role in a Broadway show, and I want to take it." I said it quickly. Peter sat back in his chair. His face softened and he leaned forward, as if his eyes were really seeing me for the first time since I walked into his office. Then he narrowed them. In that one look, he made his disdain clear—he abhorred the idea of one of his elite soloist dancers lowering themselves to an ensemble performance eight shows a week.

"Well, before you make a decision," he replied too carefully, "you should know that I've been considering you for the roles of first jumping soloist in symphony three and Russian girl in *Serenade*."

I felt my strength waver, a lot. These were roles I always wanted to dance, and he knew it. They were roles I could fully throw myself into, bringing freshness and excitement to them, and Peter knew that, too. But now, one thing was different. I had grown not just as a dancer but as a woman and an artist. My heart hurt for a second because while the words coming out of his mouth had so much appeal, I knew it was a ruse. I would never be cast in those roles. This was a game for him, and as someone who was equally competitive, I could tell that he wanted to win.

"Think about it carefully, Georgina. But just remember, I don't share my dancers."

After a few days of deep soul-searching, about facing a pay cut and the inevitable ramifications from Peter* (could Andrew Lloyd Webber offer me more?), I was walking across the bridge from Lincoln Center plaza to the Rose Building when I saw Peter approaching from the other side.

"So have you thought things through?" Peter towered over me, and my body responded almost viscerally. That moment decided it.

"I have. I'll be taking a leave. I'm going to do it."

He shook his head, acknowledging the touché and the ongoing power struggle between us. He replied, "Okay, I'll let everyone know." His expression showed a hint of confusion—like he didn't know how he was going to gain the upper hand again with his rogue ballerina. What was the best move on the chess board? Was my loyalty with him, or to myself?

---

* In fact, when I did return from *Cats*, one of the ballet masters said I would not be reprising the principal Russian role in *Swan Lake* because "you have been gone" while other dancers have been here.

Swan Dive #12

While Victoria is not a feature in the Bustopher Jones vignette, the earworm of a song about a well-fed, high-brow gentleman fat cat who goes to fancy clubs, there's a lot of cats walking around with props preening to be in his glory . . . a fish bone carcass, a magnum bottle of champagne. At this point in the number, I am to carry a gigantic tea-pot across the stage. I'm supposed to walk off with it all heel to toe like I'm a member of the aristocracy. It's cold in the rehearsal studio, so I'm wearing leg warmers. I'm heel-toeing in my jazz shoes when the lip of my woolen leg warmer caught on the heel of my jazz shoe. I AM WALKING. MY INSTRUCTIONS ARE TO WALK. But I go down so hard—my entire right side crashes onto the floor. Everyone here is an accomplished dancer, but I'm the only professional ballerina in the cast, and when asked to walk, I end up on the floor.

And I'm also the only person who has totally wiped out *while walking* in front of everyone; the entire creative team, the music director. Everyone is shocked. Legit shocked. I went down so effing hard that people are concerned. *Oh my God, is the ballerina okay?* I'm pretty sure the creative team was like, "Abort the teapot! The ballerina can't handle a prop!" So, if you're wondering, the giant teapot didn't make it into the show.

CHAPTER 25

Here, Kitty Kitty

I showed up for our first rehearsal at the new Forty-Second Street studio space. Nervous AF. How long had it been since I had a "first day at school" experience?! I defaulted to cool/demure mode, which will read laughable to the folks who truly know me. After the meet and greet with the producers and the iconic creative team, including Trevor Nunn, Andrew Lloyd Webber, Andy Blankenbuehler, Chrissie Cartwright, Kristen Blodgette, and, of course, Gilly, I felt no less intimidated.

I'd come prepared to dance. But after this epic Broadway meet and greet, I was confined to a folding chair for two straight days so I could learn everything there is to know about the origin of the musical *Cats* from our oracle, Trevor.

It was certainly informative, but any creative secrets spoken of during that time shall remain among the privileged attendees. I will, however, share a couple of choice *Cats* trivia facts. The original Broadway production involved three hundred pounds of yak hair and was once sued for $6 million by an office worker who did not appreciate having Rum Tum Tugger gyrate his pelvis in her face.

I'm used to constant motion, and sitting still for hours on end is my own personal hell—*it physically hurts*—but as desperately as I wanted to plop down on the floor and stretch, I got the feeling it wouldn't be kosher.

Exactly one and a half days later, I nearly screamed from relief when Trevor let Gilly take the helm for a few minutes. Andy was our choreographer for this show, and it was public knowledge that Gilly was upset about how that shakedown had happened at first. I happen to know firsthand that Andy and I considered Gilly our absolute favorite member of the original creative team. There was no bad blood between Andy and Gilly—no claws were out! There was an urgency to Gilly's words, as she only had the floor for a few minutes, and during that time she wanted to explain the *lore of felinity.** She gathered us together into a mush of bodies and explained the simple goal of *Cats*: "To make the audience want to go home, rip their clothes off, and fuck." Goddamn, I loved this woman. The next day, Trevor went around the room to anoint each of us by whispering three secret words that were to define our individual pussies. These were the "ineffable" parts of our cat characters, and they were to remain top secret. That being said, "innocence, romance, and unapologetic" were my supersecret words.

Then it was time for me to drop on the floor and morph into a feline. I felt like I was in a gentler, softer version of the movie *Teen Wolf*. My first thought was *Whoa, I am so not at the ballet anymore*. I had just rolled over onto my back, stretching out my legs and arms, when I heard my castmate Tyler, from *On the Town*, gag—totally disrupting the relaxed cat vibe I was really starting to feel. I curled onto my side and shot him a look (a catty one) that said, "Dude, what the fuck is wrong

---

* There is a detailed description of this conversation featured on the podcast *Another Cat's Diary*, created by fellow cat cast member Christopher Gurr, if you're curious. It's genius.

with you?" He ignored me. He arched his back and made a louder noise, more guttural and at least five times more disgusting. *Is he coughing up a fur ball? Shit. That is so next-level.* This was my very first Broadway rehearsal, and I was not going to be out-catted. I started licking my fingers, slowly and one by one, wondering if the dust and dirt I was ingesting was infused with years of Broadway magic. I dragged my hands/paws through my hair like I was grooming myself. I flipped back onto my hands and knees, grateful for the kneepads the stagehands passed out, because the floor was hard for virgin knees. I started to crawl across the room, all languid-like. I slink past Leona Lewis, a chart-topping pop singer from the UK, lying on her side mewling loudly, and nearly get knocked over by a grown man pouncing toward an invisible ball. I was in the Jerome Robbins rehearsal studio surrounded by some of the world's most talented singers and dancers, who at this moment were pretending to chase mice and shit in litter boxes. I had made it!

All of us just *being* cats—this totally esoteric, unstructured exercise where we had the freedom to do whatever made us feel catlike—was merely the first in a mountain of new artistic experiences I was about to encounter. *Cats* was one of the hardest things I've ever done in my life, and I savored every second of it. The cast of *Cats* is responsible for transforming themselves into their character on their *own*. The first time I did my Victoria makeup, which was one of the easier plots, I ended up looking kind of like a baby deer. I had to practice until I got my makeup plot right. Some other castmates practiced for hours. I was charmed although slightly puzzled when we were given shiny black *Cats* bathrobes on opening night. Another dancer enlightened me.

"It's so you have something to wear while putting on your makeup. You know, before your costume."

I looked at her, still confused.

"Um, it's so everyone doesn't have to see you naked."

Oh! For over a decade I had been riding the elevator up to my dressing room in various states of major undress after performances—

having removed and lost various items during preshow warm-up and sweat (the rule is costumes are put on and taken off at stage level). To think I could have just tossed on a bathrobe after the show? Wow. *Broadway people are geniuses.*

I got the artistic fuel I was looking for, but I don't know that I expected *Cats* to be such a major turning point in my life and in my career. Playing the role of Victoria in *Cats* was not only a fascinating artistic experience that stretched my limits as a dancer and singer and actress, but an education on the major differences between being in a Broadway show and a member of the New York City Ballet. I really didn't expect my time on Broadway to shine a light for me on the misogyny that happens at the ballet, and certainly not a flood lamp. But ballet's toxicity was soon glaring.

On Broadway, you're not expected to work when sick or injured; if you need to call out, your understudy goes on. Everyone is treated like an adult and respected. At the New York City Ballet on any given day (at least under Peter), a woman might receive the fat-shaming talk of her life (even while postpartum) or be criticized to a level of humiliation in front of everyone and be expected to be smiling and dancing for her life just moments later. Broken toes, strep throat, crushed spirit—doesn't matter, get in costume and dance. Dancers were not to miss a performance for any reason and doing so would leave you with a pit in your stomach. Will my role go to someone else? Some men of the New York City Ballet were not held to the same staunch expectations. One male dancer called out because he couldn't get past the Puerto Rican Day Parade. In reality, that parade had occurred weeks ago. Being in Peter's club definitely had its perks.

While the ballet is still my home, and a home I love deeply, the expectations of ballerinas are extreme. Broadway was about camaraderie; every stagehand, usher, and door security person was integral to the show. This was soooo not the case in the ballet world. This difference was evident from the moment I started the *Cats* audition process.

When I finished the hip-hop combo, which couldn't be more different from a pas de deux, the rest of the dancers clapped and shouted, "You *go*, ballerina!" It may sound like a small gesture, but that moment was a harbinger of things to come—performance defined by dignity and support. Being treated like a respected artist. I got to the theater one day and was told I would be swung out. I was like, *I'm doing what now? Are you adding the trapeze back into the show?* Not that I would necessarily object to that sort of change. But I had learned by then that there was another difference between ballet and Broadway. At some point during the previews, a Broadway show gets "frozen"—and no further changes are allowed to be made.

"No. Gina. We're going to give your understudy a chance to play the role. You are required to be in the theater if we need you. But just relax, let your body rest and enjoy the show."

I can't imagine the look I must have been giving Ira.

"Um, this is normal, Gina." I was still looking at him with shock or disbelief.

"Really, this is like a thing. In theater."

Well, holy shit. It took me a minute to compute what was happening. I would, um, rest and relax. Yes, okay. And my understudy would be given a chance to shine in this glorious role? And I would get paid to sit and watch the show? I am 100 percent behind this! This was definitely not how we rolled at City Ballet. I was so delighted by this unexpected development that I decided to use the opportunity to utilize my *Cats* cast member discount. I went wild. By the time I sat down to watch the show (in a *Cats* sweatshirt), I had also procured a *Cats* pillow, sunglasses, a tote bag, umbrella, and hat. I was swung out one more time the following month, but due to a bit of advance notice, I was able to plan a spectacular prank. Unique to this particular revival, Tugger (aka my dance partner for life Tyler Hanes) takes a photo with a superlucky and unsuspecting audience member in row F. I managed to get a seat in row H and execute a full transformation into Balanchine ballerina complete with pointe shoes while sitting in my seat. When it was time for Tugger to visit row F, I ran down to meet him in all my ballerina glory. The moment was priceless. The entire cast was gagged, the photograph is spectacular, and I'm sorry—I'm going to give myself props here for changing my clothes discreetly in a tiny theater seat during a live show.

Being in the cast of *Cats* was one of the most extraordinary experiences of my career. We got along so well—the overall energy was one of mutual support and respect. To be treated as an adult—to know that if I woke up one morning with a fever of 106, there would be genuine concern. Not the usual City Ballet nonsense: a) What time can you get here (the administration)? or b) Can I have her role (insert name of almost any dancer)? Each cat was so meticulously cast, too. Such a stroke of genius by the whole creative team. We were such a beautiful motley crew and perfectly put together to create theatrical magic. We bonded over the insanity that took place in the audience (oh, the cat toys, and people, please don't say "Here, kitty kitty" and urge the actors onto your laps. We are not really cats!). We were all amused when a real cat, aka Grumpy Cat, was paid $10,000 to make a cameo. We all fully committed to being cats together—and let me tell you, getting your feline on with a bunch of people is really bonding. Taking the words of my dear friend Chris Gurr, getting the opportunity to take part in a global phenomenon is also highly recommended.

But eventually Peter summoned me back. I sent a detailed email, pleading my case for continuing to perform in *Cats* and the ballet. My role was the hardest to replace, so if *Cats* needed me, I wanted to help while they found the replacement. I made it clear that there would be no conflict—any *Cats* performances I agreed to do wouldn't interfere with my schedule at City Ballet. Peter's answer was short and to the point.

Georgina, are you here or are you not here? We've gone over this—enough. Make a choice by tomorrow morning. Period.

Peter

The message was clear. After the rest of your run is over, Get Back Here; this is where you belong—even though I had so few shows to actually perform in (soloist purgatory). It didn't matter that I was essentially asking for the same thing he let a male dancer do the year prior. My rules imposed were different.

*　*　*

On January 1, 2018, seven months after allegations about Peter were brought to the forefront... seven months that I would describe as *Requiem for a Dream*–level fucked-up and traumatic, I was jolted awake by the realization that *I am a victim.*

I am a survivor of some deep emotional abuse, and all of the behaviors I have exhibited prior to that moment, in my relationships with men, actually in ALL my relationships, came down to the abuse I started being exposed to at the age of seventeen. Stockholm syndrome is also very real, and the experience of coming out of it is excruciating. The shame and the brokenness that have been ingrained into my psyche largely by the power dynamic imposed upon me by this leader is something I will battle for years to come.

The email opened with "news articles reporting largely anonymous and decades-old accusations of sexual harassment or physical mistreatment of dancers or others . . ."* and wraps up saying, "to bring an end to this disruption which has enveloped the Ballet and the School, I have decided that it's time for me to retire."

Retire? Well, how fucking convenient.

---

* As noted, Peter has denied all of these allegations.

Over the last two decades, I have grown as an artist, and I've created unbreakable bonds with my colleagues and danced beautifully. My spirit and body have been both broken and lovingly if not painstakingly stitched back together. And I'm a biracial ballerina who cofounded a globally recognized diversity initiative. Peter is gone now. If I am ever promoted to principal dancer, it will be by the new regime. I want to be a principal dancer—I don't need to be, but I *want* to be. All this time later, with so many years of Saratogas, *Nutcracker*s, and performances under my belt, I can't help but feel thwarted in that Peter and I won't have a final duel. One desires closure in defeating the monster, right? I always felt that our adversarial relationship would resolve in an epic battle of will ending in him choosing to promote me to the highest rank, and that would have been the ultimate victory for me. Would I have found the gratification that I had been aching for within that victory? I'll never know. But perhaps knowing the freedom I have experienced being released from this toxic individual is the biggest victory of all. Peter has left his mark, and it is a deep and painful one—but from this point on, the narrative belongs to me.

* * *

After *Cats*, I came back to the ballet, and while I was happy to be home, my eyes would be forever open. It was like I had "stepped out" on City Ballet and explored a different facet of what a career in the arts can be. I experienced how creativity can be unlocked when dancing in a place where positivity was the norm, and everyone, regardless of title, was valued as a collaborator rather than a commodity.

CHAPTER 26

Dancers Die Twice

Iemerge from the subway into the financial district, where life rarely takes me. These are the buildings where an obscene amount of money is earned. They gleam in glass and steel. I find the building I'm looking for. It is also massive and cold. I walk out of the elevator on the third floor for my appointment at the worker's comp office. The room is barren, at least devoid of any pleasantries. I sign my name on a clipboard, but my writing is shaky because the table is on wheels. There is one fake plant, and even the plant has succumbed to the atmosphere of misery: it's wilted—almost melted. The seating area is nearly full—with my fellow injured Americans, I suppose. I sit down to wait to see the doctor, hoping my appointment will take place as scheduled. I have rehearsal, and PT, and then acupuncture. I am doing everything in my power to heal my body so I can just get back to work.

April 25, 2017, is a date that's permanently marked in my mind. I remember thinking that day that I felt stronger than I ever had. I was back dancing the role of the Woman in Red in *Russian Seasons*, but this time with *Cats* stamina. I felt unstoppable during that rehearsal, but I was about to hit my limit. I landed after a massive jump, and my body betrayed me. A slight miscalculation of landing, an overworked body, and a shitty card deal of fate. I knew almost instantly. The magical little Doozers signaled the MAYDAY MAYDAY alarms before I had fully processed the fact that my knee had hinged the wrong way, laterally hitting the floor, then ricocheting back from whence it came with a classic pop like the sound of a Pringles can. I had obliterated my left ACL.

It was such a massive blow to the system that even though I did not fall in the classic swan dive sense, once I was down I was completely immobile. My prettily costumed body melted into a shocked slump. I was uttering the guttural obscenities that indicated *This is not a drill.* The orchestra had been playing for me (a rare rehearsal perk), and they stopped, which only happens during the worst falls, the worst injuries. My vision tunneled, and time slowed.

I remember thinking, *This is bad. This is fucking bad news bears.* I had to be carried off the stage. A humiliating process for most dancers and athletes, but what made it feel more fucked-up was the small visiting audience of high-level donors. Backstage, there was already a flurry of people gathering as I was laid on the floor, still in costume, writhing around in pain but trying to mask my disappointment. It's really hard to describe these moments. I'm on the ground looking up at my colleagues, I'm in pain, I feel ashamed, and all the while I know that their concern is only in part for me. I'm a goner. The show must go on tonight. Who will be my replacement? Even in this state I have the wherewithal to consider the consequences my injury has on the evening's performance. My only replacement is dancing two other ballets that night. *Not my problem now.* But this development was definitely of interest to some. A bunch of dressing-room mates who had been watching on the monitor upstairs had run down to my aid, but there were also a few vultures who swooped right in—they knew there was a gain to be made from my loss. This is bad form for anyone, but the blatant disrespect from principal women who should know better especially hurt.

They got me into the elevator, and the shock was replaced by reality. I fainted from the pain.

Eventually, Sebastian, one of the male dancers, carried me into a cab headed for the hospital for an emergency MRI, and that's where the real anguish began, worse than how much it hurt. I started to bargain, *Hey, maybe it's not so bad after all. I can think clear thoughts now. It's probably just a sprain, and I'll need a few days to recover. I'm a fast healer. It's all gonna be fine. Actually, I could probably do the show tonight. Hmmm, okay, not tonight but definitely tomorrow.* These are all legitimate thoughts that bounced through my head, and I guarantee any other ballerina in this situation would do the same. The fear of being sidelined is powerful. And the understanding that the body is fragile is not easy to come to. Our bodies and their ability to do amazing things are what we live for—and how we make our living.

I live in a gracious and lovely, albeit small, apartment in a brownstone building on the Upper West Side. There are many perks to my apartment. It's a stone's throw from the subway and Central Park. It has ample light, hardwood floors, and plenty of storage for my custommade tutu. But what really made my eyes light up when I saw this particular apartment was the bathroom . . . with its glorious, ultradeep, oversized old-fashioned bathtub. I knew this tub was meant for me— that I'd spend hours of my life inside it soaking my overworked muscles while drinking a glass of Syrah (my favorite bathtub wine). I made an offer, and my fifty-pound container of Epsom salts and I moved in during December 2011—nothing like throwing a real estate transaction into *Nutcracker* season.

Ballet *hurts*. Everything we do with our bodies, from relentless relevés to midair splits, is completely unnatural. The human hip was not meant to handle extremes such as putting your leg beside your face (aka développé) or standing on the very tips of your toes in shoes made of cardboard and paste. On a day-to-day basis we're dealing with anything from dropped metatarsal pain, soft corns, labral tears, or a headache from a hangover. Pain is part of our world (and a giant box of single-serve Advil packets are kept backstage at all times). But the pain we feel physically, in our strained muscles, is nothing compared to the deep gut-wrenching pain we feel when wiped out by an injury. I've heard a dancer's Achilles tendon pop onstage while I was watching from the third ring—the sound is unforgettable, like a lightning crack straight to the body. I assure you that it hurts like hell, but it will also cause an instantaneous breaking of your heart—with that snap and tear you are sidelined for one or two seasons; other dancers step into your roles while you endure months of physical therapy and contemplate your postdance existence . . . which up to that moment you've never done because you've been cocky enough to think it will never happen. Can I teach? Maybe I could finish college? What about my health care? When a ballerina goes down, we might be out forever. And unlike some professional sports athletes, we can't retire happily in a never-ending McMansion with five cars and a bulging bank account from the multi-year contract we were lucky to sign. We'd be broke, or close enough to it.

Few are the dancers who stay perfectly intact throughout their careers; I can count the ones I know on one hand. If a dancer *chooses to retire*—if the decision is not thrust upon them by a blown-out hip or destroyed Achilles tendon—they are in the lucky minority. And while injuries happen frequently, the ballet company rarely handles them with the right sensitivity and concern. Once again let me remind you of the reality of a ballerina crying backstage after a serious injury, only to have her costume literally ripped from her body so it could be put on another dancer to save the show. And in my case, a greedy little principal ballerina literally whipped out her phone while I lay immobile and texted the ballet master and (the slimiest degree of opportunism) Peter Martins himself to pitch herself for the role. (Joke was on her, though. Alexei, the choreographer, didn't think she was right for the part. HA.)

I'm pleased to say that five months after the ACL surgery, I was back on that stage, dancing the role of Anita once again. This is essentially unheard-of in my world. The journey from injury to pinning on my saucy Anita wig was the hardest I've ever faced in my life. We're talking a major surgery, months of physical therapy, neuro-vision therapy, acupuncture, painkillers the size of small children, and the absurdity of trying to convince a worker's comp doctor that I wasn't ready to go back to work because my job required that I stand en pointe for extended periods of time, often with my leg near my face. As I stood backstage before my entrance, I worried what would happen once I channeled every fiber of myself back into dance. Would my body cooperate? Would this be a triumph? Or would I end up crying backstage, knowing that this time it was all over for real?

Retirement wasn't forced on me, I reminded myself. I was still in the game, for now. I had not danced my final performance.

Anytime a dancer dances his or her final show, I am there to support and witness what I know is a hugely emotional moment. On my way to the theater for my friend Savannah's last performance, Broadway was basically a parking lot. I jumped out of the cab, running the last two blocks in heels, my dress flowing comically behind me like the flighty heroine in a bad romantic comedy. I wasn't going to miss a single second of her show, and I was willing to risk falling flat on my face (if I survived the ACL, I could handle a broken nose). By the time I reached the wings, I was gulping air into my lungs, and I was a sweaty wreck—but I made it. I tried to quiet my breath as the curtain went up. The orchestra played the familiar first few notes of Bach's Concerto in D Minor.

The music calmed my breathing further; *Concerto Barocco* is one of my favorite ballets. Savannah sailed out and hit every note with remarkable, seemingly effortless precision. My melancholy apparently wasn't deep enough to keep a smile from spreading across my face—my tribe was *killing it*. Watching the first ballet of the evening from the wings, I could viscerally feel the energy and the adrenaline of the other dancers. I also wanted to be a face of support. When I'm onstage and I see one of my colleagues watching from the wings, it's one of the most gratifying, validating experiences for me as an artist. I'm not alone in this feeling either—there's something powerful, intoxicating even, in knowing your peers respect you. It's deeply meaningful to feel the appreciation from someone who actually understands what it takes physically and mentally to nail every single move. Savannah exploded across the stage with her vibrant, enormous spirit. She was doing great, and then there it was—she caught the lip of her pointe shoe and slipped a little. This is probably unnoticeable to the untrained eye, but as the master of the toe shoe slip, I knew inside she was thinking, *Shit. Shit. Shit.*

When a dancer retires, it's a big deal . . . *really big*, especially if you're a principal dancer; they practically have a parade on the damn stage for retiring principals. A soloist or corps member won't get as much fanfare, but to me (or whoever is retiring) it's still a big deal. Retiring from ballet is nothing like a corporate retirement—where someone is presented with a sheet cake and a plastic cup of chardonnay after thirty years of dutiful service before moving on to daily rounds of golf and Florida vacations with the grandkids. Recently, a huge wave of New York City Ballet dancers have been retiring in their thirties. Generations before may have made it until their forties—dancing after forty is totally badass; think Alessandra Ferri, Whelan, and Baryshnikov. But the truth is, they aren't throwing themselves into the air the same way they used to. Bodies and spirits wane, sometimes only to be revived by the idea, the fantasy, of a normal life, accompanied by a normal schedule and a normal paycheck. *Normal* can seduce the very best of us. And duh, we also retire because our bodies start saying, "No more, please."

Every dancer knows deep in their core that their time onstage is limited. How limited is the big looming question. Will an injury end it all in one bone-crushing, muscle-tearing moment? Or will your body just slowly stop cooperating—no longer able to jump and turn or fold into seemingly impossible displays of flexibility?

That night, dancing in *Agon*, Savannah was nothing short of transcendent. She was so present, so ethereal—her last performance was a true gift to everyone watching. Her expression during her final bow, lips trembling, eyes moist, said it all to me. Her last bow as a ballerina. When I caught up with Savannah later on, backstage, she looked at our colleagues who were still dancing and simply sighed and said, "I'm going to miss this." I knew what she meant. It wasn't just the performing; it was all of it. She'd miss the rituals, the routines, the costumes, the music. She'd miss shooting the shit in the middle of a performance, how we helped each other handle the insane pressure, the madness of this crazy job that we had sacrificed everything for—leaving with nothing more than memories and a few battle scars. The childhood dream that came true, but for her, was over now.

When it's my turn to stand onstage, looking out at all the bright red velvet, the four golden rings, and the audience of 2,586 clapping and cheering ballet lovers for the last time, what will it feel like? Will it be how Michael Phelps felt when he swam his last race? Or how Kristi Yamaguchi felt during her last program? A loss of identity? Will my entire career flash in front of my eyes? From my first *Nutcracker* as a four-year-old, when I fell on my ass, to Dew Drop and *Opus Jazz* and Anita: this is all I've ever known. What will I do when I go home that night and fall asleep with the knowledge that I'll never dance on that famous stage again? Some of my magic will be lost, I know—a part of me left behind on the stage forever. But I've always felt that I leave a little piece of my soul behind as a willing sacrifice after every performance.

Because that's how it feels to be a ballerina, when all the bullshit is swept aside: complete and utter magic. And the cost of that magic is the understanding that it's evanescent. A gift simply so wonderful it's impossible to harness forever in my physical mortality. And what about my weird, freaky, loving ballet family? My fellow dancers and I have sweated, bled, and cried so hard we've gotten snot on each other's clothes. We've shared a million performances, countless drinks, a few bad boyfriends, and a hundred bad decisions. I know that beyond a select few, most of these relationships will dissolve when I acquiesce that the time has come to face *normal* and take a final bow.

But we all must discover a second season for ourselves. I've seen dancers unravel completely after retirement, at a loss for direction about how to find their place in postcompany life. Without class, rehearsals, performances, many dancers have been known to turn to drugs and alcohol. Many find their place as ballet masters and teachers—and I'm pleased to say that some of my contemporaries are embarking on equally ambitious second seasons for themselves. Savannah recently drove across the country to start her new life as a medical student. And Liko, who sat in dressing room #19 with her MCAT study guide, won herself the elusive full ride on offer now at NYU medical school.

Ballet has been my life, and I intend for it to be my life for a while longer, but I am always aware that I will need to discover my own second act. Being a curious person has given me the courage to just tip the domino—to think about what life looks like for me later on. If I'm really lucky, Broadway may have room for me—performing roles in *On the Town*, *West Side Story,* and *Cats* has felt equally as good as any ballet I've danced. And if my vessel totally gives out? I know I don't want to teach; that's not for me. I could be seduced by the idea of more on-screen storytelling.

But I've got a biting wit and a real estate license I'm not afraid to use. I might not know what my future holds—ballet, theater, more surgery, or selling overpriced Manhattan real estate—but I've survived nearly two decades at the New York City Ballet intact. I've danced my way into the upper tier. I've felt the pain. I've navigated the drama. I've even farted onstage and survived. Ballet may be an ephemeral experience, but to be able to give myself over to this special gift has been an honor. I will always be grateful for what my inner rogue ballerina has encouraged me to become. I can't imagine much else that will scare me or exhilarate me as much, but whatever is next, I'll jump right into it with all of my body and soul. Ballet has taught me that's the only way to face the uncertainty of life, and that might be the best lesson I've learned.

Acknowledgments

I knew embarking on this journey that I would need the help of a brilliant mind. Someone who could organize the mess of my life, frenetic memories, and countless stories. Helping me articulate them in a way any newcomer to ballet would feel welcome and intrigued to learn more. Paula Balzer Vitale, you have laughed, cried, drank with me, and, most importantly, been my rock through this process. I knew at bacon we would be forever friends. You have absorbed my voice and now know the darkest/most hilarious truths behind my outrageous and absurd choices, and you still let me be around your children. Thank you, Paula. Your gift is so special, and I can't wait for the next opportunity to work together.

To my family, especially my mom and dad, Cheryl and Silvino Ben Pazcoguin. Thank you for understanding my gift and the sacrifices early on. My brothers and sisters, Cory, Tony, Joe, Stacy, Christina: thank you for letting me take center stage most of the time. Christina, I will forever appreciate your amazing commentary on my foes.

Miranda Grove, we are an ocean apart but forever bonded in sisterhood and love. You are my OG ride-or-die.

To the very many people who made up the village responsible for instructing a tiny Georgina Ballerina. There are too many of you to name individually. But you know who each and every one of you is, and I owe you a debt of gratitude. Suki Schorer, you hold an extremely special place in my heart, and I thank you for always being my champion.

I would be remiss if I did not mention my partner in change and cofounder of Final Bow for Yellowface, Phil Chan. Thank you for your friendship and continual support throughout this journey into a new era of wokeness in the ballet world. Our stories are too long to be chronicled and will be highlighted to the degree they deserve on different pages to come.

To the ballerinas of color who have come before me. Your stories have shaped a blueprint for me to forge my own path through this world. I acknowledge that I stand on your shoulders and my courage is bolstered by yours, sent out into the universe generations before me. Your wisdom has helped shape my own unique story at NYCB and beyond. Thank you.

To Diana. Your care, wisdom, and fire saved me when my own was in danger of being snuffed out.

To the many other women—Chita, Carmen, Donna, Nikki, Catharine, and Claudia, just to name a few—who have demonstrated to me that the power of uplifting women is stronger than ever wanting to compete with and defeat them.

To the men in my life who have lifted me up, respected my wildness, protected my vulnerability. You guys are warriors of the highest honor.

To the various people who make my home at Lincoln Center something much more than a workplace. From orchestra members to security guards to Local 1 to stage managers to ticket sales to beloved dressers and hair and makeup—you guys are a treasure to me.

To my select team of miracle workers who rebuild Humpty Dumpty when she Swan Dives: Marika Molnar, Scott Kuhagen (aka Unicorn),

Julie Segall, Götz Lehle, Anna Vollmar, Emily Smith, Dr. Roy Siegel, Dr. Bauman, Dr. Rodeo, Sean Hampton, Ash Parker, and Brian Carberry. I would quite literally be a mess without you.

Thank you to Phil Rosenthal for putting me in touch with Brandi Bowles at UTA. You heard something in my stories and encouraged me to take a leap in the dark.

Brandi, thank you for fighting for me every step of the way!!!

Thank you to everyone at my publisher, Henry Holt, for believing in this book. Thank you to Libby Burton to seeing what this book could become from the very beginning and to Madeline Jones for taking over and helping us get this book to the next level. I'd also like to thank Ruby Rose Lee, Sarah Crichton, Amy Einhorn, Maggie Richards, Janel Brown, Patricia Eisemann, Marian Brown, Caitlin O'Shaughnessy, Allison Carney, and Christopher Sergio. Thank you to Georgina Morley and her team at Picador in the UK.

And to the select few early readers, Michele, Roger, Yisell, Karla, and Margo. I am so grateful to you guys for your insight. Matt Karas, you are a gifted lensman, and I love what you captured for the cover.

To my nearest and dearest of friends: T. R. J. T. S. Y. L. C. H. R. E. C. You guys will forever make me laugh, and you keep my ego in check.

To my NYCB family: my colleagues, bosses, and ballet rehearsal directors. We are embarking on a new era and I am so thankful for the good, the bad, and the absolutely hilarious we have experienced as a unit. It takes a special group of individuals to weather what we have, and I am so proud of us for doing our collective work to create change at NYCB and of the company's renewed determination to embrace that change and to become an institution that welcomes and amplifies the voices of all races, ethnicities, and cultural identities.

I know some of you aren't going to be very happy with me, but I have to say even to those people I've "read" within an inch of their life that you all have shaped me into the Rogue Ballerina. I can't wait to share the stage with you again.

About the Author

Georgina Pazcoguin, "The Rogue Ballerina," has danced with the New York City Ballet since 2002 and was promoted to soloist in 2013. A steadily rising star, she is an ambassador of her art on many platforms, crossing over to Broadway, TV, and film. In addition to her many appearances at NYCB, including a celebrated portrayal of Anita in Jerome Robbins's *West Side Story*, her credits include the award-winning film *NY Export: Opus Jazz*, Ivy in the Broadway revival of *On the Town*, and Victoria in the Broadway revival of *Cats*. Georgina is a passionate activist for the Orphaned Starfish Foundation and the cofounder of the globally recognized diversity initiative Final Bow for Yellowface. She lives in New York City, and a half hour with her will shake your stereotype of uptight ballerinas to bits.